35—00

START AND THE FUTURE OF DETERRENCE

Also by Michael J. Mazarr

*MISSILE DEFENCES AND ASIAN-PACIFIC SECURITY
SEMPER FIDEL: AMERICA AND CUBA, 1776-1988

* Also published by Macmillan

START and the Future of Deterrence

Michael J. Mazarr

Fellow in International Security Studies,
Center for Strategic and International Studies,
Washington DC

MACMILLAN

First edition 1990

Published by
MACMILLAN EDUCATION LTD
Houndmills, Basingstoke, Hampshire RG21 2XS
and London
Companies and representatives
throughout the world

Typeset by
Footnote Graphics, Warminster, Wiltshire

Printed and bound in Great Britain by
WBC Ltd, Bristol and Maesteg

British Library Cataloguing in Publication Data
Mazarr, Michael J., *1965–*
START and the Future of Deterrence.
1. Nuclear warfare. Deterrence
I. Title
355'.0217
ISBN 0–333–52392–X

To Jennifer
my best

Contents

Acknowledgements

Many friends and colleagues have given generously of their time to read drafts of different chapters of this volume. All have earned my thanks and respect; none are responsible for any errors of fact or judgement that remain. Dr Stephen Cimbala read chapters 1–4; Dr Robert Jervis, chapter 2; Dr Loren Thompson, chapters 6 and 8; Dr William Kincade, chapter 4; Dr Anthony Cordesman, parts of chapters 3 and 7 in an earlier form. Chapter 5 was reviewed in an earlier, shorter draft by Robert Hunter and Michael Moodie at CSIS; in its longer version it was read by Robin Niblett and Paul Cole.

One last, special word of thanks to my boss at CSIS, Dr William Taylor. While he did not participate in the drafting of this volume, Bill Taylor is an extraordinarily wise, supportive and loyal boss. His support was indispensable for the completion of this book.

Portions of chapters 3 and 7 are taken from 'On Strategic Nuclear Policy', *SAIS Review* 9 (Winter-Spring 1989). Thanks go to *SAIS Review* for allowing us to reprint this material.

I would also like to express my debt to Robert Harris, who did a large amount of research and an even larger amount of thinking to help me prepare the section on cruise missiles. Robert was at the time a Dartmouth undergraduate who will make a superb policy analyst sooner than he thinks.

Glossary

ABM	anti-ballistic missile
ALCM	air-launched cruise missile
BMD	ballistic missile defence
C3I	command, control, communications and intelligence
CEP	circular error probable
counter-force	nuclear strategy of striking against enemy military forces, particularly nuclear weapons
counter-power	nuclear strategy that directs strikes against enemy non-nuclear military and military-related targets
counter-value	nuclear strategy calling for strikes against enemy value targes – cities, industry, etc.
EMP	electromagnetic pulse
FOFA	follow-on forces attack
ICBM	intercontinental ballistic missile
INF	intermediate-range nuclear forces
MAD	mutually assured destruction; both a situation and a strategy
MBFR	Mutual and Balanced Force Reduction talks
MIRV	Multiple Independently targetable Reentry Vehicle
NNSW	non-nuclear strategic weapons
OMG	operational maneuver group
POMCUS	prepositioned overseas materiel configured in unit sets
SDI	Strategic Defence Initiative
SIOP	Single Integrated Operational Plan
SLBM	sea-launched ballistic missile
SLCM	sea-launched cruise missile
SNF	short-range nuclear forces
SRAM	short-range attack missile

List of Figures and Tables

1 The Status of Deterrence: START and Other Factors

Nuclear deterrence and US nuclear strategy entered some time ago what is at once an intellectual stagnation and a political crisis. Until recently there has been little prospect that new ideas would emerge to help resolve what had become telling faults in the edifice of traditional deterrence theory and practice. While public concern with nuclear weapons remained significant, the threat of war had receded enough so that popularly forced radical change seemed unlikely.

Yet change is certainly needed. As recognised by a recent report, 'Current U.S. nuclear policy is directed toward three objectives: deterring conflict, controlling escalation should deterrence fail, and terminating conflict on terms favorable to U.S. political objectives'.[1] US nuclear forces and doctrines currently serve the first of those three purposes adequately, the latter two scarcely at all. Worse, the goal toward which so much of US force structure and strategy is directed – extended deterrence of Soviet nuclear and conventional attacks on Europe – has been placed effectively out of the reach of US planners. US nuclear forces are planned and procured in a virtual strategic vacuum, without adequate guidance as to what their purposes will be once acquired.

Solutions must be found for these problems, and the central theme of this book is that existing trends, if they continue, will lead in just such a direction: to the resolution of many of the dangers and contradictions of the nuclear era. The recent improvement in East-West relations, if it continues and is accompanied by strategic arms control (the central assumption of this volume), will create an environment in which anything but the most minimal deterrent postures would be publicly unacceptable. The West will not be able to continue doing nuclear business as it has been, a point brought home forcefully by the recent intra-NATO squabbles over Lance modernisation and short-range nuclear force (SNF) arms control. Something has to change, and that something will probably be the nature of deterrence itself as well as the way the superpowers go about ensuring it.

This volume contends that deterrence is evolving, but only slightly, more at the margins than at the core. The stability of the nuclear balance will continue to improve in the years ahead, provided several assumptions of this volume (most critically that a START treaty will be ratified and that US nuclear modernisation will continue) are borne out. If so, those steps will complement a process of 'nuclear learning', described in chapter 9, that is underway between the superpowers, in which both come gradually to accept common bodies of knowledge on the basics of stable deterrence. The result is a continuation and strengthening of basic, central deterrence and the reinforcement of the general perception that large-scale war in particular, but not only that which would cause or risk nuclear escalation, is an anachronism.

Guided by that basic recognition, this volume contends, deterrence will evolve in the next century into a more defensive, co-operative form rather than traditionally provocative offensive force structures and doctrines. Both superpowers will use mobility, concealment, limited strategic defences (primarily of nuclear weapons), and other means to deny the other the capability to conduct reliable counterforce strikes. Arms reduction treaties, and perhaps operational arms control agreements as well (such as a comprehensive test ban treaty), will restrain and reverse the quantitative and perhaps qualitative evolution of nuclear arsenals.

These trends will probably not be continuous. Indeed, all indications are that the Bush administration's new war plan, SIOP-7, attempts to deal with the declining feasibility of counterforce, not by seeking alternative strategies, but by pouring tens, eventually hundreds, of billions of dollars into sophisticated new systems to locate, track, target and destroy mobile missiles and other difficult-to-hit nuclear systems. If some of the salutary trends currently underway in international politics – the Gorbachev phenomenon, for example – are reversed, the trends discussed above would be partially, if not totally, undermined.

Still, the assumption, and in a way the argument, of this volume is that those trends *will* continue, and that deterrence eventually *will* evolve into more promising avenues. To support that hypothesis, this volume examines many aspects of the problem of nuclear deterrence, and attempts to interrelate them along the way. This first chapter establishes the groundwork by discussing some of the trends in the strategic nuclear environment causing the shifts suggested earlier. Chapter 2 examines critically theories of what is required for deterrence, to find some basic notion of deterrence that would fit a new era of deterrence theory and practice. Chapter 3 proposes nuclear balances that might achieve deterrence based on the theory outlined in the previous chapter, and chapter 4 considers the targeting policies required to support the theory. Chapter 5 discusses the future of extended deterrence, and chapter 6 is a survey of Soviet nuclear doctrine, explaining how it is not inconsistent with a shift in deterrence to more defensive lines. Chapter 7 deals with a number of other issues, such as strategic defence and arms control verification, and chapter 8 examines the effects of non-nuclear strategic weapons. Finally, chapter 9 attempts to draw all the analysis together into a coherent whole.

CLARIFYING THE ISSUES

At the outset, it is important to define and discuss several of the most critical concepts used in the analysis that follows. Discussions of nuclear strategy are commonly criticised for their use of 'jargon'; yet one writer's jargon is another's precise term, and a number of notions in the deterrence literature are so well-formulated that it is next to useless to attempt to put them into 'plain' language. This section will undoubtedly sound simplistic to experienced nuclear theorists, but might be useful to those who are not nuclear 'afficionados'.

Initially we must understand the concept of deterrence. In its most basic sense, the term implies deterring another party from doing something one does not wish them to do. In the nuclear context it means deterring any use of nuclear weapons. Nuclear deterrence, moreover, has two aspects: *simple* or *central* deterrence, which contemplates deterrence of nuclear attacks against the country concerned (for our purposes, the United States); and *extended* deterrence, which is the pledge of nuclear use to deter other events, such as nuclear or conventional attacks on our allies.

Extended deterrence is in turn related to another concept, *flexible response*. This is the basic declared US strategy for the use of nuclear weapons, outlined in a secret NATO message of 1967. As it is publicly known, flexible response threatens the first use of nuclear weapons in response to aggression or, potentially, provocation. It has therefore led to a proliferation of limited nuclear war plans, which are examined more fully at the beginning of chapter 4.

The nature of deterrence and of nuclear weapons has also fostered an evolution of the term 'strategic'. In its basic sense, the word means nothing other than 'of or pertaining to strategy'. Yet in the modern era, the term 'strategic' has almost come to be synonymous with 'nuclear'. In large part this is due to the use of strategic in a geographic sense, referring to weapons with 'strategic' or interconti- nental range; until now the only prominent weapons with such capability have carried nuclear weapons. (This may change; chapter 8 examines the growing field of *non-nuclear* strategic weapons.)

Deterrence is achieved by targeting nuclear weapons against an adversary, and how that targeting is accomplished is an issue addressed by doctrines and terms. *Countervalue* targeting consists of aiming nuclear weapons against cities, industries, transportation centres, and other population-intensive 'value' targets that form the sinews of society. *Counterforce* targeting calls for threats against enemy military forces rather than civilian targets; those military forces can be either nuclear or conventional or both. Naturally, there is some level of overlap: a transportation hub or military industry could be on both lists, and in fact current US target lists (as they are known in unclassified circles) contain elements of both.

But what is the purpose of these nuclear threats? What would the United States want to do with its nuclear forces in a war? That question is addressed by another set of doctrines. A *minimum deterrent* posture argues that, since only a madman would fail to recognise that any nuclear use could escalate to worldwide destruc- tion, deterrence is a reasonably easy task; the United States must simply deploy a few hundred weapons, capable of annihilating Soviet society, and engage in largely countervalue targeting to ensure that any Soviet attack would result in a retaliation that would destroy Soviet society. Other analysts reject that claim, contending that the Soviets plan to fight and win a nuclear war and would only be deterred by the fear of losing a war; mere threats to punish them with a minimum deterrent are insufficient. Such analysts subscribe to *nuclear warfighting* doctrines. Chapter 2 will examine these doctrines in more detail.

It is not too difficult to see how these ideas could influence the acquisition of nuclear weapons. Minimum deterrence proponents need only a small, very survivable nuclear force, perhaps a couple of dozen submarines. Warfighters contemplate much more ambitious nuclear forces: counterforce-capable missiles (because if one is fighting a nuclear war one must destroy the other side's nuclear forces), the ability to maintain command and control of nuclear forces during a war, strategic defences to ward off an enemy's strikes, and so on.

Minimum deterrence and warfighting parallel two other concepts of deterrence, *deterrence by punishment* and *deterrence by denial*. These two notions are merely other ways of describing the two general strategies outlined above. Deterrence by punishment contemplates deterring another party with the threat of massive societal attacks, that is, punishment. Deterrence by denial seeks to build forces and doctrines capable of denying an opponent his war aims.

In the end this distinction reflects a difference of opinion on the nature of the nuclear era. Minimum deterrence proponents generally argue that nuclear weapons have radically altered the nature of warfare; whereas before wars could be fought and won, now any major conflict would be so destructive that societies on both sides would be destroyed. Given that fact, there is no need to possess subtle nuclear war plans, since the mere threat of a nuclear war is its own best deterrent. And such analysts oppose the deployment of any weapons, such as strategic defences, that threaten to upset the mutual vulnerability that has come to guarantee the peace.

Most warfighters, on the other hand, believe that nuclear weapons are merely another class of weapon to be used in warfare. Most critically, they contend that the *Soviets* believe this, and that therefore any other strategy will fail to deter them. Warfighters see the nuclear revolution as an altogether more modest phenomenon than minimum deterrers.

This volume, as will become apparent in the chapters to come, argues for a compromise position between minimum deterrence and warfighting, and contends that developments in the strategic nuclear environment are indeed urging the superpowers toward such a compromise. I accept the notion that nuclear weapons have revolutionised the nature of warfare, but argue also that, in part because of the fact that general nuclear war is so unthinkable, in some cases limited nuclear options might appear feasible; if it is insane to start a nuclear war, it might be insane to escalate in response (or even to respond) to limited nuclear attacks. In those cases, the superpowers need more flexible forces and more ambitious nuclear plans than those suggested by minimum deterrents proponents. These ideas will be fleshed out more fully in the next chapter.

There is indeed a third major nuclear doctrine, one to which this volume will turn for the general outlines of its own proposed strategy: *countervailing deterrence*. In its most basic sense it calls for a capability to match the nature and destructiveness of any enemy attack to the degree required for mutual deterrence. It would suggest that the United States must be able to respond to a major Soviet nuclear strike, limited Soviet strikes or Soviet conventional attacks on their own terms and with sufficient force to guarantee that no Soviet move could gain them militarily or politically significant advantage. It does not require a full warfighting, war-winning capability, but merely the capacity to respond in kind to Soviet attacks.

The United States in fact adopted something called the 'countervailing strategy' during the Carter administration. Unfortunately, since then the trend of thinking in official circles seems to be to develop a countervailing deterrent with a warfighting slant – not just to retaliate in kind, but to retaliate to win in protracted nuclear exchanges. This emphasis, and the counterforce targeting it implies, ought to be given up, as chapters 2 and 4 will argue.

The term 'countervailing strategy' hence carries a bit too much definitional baggage to be used profitably in this volume. The difference between the strategy advocated here and the existing countervailing strategy suggest that perhaps a new term is called for. I will term the general strategy predicted and advocated in this volume *co-operative reciprocal* deterrence, a term chosen, not to suggest that the theory it describes carries any novel aspects, only to distinguish it from existing concepts. It is co-operative in the sense that, following it, both sides would deploy mobile missiles, missile-carrying submarines and other hard-to-detect weapons while eschewing to a great degree counterforce capabilities, in both systems and doctrine. It is reciprocal in that it depends for deterrence, not on the capability of either side to defeat the other in war, but merely on the ability to respond in kind. These notions will be explained at greater length later.

Then there are the often-used terms, *assured destruction* and *mutually assured destruction* (or MAD). The latter describes the current strategic relationship, in which both sides are vulnerable to the other's first or second strikes; this vulnerability means that any attack will be met with a destructive retaliation. Assured destruction, however, has historically been used to describe both a situation and a strategy: the situation of MAD, and a specific nuclear strategy designed to take advantage of that fact (which, as one would expect, parallels the minimum deterrence/countervalue school). As such it has been defined as the 'capacity to retaliate and inflict unacceptable damage upon the Soviet Union's economy and population after a preemptive attack'.[2]

Finally, there is the notion of *stability*, a concept that is examined at the outset of chapter 3. Suffice it to say here that it is the minimum goal of all the strategies outlined above, though different strategies necessitate different versions of stability. Most basically, stability consists of the possession of a secure retaliation, to guarantee that neither side could launch a first strike and go unmolested.

THE START TREATY

This study makes a number of assumptions and arguments about the future strategic environment. One assumption is that a START treaty along the lines of the one currently under negotiation will be signed and ratified, a development that, as the following chapters will lay out, would have significant implications for strategic stability. The basic elements of the START treaty are summarised below.

- **6000 Warhead Limit**. Each side would have to reduce its strategic nuclear arsenal, currently about 10 000 warheads apiece, to 6000 total warheads. In fact, as currently written, the treaty allows for 6000 *counted* and about 8–9000 *actual* warheads: it counts each bomber that carries gravity bombs or short-range attack missiles (SRAMs) as one warhead no matter how many such weapons they actually carry, a loophole in the 6000 limit. As two analysts of the treaty have concluded, if either side deployed 200 bombers carrying bombs or SRAMs, each with 14 weapons, 'it could field a force carrying 5800 ICBM and SLBM RVs [warheads] and ALCMs plus 2800 bomber weapons (200 × 14), for a total force of 8600 actual weapons'.[3] This method of counting ALCMs might be changed, however, in the final START agreement.

- **Sublimits on ICBMs and SLBMs**. START would also restrict each side to 4900 combined ICBM and SLBM warheads. It therefore requires each side to deploy at least 1100 warheads on bombers (including ALCM-carriers) or similar non-ballistic missile systems. The treaty also calls for an effective cut of 50 per cent in Soviet heavy missiles: it places a sublimit of 1540 on heavy ICBMs (that is, ICBMs with large throw-weight – only the SS-18 is currently so classed), forcing the Soviets to dismantle half of the 308 SS-18s they currently have deployed. This would 'likely reduce overall Soviet missile throw-weight from 5.6 to approximately 2.4 million kilograms'.[4]

- **Limit on Delivery Vehicles**. START will place a cap of 1600 on the number of delivery systems (missiles and bombers) that each side can deploy. This requirement, when combined with the warhead limits, has ambiguous implications for crisis stability: by allowing each side to field 6000 (in fact really almost 9000) weapons and only 1600 targets, it institutionalises the unstable warhead:target ratios present since the MIRV era. On the other hand, allowing 6000 delivery vehicles might pose severe verification problems (to determine how many warheads each carried), and in any case the roughly 4:1 warhead:delivery vehicle ratio imposed by START is not as bad as the 10:1 ratio present in some modern systems, including the MX, D-5, and SS-18 missiles.

● **Unresolved Issues**. A number of issues remain to be resolved. First, the Soviet Union continues to demand a ten-year reaffirmation of the ABM Treaty, and the United States continues to resist. A possible compromise has been opened, however, by the appointment of Brent Scowcroft as National Security Adviser; before his appointment, Scowcroft had commented that such a decade-long ban on deployments of missile defences would not substantially impair the SDI program. Indeed, Soviet Foreign Minister Eduard Shevardnadze in 1989 meetings with the Bush administration arguably de-linked SDI from START, though the implications of the Soviet statements were somewhat unclear. It does, however, appear as if SDI no longer stands as a firm barrier to an accord.

Second, there is the issue of sea-launched cruise missiles, a subject discussed in some detail in chapter 7. US negotiators have so far opposed any limits on the weapons in START, considering an SLCM cap to be unverifiable. The two sides did agree at the Washington summit of December 1987 to seek limits on SLCMs outside START. The Soviet side desires sublimits on SLCMs with ranges over 600 miles of 400 nuclear SLCMs to be carried only on two classes of submarine and one surface ship, and 600 conventional SLCMs on agreed platforms. More recently they have suggested a total ban on all nuclear SLCMs.

Third, in regard to air-launched cruise missiles (ALCMs), the United States seeks to exclude all long-range, conventional ALCMs from limits, and suggests that nuclear ALCMs must have a range of over 1500 miles to count. US negotiators have proposed a value of ten ALCMs arbitrarily assigned to all ALCM carriers. The Soviets desire all ALCMs with a range of 600 miles or more counted, whether coventional or nuclear, and want maximum counting, not an arbitrary ten rule.

Fourth, both sides are still discussing what they will do with non-deployed missiles (missiles in storage rather than deployed in silos). The Soviets apparently intend to use non-deployed missiles as reloadable, refirable weapons to give their silos a multiple-shot capability. Both sides have agreed to limit non-deployed missiles but are not yet certain how.

Fifth and finally, the United States continues to suggest an additional sublimit of 3300 ICBM warheads. Viewing such fast, powerful weapons as inherently destabilising, the US side would like to reduce reliance upon them. The Soviets, however, while noting that they would not plan to deploy more than 3300 ICBM warheads under START in any case, have objected to the separate sublimit and would prefer merely to formalise the limit of 4900 ballistic missile warheads.[5]

OTHER DEVELOPMENTS

In addition to the START treaty, a number of other developments will affect the strategic environment in the next decades. Four are summarised here: public opinion, the nuclear winter phenomenon, advances in weapons technology, and the infeasibility of major war.

Public Opinion

A number of analysts have recognised that, since 1945 and especially beginning in the late 1970s, public opinion has been playing an increasingly significant role in the formation of nuclear policy in the West.[6] Indeed, Philip Bobbitt, in his interesting history and critique of nuclear strategy, devotes an entire chapter to the notion that the 'social' dimensions of deterrence have been overlooked. 'The next cyclical vulnerability in the central relationship to be manifested in the extended theatre ... arises from public alienation from deterrence itself, and ... this alienation also threatens to render the American nuclear strategy inexecutable'. Nuclear strategies are not credible without public support; deterrence 'no longer takes place over the heads of the publics involved and ... public consent must be won if nuclear strategies are to be executable and therefore credible anywhere outside the simulations room'.[7]

The evidence that Western publics are becoming dissatisfied with at least the practical manifestations of nuclear deterrence, both extended and simple, seems clear. Bobbitt points to the public pressure on the nuclear freeze, deep cuts in strategic weapons, no-first-use doctrines, and others. We might add the violent reactions to the neutron bomb and the INF deployments in Europe. Recent developments in West Germany forcefully support this argument: despite the absence of large-scale protests, the increasingly resonant public opposition to nuclear weapons has persuaded the government to adopt positions contrary to those of other NATO members.

Just how public opinion might alter nuclear policies is suggested by the results of a series of recent polls on the issue. Most basically, the American public does not support the US pledge to use nuclear weapons first in response to conventional aggression. Over 50 per cent of the public favoured a no-first-use pledge, which only 37 per cent opposed. One poll concluded that 'even when the first use doctrine is carefully explained, Americans *refuse to believe the U.S. government would ever implement the policy*'.[8]

Current US nuclear doctrine is also called into question by the purposes for which Americans would endorse nuclear use. The only clear support for such use backs a response to an all-out Soviet nuclear attack; thus some 60 per cent of Americans believe the only purpose of nuclear weapons is to deter nuclear war. Even in this case, however, while 90 per cent of those polled believed that the United States *would* respond to an all-out Soviet attack with a large-scale nuclear response, only 77 per cent said that it *ought* to. Only 46 per cent of those polled said that the United States ought to use nuclear weapons even if US troops were attacked with nuclear weapons; 40 per cent argue that US planners ought to find other means to respond.

The most telling figures emerge, however, when questions are asked regarding the US extended deterrent pledge. If the USSR invades Western Europe, only 11 per cent of Americans polled would favour the use of nuclear weapons to stop them; 79 per cent argue for a search for other means. Another survey found that Americans oppose by an 11-to-1 margin the use of nuclear weapons to defend Europe.[9]

Other aspects of public opinion have implications for US nuclear weapons policy. Significant majorities favour the modernisation of the US nuclear force. Most Americans have also come to have significant faith in deterrence: over 60 per cent believe it will always work, and even more believe it will work for at least another quarter-century. These opinions will help to undermine protracted war-fighting schemes and extended deterrence and to bolster central deterrence.

Nuclear Winter

Another important barrier to unfettered nuclear planning has been introduced by the advent of detailed theories on the nuclear winter phenomenon.[10] More recent analyses have discounted the apocalyptic conclusions of earlier ones, but it remains indisputable that large-scale nuclear attacks will do severe damage to the environment by raising large clouds of dirt, smoke and other debris and thereby lowering the earth's temperature. How bad the damage will be is unclear, but the certainty of some detrimental impact, and at least some risk of global suicide, are both very real.

As various writers have recognised, the fact of nuclear winter carries several implications. First, it significantly reinforces the basic deterrent to nuclear war. Even if one side were to attack another and disarm it, it *could* do severe damage to itself through the global cooling effect described above. Thus any nuclear strike by its very nature risks suicide, regardless of the size of the retaliation.[11] Attacks against non-urban targets are preferable to attacks against urban targets, moreover, insofar as the former release less debris into the atmosphere than the latter.

Advances in Weapons Technology

Meanwhile, the accuracy and speed of nuclear weapons have been increasing. Circular errors probable (CEPs) of ballistic missile systems have been reduced to dozens of yards, and of cruise missiles to a few yards. Cruise missiles are growing faster, and fast-burn boosters can increase the speed of ballistic missiles as well. Such improvements in accuracy have actually allowed (and encouraged) a decline in the explosive power of nuclear warheads. At the same time, conventional munitions are becoming more powerful, both in pure explosive power and in anti-personnel or anti-tank effect. These facts suggest both that nuclear weapons are becoming more discriminating and that non-nuclear strategic weapons are becoming more useful to fulfill roles previously assigned to nuclear weapons, trends that will be examined in chapters 2 and 8.

The Unfeasibility of Major War

The final trend to be examined here, which will be treated at greater length, is the apparent fact that large-scale warfare has become an anachronism. The massive destructive power of nuclear weapons has finally, it seems, convinced the superpowers that war, as an instrument of national policy used to achieve political ends, is a self-defeating enterprise. Advanced conventional weapons are rapidly approaching low-yield nuclear weapons in destructiveness, moreover, and large-scale conventional war might be impossible to win; forces on both sides would be annihilated. Even medium-intensity wars have proven useless.

Are these perceptions correct? Probably so, but not necessarily only for those reasons. Major war has indeed lost its utility as a political instrument, and this fact will become apparent to more and more nations in the decades ahead. The corollary is that military power is declining (perhaps slowly) as an index of national power and economic and diplomatic savvy will count for much more in the next century. Yet the reason is not just the risk of nuclear escalation or the power of conventional weapons, but a combination of those and the nature of deterrence. And those conclusions do not suggest that war is impossible – only that it is not a rational act. Unintended wars launched by some men and intended wars begun by lunatics or zealots could still occur, and provision must be made to end them if they begin.

THE DISUTILITY OF ARMED FORCE

The notion that military force does not buy as much national power as it used to is far from an original notion. Princeton professor Klaus Knorr, for example, argued in his 1966 book, *On The Uses of Power in the Nuclear Age*, that the use of military force was no longer a profitable instrument of national policy. Using an equation of *value* and *cost*, Knorr contended that war had become less valuable and more costly. On the value side, the premium on territorial conquest had certainly declined, because most states recognised that the development of domestic strength in such forms as education and scientific and technological progress were the keys to national power. 'Military power may be required for the protection of wealthy societies, but the way to national riches is investment in new capital, better education, and technological research and innovation, rather than in armies, navies, and air forces.'[12] (The relevance of this statement to modern Soviet and Chinese reforms, to cite but one example, is obvious.) It might be added that the development of the world economy has rendered conquest unnecessary; states can now acquire by trade those resources and products they would in the past have had to fight for.

Still, there are many uses for military power besides territorial conquest – psychopolitical uses, bullying of lesser powers, and others. Thus Knorr contended that the primary reasons for a decline in the value of military power could be found on the cost side of the equation. Knorr isolated five significant restraints on military power: legitimacy, international opinion, guerrilla wars, the David and Goliath syndrome, and the development of nuclear weapons.[13] The use of military power had lost its legitimacy, Knorr argued, in the community of states. Nations viewed as militarily aggressive were seen in a pejorative light. And, while not holding anything close to a veto power over the behaviour of nations, the international community could certainly punish offenders, through economic sanctions and other means.

The refinement of guerrilla and insurgent tactics had also helped undermine the utility of military force, wrote Knorr. Even powerful nations could not be confident of victory in small wars, because insurgencies were proving nearly impossible to defeat. The US experience in Vietnam and the Soviet experience in Afghanistan substantiate Knorr's argument. Terming this phenomenon the 'David and Goliath' syndrome, Knorr located its cause primarily in the restraints on military power outlined above. More recent evidence would urge qualifications of this rule – Grenada and Panama are two cases in which superpowers were not restrained by the barriers to warfare – but the general rule seems valid.

We might add one point to Knorr's analysis, or actually stress one argument that he makes but does not emphasise: the role of domestic popular opinion in restraining military adventurism. Writing before the US defeat in Vietnam, Knorr can hardly be blamed for placing his emphasis elsewhere. But since 1970, the 'Vietnam syndrome' has arisen to strike down any plans for large-scale US interventions abroad. Indeed, even the Soviet Union appears to have acquired a public relations problem of sorts in Afghanistan. Public opinion acts as a brake on large-scale military adventurism in all states, and democratic ones in particular.

DEVELOPMENT OF WEAPON TECHNOLOGY

The development of weapons technology brought these trends leading to the inutility of military force to their apex. Until recently, weapons were insufficiently powerful to threaten mutual destruction if employed in large numbers. The first weapon that broke such a barrier was the chemical bomb. Writers in the 1920s and 1930s suggested that a new war would wipe out civilisation, largely because of the effects of chemical weapons; H. G. Wells wrote a 1940 screenplay in which one character lamented, 'If we don't end war, war will end us'.[14] Efforts to control these weapons emerged immediately after the war, and there is little evidence that any belligerents in World War II seriously contemplated their use on a large scale. The logic of mutually assured destruction had already come into play.

Nuclear weapons, of course, brought that logic to fruition. The vulnerability of societies guaranteed that any war could result in mutual suicide, a fact that has deterred major conflict between nuclear weapons-holding states for four decades. No one could start a war because no state could ensure it would not be destroyed in that war.

Knorr, following Bernard Brodie and others, recognised the revolutionary implications of nuclear weapons. Their destructive power, the dominance of offensive over defensive systems, the unacceptable uncertainties of nuclear conflict, and the global reach and speed of nuclear weapons combined to render any form of nuclear war infeasible from a military standpoint. These changes, Knorr explained, 'tend to restrict, singly and together, the usability and hence the political utility of national military power in various ways'. As long as mutual vulnerability prevailed, he argued, national interests would never justify resort to nuclear warfare. 'It is hard to think of conflict objectives valuable enough to justify the deliberate initiation of large-scale nuclear war', he wrote. 'The disproportion between the military means and any conceivable foreign policy objective is so vast that such an act would be irrational.'[15] Wars can no longer have political ends that would justify them; if the result is mutual destruction, any political goals would be vitiated.

In fact, some argue that MAD, which has long held at the chemical/biological and nuclear levels, is becoming increasingly relevant to coventional warfare. This is seen to be true for at least two reasons. First, increasingly accurate and powerful conventional munitions will eventually be able to promise mutual societal annihilation. Soviet analysts have recognised this potential for some time; chapter 8 will examine specific Soviet doctrinal writings in this regard. Second, there is the familiar argument that any large conventional war could easily escalate to the nuclear level, and that therefore conventional adventurism is ruled out; Knorr viewed this avenue as a more probable route to nuclear conflict than promised escalation.[16]

ARE NUCLEAR WEAPONS RELEVANT?

Yet some analysts have challenged the notion that nuclear weapons are at all relevant to the decline of war as an institution. One such writer is John Mueller. In *Retreat from Doomsday: The Obsolescence of Major War*, Mueller contends that it is psychological, not military technological, factors that have rendered war infeasible. 'The long peace since World War II', Mueller argues, 'is less a product of recent weaponry than the culmination of a substantial historical process. For the last two or three centuries major war – war among developed countries – has gradually moved toward terminal disrepute because of its perceived repulsiveness and futility'. Nuclear weapons, Mueller concludes, 'have not had an important impact on this remarkable trend'.[17] Rather, Mueller believes that war has been revealed as unworkable because it is filthy, cruel, brutal, and often economically ruinous; the top priority of nations today, he says, is prosperity. Mueller attributes the wars that have happened to fanatics that have bucked this trend: Hitler, the Japanese warrior class, and others.

But Mueller's thesis is fatally flawed, and its shortcomings betray the continuing importance of nuclear deterrence. For Mueller's 'psychic' barriers to war can be overcome; the fear of nuclear devastation cannot. Most important is the fact that Mueller's assertions regarding the opposition to war in civilised societies are unprovable. There are many reasons nations might not have gone to war besides the fact that they find it horrible – that they lack any pressing reason, for example. It is quite simply *impossible* to deny adequately the effects of nuclear weapons on peace since we can never know what the post-war world would have been like without them.

In many ways Mueller's argument has little meaning; war could still happen despite what he says. The manner in which wars start is the critical consideration here: if they can begin despite the fact that everybody recognises their evils, then his thesis is meaningless. And they do indeed, as he himself points out. European powers stumbled into their late nineteenth-century fracases despite the fact that all remembered clearly the effects of the pre-1818 conflicts. The question is, can war still occur?

The answer is, of course, yes, in part because the *reasons* or motives for war, currently absent in the developed world, could recur. Mueller cites Mahan to the effect that nations go to war because of 'ambition, self-respect, resentment of injustice, sympathy with the oppressed', and these motives could again foster conflict. Movies like the Rambo series have taken over from books the task of glorifying their war spirit. Fanatical individuals could come to power; miscalculations in crises could spark war; a shift in values could again subordinate killing to other goals. Edward Luttwak has remarked that it is exactly when war is viewed as absurd that it becomes likely, because people will stop taking its risk seriously.

Yet Mueller admits all this in a remarkable section in which he essentially suggests that all the factors leading to the *de facto* outlawing of war could change.[18] 'Genocide has happened several times since Hitler: another Hitler-style war is not impossible', he concedes. Nor, the same logic suggests, is another Sarajevo-style war, or a Pearl Harbor-style war, or a Fort Sumter-style war. Wars can still happen, it seems.

Mueller's next step is an odd argument: war, he contends, has become more than rationally unthinkable – it has become 'subrationally unthinkable'. 'An idea becomes impossible not when it becomes reprehensible or has been renounced', he writes, 'but when it fails to percolate into one's consciousness as a conceivable option'. That is, war becomes impossible because it never occurs to anybody any more. Mueller uses an example of a person on the fifth floor of a building deciding whether to get down by the stairs or a quick leap from the window: jumping from the window, he suggests, would never occur to the person.

Yet if the conditions working to make war rationally unthinkable change, so would those making it subrationally unthinkable. If an economic crisis gripped China, for example, throwing the country into chaos and threatening the regime, it is easy to see how the government might feel a need to invade Vietnam (again) or South Korea (again) or take some other act. War will always exist as an option; nobody will 'forget' it.

Most important, Mueller's example betrays both the flaw in his logic and the main argument here. For jumping out the window and going to war are not necessary analagous: a nation going to war must assume that it will at least survive the war and at best win, whereas a leap from the window guarantees death. On the other hand, modern war has indeed become suicidal, which makes Mueller's example more telling, but only because of the advent of nuclear weapons, whose effects he denies. (Indeed a common refrain about nuclear weapons is that they have, in Herman Kahn's phrase, made war 'unthinkable', and a common critique of counterforce systems is that they make war once again 'thinkable'.)

If Mueller is wrong, why has war declined as a foreign policy instrument? Actually he is not entirely incorrect; after all, it is one of the central themes of this study that major war has indeed become an anachronism. Much of what he says is true: war has indeed acquired a bad name in the modern era, both because it is brutal and because it often does not work. Other reasons outlined by Klaus Knorr above, including domestic and international public opinion, work to achieve the same effect. As Mueller recognises, deterring a country from going to war is a very complex proposition and often involves far more than pure military preparations by its adversaries. Preparing for war to prevent war is sometimes a necessary but seldom a sufficient condition for peace. War has also become less popular because there has been less need for it. The incentives for war, as Knorr recognised, have declined as the costs have risen.

Where Mueller goes wrong, however, is in denying that war has remained unpopular in the post-1945 era primarily, though not completely, due to the existence of nuclear weapons. Mueller even argues that conventional war probably will not escalate to nuclear war, and limited nuclear wars need not escalate to total Armageddon; therefore the fear of escalation should not have deterred conflict. [19]

In fact, nuclear weapons have been quite indispensable to the maintenance of peace in the post-war era. This was recognised by early analysts such as Bernard Brodie, and it remains true. As Robert Jervis puts it, 'Nuclear weapons have led to the replacement of brute force by coercion, or, as it is more frequently put, of defense by deterrence'. The absence of war after 1945 and other aspects of peace, Jervis concludes, 'all flow logically from the nuclear revolution'. [20]

For Mueller, though, the implication of his arguments is that, because the mere risk of general war (not nuclear war) is bad enough, there is no real need for nuclear deterrence; at least, deterrence based on current ideas of stability, which call for a reliable second-strike capability. He seems to suggest that a minimum deterrent, or something of the sort, would preserve the peace, though the idea is not very well defined. He refers to critiques of nuclear deterrence by writers such as Jervis, who suggest it might not be necessary because other factors deter war; and he suggests that a *policy* of deterrence can never be proved to have worked because one can never know if a nation would truly have gone to war without it.

These are incorrect and dangerous ideas. Nuclear deterrence remains the centrepiece of the post-war order. As suggested above, nuclear weapons have been critical to the evolution of thinking on the infeasibility of war; but if that situation is to remain, nuclear weapons must be deployed and operated in such a manner as to keep the notion alive that they could never be used successfully as instruments of warfare. How this might be achieved, through the notion of stability, will be defined and discussed directly in the next two chapters and, to a degree, in the rest of the volume.

A secure nuclear deterrent in the form of stable mutual retaliatory capabilities therefore remains essential to peace. This is true for several reasons. First, to the degree that one side or another obtains what it perceives to be a militarily useful advantage at the nuclear level, war becomes more possible; nuclear weapons could again fall into the realm of usable or 'thinkable' weapons.

Mueller also critically fails to recognise the nature of the nuclear balance. It is in many ways a unique military situation: each side has the potential to destroy, through nuclear attack, the other side's nuclear and conventional forces within hours. Mueller points out that this is the nature of nuclear weapons but does not draw the proper implication. That is that in a crisis, a country with vulnerable nuclear forces exists under the threat of imminent disarmament and/or destruction. The incentives to go to war have suddenly and danger-ously shifted: no longer is it always a slow, deliberative decision over many weeks or months (although it could be that way); now decisions must be made in a matter of hours or minutes. In a severe crisis, the stronger side might be tempted to strike first, the vulnerable side to strike first before it is attacked; and knowing the latter incentive, the stronger side might feel required to pre-empt an attack by the weaker. In short, nuclear weapons massively increase the pressures to go to war in a crisis to avoid imminent destruction in a manner unique in the history of warfare. The only way to guard against this is with a stable balance that is minimally susceptible to crisis pressures.

In their analysis of the START treaty, RAND analysts Edward Warner and David Ochmanek recognise this fact. 'States do not always begin wars', they write, 'in order to achieve objectives whose value is judged at the outset to exceed the expected costs of the war'; rather, 'states may attack one another because their leaders believe they have no alternatives that are more attractive (or, more to the point, less unattractive) than going to war'.[21] Robert Jervis once again says it well: difficulties in outlining an 'advantage' to nuclear superiority, he notes, reflect

> the difficulty in conjuring up a sufficient cause to start the conflict. To focus on what political objective might warrant unprecedented Soviet aggression leads to the realization that desperation, rather than hope, is the likeliest cause of a nuclear war. Russia is more likely to be pushed into striking by the fear of what will happen if she does not than pulled by the attraction of positive gains.

Or in other words, 'To erode the other's power too much may produce short-run gains, but it may also push the other closer to war'.[22] Crisis instability can create exactly those motives.

Nuclear deterrence, it seems, is an inadequate but extremely necessary condition of peace. A stable nuclear balance is required to maintain the relative stability and caution so characteristic of the post-war order.

IMPLICATIONS OF THE START ACCORD

The rest of this volume attempts to outline the way a stable balance can, and potentially will, be constructed in the context of a START treaty. The central argument is that the treaty would complement the general evolution outlined above toward the infeasibility of war. A myriad of possibilities suggest themselves, some stabilising and some not. But overhanging the detailed analysis to follow is one overwhelming fact: the START treaty heralds a new, possibly final, stage in the nuclear competition, a stage in which the military utility of nuclear weapons has been firmly rejected and in which both sides recognise the basic stability of a continuation of mutual vulnerability at much lower levels of weapons. In short, START signifies an acknowledgement by the superpowers that deterrence is a fact and that nuclear weapons have inaugurated a revolution in military affairs (as the Soviets call it).

This conclusion carries several implications of its own. Most important, it will become essentially impossible to contemplate a successful nuclear war. The notion that a limited nuclear war could be fought, and perhaps even won, was always suspect, and it has become increasingly apparent that the same assured destruction rationale applying to general war applies to limited wars as well. As chapter 4 will explain, moreover, counterforce strikes at an opponent's nuclear assets are becoming less and less feasible.

As noted earlier, this volume contemplates the establishment of a nuclear strategy along countervailing lines. Co-operative reciprocal deterrence has no clear implications for conventional war. Some analysts contend that the same risk of escalation to societal destruction which deters nuclear war deters large-scale conventional war as well. Others contend that strategic stalemate and mutual self-deterrence – unwillingness to use nuclear weapons because of the risk of escalation – makes conventional war more likely by erecting a firm barrier between nuclear and conventional war.

This is not to say, however, that nuclear or conventional war could not occur. As suggested above, wars perhaps occur most often for reasons that were not foreseen. There is no reason to expect conflict in the nuclear age to be any different, except insofar as the danger of nuclear escalation reduces risk-taking. Accidental or unintended nuclear war may be extremely unlikely, but the risks involved demand a consideration of policies, including limited nuclear operations and war termination strategies, to deal with that eventuality.

In the past, severe risks may have resided in such attempts. The evolution of American strategic doctrine is a testament to the fact that recourse to limited nuclear options may well lead to the belief that nuclear weapons are usable to achieve political ends, and thus to the acquisition of a counterforce, war-fighting, damage limiting doctrine – the notion that a country can fight and win a nuclear war while partly limiting damage to itself in the process – that heightens tension and threatens to undermine crisis stability. Yet under START a similar risk could be avoided. If complemented by mutual force modernisation, START ceilings would rob both sides of a counterforce capability sufficient for a first strike as well as the right to pursue such a capability. It would also institutionalise the mutual vulnerability that lies at the heart of deterrence. Under START, therefore, each superpower could enunciate very restricted potential responses to a limited nuclear attack, thereby building a credible bridge between peace and all-out war to help deter limited attacks.

As a result of all of this, US nuclear doctrine and force structure must be reassessed. The acquisition of a counterforce strategy and arsenal, long viewed by many as unnecessary and unwise, will finally be practically impossible, rendering the debate moot. The challenge for the United States will be to assume a posture more similar to assured destruction while retaining some flexibility, form a coercive strategy to effect war termination if hostilities begin, and acquire a highly survivable deterrent. How that might be done will be spelled out in the following chapters. It must be emphasised at the outset, however, that modernisation of the US deterrent (including its command, control communications and intelligence (C3I) aspects) will be critical to deterrence. As chapter 3 will suggest, a START treaty pursued without accompanying modernisation might be detrimental to US security.

2 The Requirements of Deterrence

As hinted at in chapter 1, the future strategic environment will be extraordinarily complex. One basic fact seems apparent, however: the world has arrived at a point where major war remains an infeasible and irrational policy option. Rather than war being a continuation of politics by other means, politics and economics have become surrogates for war, at least between major powers. The key question to be addressed by this book is how nuclear deterrence, a critical linchpin of the trend making war infeasible, will evolve in that context.

The nuclear stalemate could be resolved in a number of ways.[1] Potential nuclear futures range from war to a technical fix to world government to a simple continuation of deterrence success. It is the contention of this volume that the last outcome is the most probable: deterrence will not be superseded and will continue to work. And more than that, the superpowers and other nuclear powers may move away from *competitive* deterrence to *co-operative* deterrence, in which the goal is clearly preservation of the peace. As noted, that co-operation would be both explicit, in the form of arms treaties, and tacit, in the form of deploying systems that deprive each side of counterforce capabilities, avoiding deployment of destabilising new counterforce weapons.

Such a resolution of the deterrence debate is also critical given the increasing relevance of public opinion noted in the previous chapter. As Johan Jorgen Holst has argued, societies generally support an extended military effort 'only when it is associated with an alternative vision of a more cooperative arrangement than an open-ended military competition'.[2] As we shall see, the START treaty provides the basic framework on which can be built a perpetually stable deterrent relationship that continues to rule out major war of any sort as a rational policy option. And, as chapter 9 will suggest, the process of 'nuclear learning' will contribute toward that end.

Yet deterrence is not a simple process. Faith in the security of central deterrence has always suffered from the flaws outlined by proponents of limited nuclear options. If the use of chemical or nuclear weapons is indeed so hideous, then conventional wars could be fought without recourse to them; nations will be deterred from using such weapons of mass destruction. And therefore, threats to use nuclear weapons to deter, say, conventional attacks are not credible, and limited nuclear options are possible. By precluding general war, the destructiveness of nuclear weapons seems to open the door to limited conflicts.

The factors deterring the use of chemicals during World War II, for example, are complex. But the point is that the threat of the effects of their use was sufficient in whatever form to deter resort to them, and was sufficiently distinct from conventional munitions to decouple the two weapons. The risk of escalation to chemical weapons did not deter a conventional war, and so it could be with nuclear weapons. The clean logic of the uselessness of military force seems to be disrupted by the potential for limited conflicts, both conventional and nuclear. War, after all, may not be obsolete, and arguments such as these account for the evolution of limited options in US strategy.

THE PARADOX OF DETERRENCE

Trying to solve both problems – deterring both general and limited wars – has proven difficult, for it runs afoul of what could accurately be termed the 'paradox of deterrence'. Deterrence contains many dilemmas and paradoxes, of course; but for the purposes of this volume one will be referred to as 'the' paradox, akin to what Glenn Snyder calls the 'stability-instability paradox'.[3] It involves the relationship between pre-war deterrence and intrawar deterrence (deterrence within wars, as for example of nuclear first-use during a conventional war). Simply put, *those systems and doctrines best at deterring an opponent from initiating hostilities guarantee escalation once a war has begun, and those which help control or terminate wars already underway appear to increase the risk that war will break out in the first place.* In an era in which the destructiveness of large-scale conflict best deters its outbreak, anything that helps establish limits on the bounds and damage of a war makes it more likely; by guarding against the possibility of nuclear war, we increase its likelihood. And this appears to render impossible the simultaneous achievement of the three official goals of US nuclear policy – deterring, controlling and terminating a nuclear war.

For example, missile defences, civil defence, counterforce weapons, tight control of nuclear weapons, and especially limited war doctrines all have the potential to limit the destructiveness of war. Yet those same doctrines and systems, precisely because they offer either or both sides the potential to fight a nuclear war without committing suicide, are provocative and degrade crisis stability, increasing the incentive to strike first in a period of high tensions. On the other hand, the nuclear systems and doctrines most likely to frighten an opponent into terminal caution (massive and inaccurate city-busting warheads, launch-on-warning policies, weakly controlled nuclear systems, spasm launches) are those that will ensure that any war will end in the destruction of the globe.

Richard Betts has recognised this phenomenon with regard to NATO's deterrent. There are 'inconsistencies in NATO doctrine', he explains, 'between what is best for deterrence and best to do if deterrence nevertheless fails. As long as nuclear war is unthinkable, what is right for deterrence is wrong for defense, and what is wrong for war is right for peace'.[4] Elsewhere Betts has written that 'A great paradox of the nuclear revolution is that such weapons reinforce peace most when their capability for destruction is greatest. The more awesome the consequences, the less risk there may be'.[5]

Many other analysts have described the same phenomenon. One writes that 'It cannot be emphasized forcibly enough that to prepare to fight and win a nuclear war ... in case deterrence should fail is a self-fulfilling prophecy, because it erodes the distinction between deterrence and defense strategies'.[6] Michael MccGwire has commented similarly on the 'contradictory assumptions' of deterrence: 'that it is the possession of nuclear weapons and the demonstrated ability and will to use them that matter; but that these weapons will nonetheless never be used'.[7] John Mueller writes that 'In an effort to enhance crisis stability a country may try to improve its second-strike capability by building up its military forces', but that country's opponent may find the strategy provocative, 'concluding that the buildup is actually a prelude to an attack'.[8]

Scott D. Sagan has discussed what he terms the 'usability paradox', which introduces the element of accidental war into the paradox of deterrence. The two key objectives of US nuclear policy – 'to deter aggression against the United States and its allies and to prevent accidental war' – require that 'US nuclear forces be usable, but not too usable'. To deter, weapons must be usable enough to 'convince the Soviet Union that a potent U.S. nuclear response would actually be forthcoming' in the event of a Soviet attack. But to prevent accidental nuclear war, US weapons must be relatively tightly held. A conflict exists, therefore, not only between general deterrence and deterrence of *limited* wars, but between general deterrence and deterrence of *accidental* wars.[9]

This paradox of deterrence is both the product of mutually assured destruction and its guardian. It is unique to the nuclear era precisely because peace has become more a 'child of terror' than of war-fighting preparedness; developments that undercut the absolute vulnerability of both sides' societies are in fact threats to stability, the inverse of the pre-nuclear era relationship between security and peace. These unhappy but clear facts have also obstructed the development of a reasonable alternative to assured destruction. The latest case in which the paradox awoke to strike down a challenger to assured destruction was in the debate over SDI.

The paradox is related to another commonly discussed dilemma of the nuclear age. A deterrent threat using nuclear weapons is inherently incredible, some suggest, because once one side had launched a nuclear attack, the other might find little reason to respond. If a purely deterrent threat fails, and if the same threat is no good for defence or war-fighting, then the threat itself is by nature incredible.[10] As physicist Carl Friedrich von Weizsaecker phrased it in 1957, 'The bombs fulfill their purpose only if they never fall. But if everyone knows that they will never fall, they do not fulfill their purpose'.[11] This dilemma is merely the other side of the coin of our paradox: it is in attempting to acquire forces able to convince an enemy that one *would* fulfill an incredible threat (this dilemma) that one risks destablising the balance (the paradox).

An important distinction must be made here. There is a difference between trying to deter *conventional* conflict with nuclear weapons and trying to deter *limited nuclear* warfare. Extended deterrence speaks primarily (but not solely, as we will see below) to the former requirement, the attempt to deter a Soviet invasion of Europe, for example, by threatening intended or unintended escalation to strategic nuclear war. The paradox of deterrence complicates the latter goal, recognising that forces and doctrines that help limit a war are those that might make war more likely. And the paradox is especially troubling insofar as it seems to rule out a 'happy ending' to deterrence.

REQUIREMENTS OF PRE-WAR NUCLEAR DETERRENCE

It is one of the key contentions of this volume, however, that developments in the strategic environment will make possible a stable, co-operative deterrent conclusion to the arms competition. At this point, we are left with two tasks related to the deterrence of nuclear conflict – to deter war and to control and terminate a war if one begins – and a dilemma that seems to render impossible the near-perfect achievement of both simultaneously. What doctrines or forces would help us escape from the paradox?

At the extremes, there are two schools of thought on the issue of deterrence. On one side are those analysts who contend, as Lawrence Freedman phrases their argument, that 'nuclear weapons have no other role but to deter the use of those of the adversary'.[12] One implication is that extensive targeting and warfighting plans are unnecessary because the risks inherent in a nuclear war, and the fear of losing one, deter resort to it.[13] The result is a minimalist deterrent strategy relying on deterrence by punishment. Another implication, as Freedman explains, is that 'the United States can no longer with credibility promise its allies that it will initiate nuclear war on their behalf – even if they face a potentially mortal conventional attack', since the stakes of a nuclear war outweigh those of a conventional defeat.[14] Writers subscribing to approximations of these ideas include McGeorge Bundy, Morton Halperin, Robert Jervis and Robert McNamara.[15]

Opposed to proponents of minimal deterrence and its variants are those who believe, as Freedman notes, that 'the quality of deterrence is a function of the quality of nuclear war plans'.[16] Nuclear weapons do have utility, political as well as military, such analysts contend; many of them argue for deterrence by denial of enemy war aims, since traditional notions of victory and defeat retain relevance in nuclear conflict. The usability of nuclear weapons allows the United States to threaten nuclear strikes to protect its allies. In extended nuclear exchanges, targeting policy becomes very important, and strategic defence might be advisable. Writers ascribing to such views include Colin Gray, Paul Nitze, Keith Payne and Fred Iklé.[17]

This study examines a hybrid of the two. Its purpose is both descriptive and prescriptive, to outline the essentials of what US strategic force structure (and the nature of deterrence itself) will probably be under START, and to argue for certain modifications to ensure that a very promising future is managed well.

In essence, deterrence will evolve in the 1990s in response to two fundamental facts, which the START treaty helps to uncover. First, the deployment of increasingly survivable nuclear forces on both sides and the establishment of limitations on warheads will put the final nails in the coffin of force vulnerability problems and strategic nuclear war-fighting schemes such as those embodied in the current countervailing strategy. Second, the United States and the NATO alliance will come to terms with the notion that the intentional employment of American nuclear weapons in response to conventional aggression is an inadequate, if not totally bankrupt, deterrent. Yet, as we shall see, this is not to say that nuclear weapons could never be used, only that the circumstances for such use are extremely unlikely.

The co-operative reciprocal deterrent advanced here is a heavily modified version of the present US countervailing strategy, tempered with large doses of assured destruction. Its essential strength resides in the fact that both societies remain vulnerable to a devastating retaliation, a retaliation that will be aimed, not at cities or other value targets, but at military ones. The collateral effects of such an attack, especially given some necessary targeting of military-industrial complexes, will be such that a society hit with such a blow would be irreparably damaged. The threat of retaliation from secure forces has been the basis of deterrence for 40 years and will continue to be so, and the simple fact that no national interest save the pre-emption of an imminent nuclear strike would ever recommend the initiation of nuclear war will continue to deter one.

As noted in chapter 1, countervailing strategies are not necessarily war-fighting strategies, and do not necessarily presume that the United States must threaten the Soviets with defeat in order to deter them. A more modest countervailing deterrent is contemplated here: the threat to employ nuclear weapons in response to any form of nuclear use by an opponent, with the goals of deterring their use before war and during war and of terminating their use if it begins. Philip Bobbitt has summarised the general parameters of the countervailing strategy, which mirror the basics of that suggested here.

> The countervailing nuclear strategy ... promises to impose costs on any Soviet aggression such that no political objective of that aggression could, by any calculation, be worthy of further pursuit. Thus it does not depend on superiority or even absolute equivalence ... It imposes mounting costs, always leaving the adversary the option of withdrawal to a point which is more favourable to it than continued conflict. [18]

Richard Betts similarly defines the countervailing strategy as 'a flexible range of selective force employment options', including 'an increased capacity to destroy military forces and command centers, to match or counter a number of conceivable Soviet attack plans', to deny Soviet objectives in such plans, 'and to retain substantial forces in reserve'.[19]

Probably the most thorough explication of the countervailing strategy can be found in Harold Brown's FY 1981 *Report to Congress*.[20] 'For deterrence to operate successfully,' Brown argues,

> our potential adversaries must be convinced that we possess sufficient military force so that if they were to start a course of action which could lead to war, they would be frustrated in their effort to achieve their objective or suffer so much damage that they would gain nothing by their action. Put differently, we must have forces and plans for the use of our strategic nuclear forces such that in considering aggression against our interests, our adversary would recognize that no plausible outcome would represent a success – on any rational definition of success.

That describes very well the strategy advocated here. It is important to note Brown's reference to *either* directly defeating aggression and denying war aims *or* inflicting damage sufficient to deter aggression; he thus admits that a pure deterrence-by-denial capability is unnecessary.

Like this volume, Brown accepts the uncontroversial point that a 'survivable and enduring retaliatory capability' is the central require-ment of deterrence. Brown also explains, in a manner to which this analysis is very sympathetic, that countervailing strategies are merely slightly more ambitious forms of assured destruction. That doctrine, he notes, 'is the bedrock of nuclear deterrence' and will in many respects remain so. But it is not sufficient 'in itself as a strategic doctrine. Under many circumstances large-scale countervalue attacks may not be appropriate – nor will their prospect always be sufficiently credible – to deter war.

Problems with existing US nuclear strategy arise when one begins to consider just what sort of attacks one would contemplate to enforce the countervailing strategy. It is possible to interpret its requirements so broadly (and Secretary Brown perhaps opened the door to such interpretations with his injunction to deter Soviet attacks 'over the broadest possible range of scenarios') that one begins to acquire the sorts of war-fighting forces and doctrines dangerous to peace. That, unfortunately, was the fashion in which the Reagan administration interpreted US policy, which seems still to be edging closer to notions of war-fighting than countervailing deterrence. In many respects, then, co-operative reciprocal deterrence mirrors neither assured destruction nor war-fighting, but could include greater or lesser elements of both depending upon the emphasis in US strategy. Today that emphasis is too heavily skewed in a war-fighting direction.

In particular, the US countervailing strategy now emphasises two notions that should be abandoned. One is the idea of a protracted war. In order to deter the Soviets from considering an extended nuclear conflict, some suggest, the United States must possess the capability to engage in one itself. This is true in an extremely limited sense; as we will see, the United States ought to possess the force structure and C3I capable of engaging in very modest limited nuclear operations. More generally, however, protracted nuclear war is impossible (due to C3I limitations), unnecessary to deter war (as we will see below), and fruitless (since the Soviets seem to follow a massive retaliation-like policy for general nuclear war, rendering US plans for graduated combat meaningless).

The other aspect of countervailing deterrence that will and must be surrendered is its contemplation of extended deterrence tasks for US nuclear weapons. As chapter 5 explains, the US pledge to respond to Soviet conventional adventurism with nuclear weapons is being undermined by various developments, especially arms control. Extended deterrence is in the process of a slow death, and its passing will relieve US nuclear forces of the burden of threatening the incredible.

EXISTENTIAL DETERRENCE

Yet many would deny the need for detailed war plans. Indeed the notion that nuclear weapons, by their nature, deter any thought of their own use is not a new one. Just weeks after Hiroshima, Bernard Brodie wrote that, while military men had previously attempted to win wars, henceforth their sole purpose would be to deter them. Lawrence Freedman has described this notion of existential deterrence:

the idea of *existential deterrence* as developed by McGeorge Bundy is proving to be extremely attractive: 'As long as each side has thermonuclear weapons that *could* be used against the opponent, even after the strongest possible preemptive attack, existential deterrence is strong and it rests on uncertainty about what could happen.' What is attractive is the suggestion that the deterrent effect is almost wholly impervious to the location and capabilities of nuclear weapons and the doctrines that would notionally govern their use. All that is required is the availability of some nuclear weapons that *could* be used in anger.

Under such a strategy, he explains, 'Forces are to be judged by essentially negative criteria: they should not be vulnerable, provocative, disruptive of arms control, or prone to accidental detonation'. So long as those requirements are met, minimum deterrers would not care much about what sort of forces and doctrines are established.[21]

Deterring an opponent from initiating the use of nuclear weapons under normal circumstances does appear rather simple. This is true for at least two reasons. First, as noted above, superpower national interests would never call for such a step. The stakes involved in a nuclear exchange are absolute national survival, and the superpowers do not possess conflicting interests even approaching that level. Even if it is assumed, for example, that the Soviets desire the subjugation of the United States, it would be irrational for them to initiate nuclear war to achieve that end because that interest is outweighed by national survival. If war is indeed a political act, its consequences must not be so severe as to outweigh any possible political gain; yet that is exactly the case with nuclear conflict.[22]

This fact suggests an initial requirement for generic deterrence: preserving the survivability of both sides' retaliatory deterrents. McGeorge Bundy, for example, notes that only a loss of survivability would undermine existential deterrence.[23] Only the prospect that one's own forces are vulnerable and/or that one's retaliation could be defeated (by either a pre-emptive strike or defensive measures) carries implications for national security serious enough to warrant consideration of the initiation of nuclear war. So long as one can always pledge a devastating response, one can be reasonably certain that an opponent does not possess any interests or motives sufficient to inspire him to strike. This perception must, moreover, be robust enough to withstand the pressures of crises.

Countervailing assured destruction obtains much of its robustness from the imputed fact that existing arsenals guarantee a retaliation sufficient to deny an aggressor *any plausible definition of victory*. On the one hand, this is true because of the risk of assured destruction, the strong possibility that the initiation of nuclear war will lead to the absolute destruction of both sides; this is deterrence by punishment. Deterrence by denial, however, suggests that threatening destruction of society in retaliation might not be credible; the latter theory aims to deter by *denying victory* rather than *promising annihilation*.

DETERRENCE BY DENIAL?

Some analysts therefore contend that the United States must deploy a nuclear arsenal capable of threatening, not merely retaliation and punishment for an attacker, but the *denial of victory aims*. What exactly such aims would be in a nuclear war is not entirely clear, although chapter 4 will hazard a few guesses. Nevertheless, the rule is clear: the Soviets will not be deterred by an assured destruction threat, it is argued, because they believe they have forces capable of prevailing in a nuclear war; they must be threatened with *defeat* rather than *destruction*.

The point of such arguments is not that destroying a nation would not defeat it. The point is that in peacetime threats merely to annihilate another nation in retaliation for an attack, rather than destroying its military forces, might not be credible. Some argue that this is true because an attacker could hit a defender's military forces and then hold the defender's cities hostage, preventing a retaliation. If all the defender can do is retaliate against the attacker's society, he may be prohibited from doing so because such an attack would call down the attacker's second strike against his cities. But if the defender has a survivable counterforce capability, it is argued, he can hit back and continue to hold the attacker's cities and other value targets hostage as well. (Co-operative reciprocal deterrence would provide means of doing that without obtaining a full counterforce capability, as we shall see.)

Yet acquiring forces able to threaten the ability to win a war (such as counterforce weapons, secure C3, and strategic defences) can be dangerous. Such a policy violates the golden rule of stability: promise an opponent his retaliation and rest secure that he has no national interests sufficient to force you to utilise yours. Crisis stability thus suffers, because in periods of heightened tensions both sides fear that if they do not launch their vulnerable deterrents first they will never have an opportunity to launch them at all. We uncover here a variant of the paradox of deterrence – attempting to acquire forces able to 'win' a nuclear war increases the risk that they will have to be used.

Nor is deterrence by denial *necessary* for deterrence. Initially, highly survivable nuclear forces can render the issue moot by undermining the perception of either side that a first strike would be cost-effective. For example, if one side deployed a thousand single-warhead mobile missiles only vulnerable to a barrage attack of 10 000 warheads and neither side possessed that many, fears that the other side will have thoughts of victory are obviated. This will be roughly the situation under START, as chapter 3 will explain.

Theoretically, too, on closer inspection the requirements of deterrence by denial are already met. Initially it must be recognised that, in the nuclear age, denying 'victory' in a general nuclear war is not at all difficult. Any retaliation that flattens the attacker's society, as any significant retaliation will do, denies victory by any plausible definition. Even if the aggressor retains a few dozen weapons after all the exchanges are done, even if battered remnants of his conventional forces regroup for an offensive, even if he (the leader) is still alive, his country would have been flattened and his people annihilated. As Richard Betts suggests, 'no national interest can be served if conventional war were to lead to a large-scale nuclear war that killed half or more of the country's population'.[24] In the nuclear era, deterrence by punishment and deterrence by denial have blended together into a single seamless web of retaliatory destruction.[25]

Even in a purely military sense, the notion that finely-tuned military doctrines and balances would survive a nuclear conflict even as societies were destroyed seems clearly incorrect. Conventional forces, military bases and ports, military-industrial assets, transportation hubs, and other non-nuclear targets would not be immune in war, and chapter 4 will suggest that they should be in the primary targets of a US retaliation.

In the future, moreover, it will become increasingly difficult to target an opponent's nuclear forces in any case. As chapters 3 and 4 will explain, the deployment of mobile, easily hidden ICBMs, incredibly quiet missile-carrying submarines, increasingly stealthy aircraft, and secure warning and command and control systems will make it impossible for either side to contemplate a truly effective first strike. The potential for counterforce attacks ought therefore to continue to dwindle in the years ahead.

Finally, let us take the discussion out of the abstract for a moment and refer to the specific country the United States is intent on deterring: the Soviet Union. It is said that the Soviets ascribe to deterrence by denial, and that as long as they do we must also, because threats of deterrence by punishment will not be believed. The Soviets, however, view their own acquisition of denial capabilities as merely the optimum means to deterrence: the *best* way to deter an opponent is to demonstrate an ability, not merely to punish an aggressor, but also to win the war. For them, the acquisition of a denial capability was merely a logical extension of the desire to avoid a war, though they admit that deterrence by punishment can work. The Soviets, therefore, have always recognised that the two kinds of deterrence, while distinct, overlapped in the nuclear age; merely because they tend toward one side of the equation does not suggest that they do not believe the whole. Their more recent acquisition of mobile missiles and better SSBNs also reveals a recognition of the value of survivable forces.[26] Chapter 6 will examine these ideas in more detail.

THE QUALITY OF DETERRENCE

The key, therefore, to denying victory is not the deployment of counterforce capabilities, but merely a guarantee of a retaliation. Here we run up against two problems, however: what the retaliation should be targeted against, and how it could be ensured. It is in these tasks, in fact, that we begin to see the requirement for a high-quality deterrent. Until now the argument of this chapter has largely paralleled that of the minimum deterrence school: that existential deterrence, residing in the overwhelming destructive power of nuclear weapons, serves adequately to deter war on a day-to-day basis, and that it is impossible to perform grand strategic-level war-fighting with nuclear weapons. Deterrence by denial is therefore unnecessary. We will now take a step toward the deterrence-by-denial analysis camp to point out that circumstances could arise in which credible plans for the use of nuclear weapons would be required, either to deter their first use or to terminate their use at a very low level.

Indeed, there is some contradiction in the arguments of the minimum deterrence school. Some chance certainly exists that tensions could rise to the point, during a crisis or a conventional war, that some major power contemplates the use of nuclear weapons. Minimum deterrence proponents contend that the horrible nature of the weapons would prevent resort to them, but even they must admit some tiny chance that it would not. Given this tiny chance, and given the horrible consequences rightly emphasised by such writers, are we not duty-bound to find credible ways to threaten actual nuclear use, if these would contribute to deterrence in a more tense period? Traditionally, the problem with such efforts is that they run afoul of the paradox of deterrence and increase the risk of war. As will be explained below, however, the nuclear balance and nuclear doctrines are evolving to the point where flexible options can be pursued without endangering peace.

But there are other failings with a minimum deterrent besides the fact that it is unnecessary to preserve crisis stability. Foregoing a large retaliatory force, for example, risks undermining the very heart of deterrence. Presumably, existential deterrence is at least in part a function of the number of nuclear weapons that would actually go off if something went wrong. If each side only possessed 500 bombs, existential deterrence would suffer significantly, especially given that each side might be confident of knocking out 300 or so in a first strike and another 100 or more with strategic defences.

A minimal deterrent strategy also ignores much of Soviet military doctrine. As noted above, there is no need for a deterrence by denial strategy, and chapter 6 will argue that the threat posed by Soviet doctrine, which aims only to deter war, has been overblown. But still, we must assume (and, incidentally, a sympathetic view of Soviet intentions requires us to assume) that a nuclear war would come about, not in a bolt-from-the-blue assault, but only as the product of incredible tensions. In such a situation, traditional Soviet emphasis on war-fighting capabilities might indeed increase their proclivity to contemplate a first strike. Even the Soviets would under almost no circumstances prefer nuclear war to any alternative, but the qualifier in that statement admits of some cases (one to be discussed below) where strategic nuclear use might seem necessary. In such a situation the West will need far more than a minimum deterrent to keep the nuclear peace.

Nor is a minimal deterrent fully credible. If only a few dozen retaliatory blows are guaranteed, they must be directed at value targets to have any coercive effect. But this falls prey to the other dilemma of deterrence, which holds that a purely deterrent threat with no military value is incredible because, once it had failed to deter, there would be no purpose in invoking it. It seems irresponsible to rest peace on the fragile notion of a more minimal deterrent retaliatory strike from the presumed anger of a defender. Lawrence Freedman has pointed out that if a first-strike is not credible, neither is a purely punishment-oriented retaliatory blow: 'If one side actually launches a strike   then the same problem of disutility applies to the victim's decision on whether to launch the retaliatory strike', unless the adversary has no reserve. If the attacker can promise a second strike to follow a defender's retaliation, there may be little point in retaliating. 'As a result, second use appears less likely and first use becomes more rational. If each successive nuclear volley equally lacks utility (until one side is physically incapable of response), then there is no logical motor to the process of escalation.'[27] The way to get around this, of course, is to invest a retaliation with some purpose – which requires credible war plans.[28]

But what conditions might arise under which nuclear use would be credible? This analysis is not meant to provide an exhaustive answer, but two scenarios come immediately to mind. The first is threatening nuclear options to deter Soviet first use against NATO. Extended deterrence is a two-fold problem – deterring Soviet conventional *and* nuclear aggression against NATO. The former requirement can be satisfied by conventional parity and some risk of nuclear escalation, but the latter must be deterred by credible nuclear options. (Chapter 5 suggests just such a limited role for US extended deterrence pledges.) If the Soviets began plunking bombs on NATO's main ports and POMCUS sites, for example, what would an America with a 500-warhead minimum deterrent do?[29]

Another scenario is this: as an East-West conventional war progressed, a desperate Soviet Union confronted with rebellious nationalities and mutinous allies might begin losing ground to NATO. If the United States' Pacific forces and allies joined the fray, the Soviet leadership would be faced with the very real prospect of defeat. In this circumstance, Soviet strategic nuclear use seems at least possible and perhaps even likely, unless the United States possesses credible forces and doctrines that convince the Soviets they can gain nothing from such an attack.

Advocates of minimum deterrence would undoubtedly object that, even in dire conditions, rational leaders would not resort to nuclear weapons use. But we cannot count on this. Under normal circumstances, even the prospect of a few dozen nuclear warheads falling on one's soil would discourage a first strike. But if the Soviet Union were about to lose a conventional war, for example, it might consider its nuclear options more closely. It is after all the deterrence of nuclear use in such circumstances, and not on a day-to-day basis, that must be our key task; if we arrive in a crisis to find ourselves with forces and doctrines suited to the commonplace but inadequate for higher tensions, it will be too late. Establishing more robust deterrent forces and doctrines would not have as its goal the acquisition of a nuclear war-fighting capability, which is unnecessary. What it would do is maximise the deterrent value inherent in nuclear weapons by convincing even the most desperate leader that there are always better alternatives to nuclear use, including, in some cases, surrender.

Other potential, if unlikely, scenarios for nuclear use at levels below the strategic will be examined below and in later chapters. The point is that deterrence resides not just in the *existence* of nuclear weapons or in their ability to retaliate, but in their capacity to hit back *credibly*. The requirements for such retaliation are more ambitious than minimum deterrence advocates would suggest, but less than the war-fighters aver. The trick is to find a middle ground that does not run up against the paradox of deterrence, that neither makes war more likely nor abandons any hope of credible limited options. Two initial requirements for such options, as noted, are credible targeting plans and secure retaliations.

In terms of targeting policy, if a nuclear retaliation is not targeted against an enemy's nuclear forces, what will it be directed against? A clue is provided by the analysis of victory above: nuclear retaliation can destroy non-nuclear targets including conventional forces, military bases, equipment stores, military-industrial assets including nuclear weapons production sites, transportation hubs, and other non-nuclear weapons targets. Such 'counterpower' targeting would deter hostilities by threatening to annihilate all an aggressor's military assets besides his nuclear forces and by raising the dark possibility of inevitable if unintended collateral damage on a massive scale. Chapter 4 explains the basics of such a targeting strategy.

It must also be recognised that the acquisition of such capabilities can be accomplished without enormous danger. Probably the greatest single argument for resort to a minimum deterrent force has been that such a move would presumably end the arms race and reduce the risk of war. As we have seen, the paradox of deterrence has worked to undermine the stabilising effect of limited nuclear options and the forces that supported them. Under a START regime, however, the quantitative arms race would already have been halted; the following chapters outline in detail how a stable balance could be constructed given START-like limits. Given the policies this volume assumes will arise (and those that it advocates – in many cases the two categories overlap), there will be no need to adopt a minimum deterrent because its goals would be mostly achieved.

INTRAWAR DETERRENCE

So it seems that the requirements of pre-war deterrence will continue to be met, given certain conditions. Both sides must maintain survivable forces, as well as secure C3I to preclude the possibility of decapitation attacks. The general fact of mutual vulnerability to retaliation must be preserved, something that seems to deny the usefulness of large-scale defensive systems.

But what of the need to deter limited nuclear options (LNOs)? If the analysis above is true, strategic nuclear war may well be a discrete, self-deterring phenomenon, in which case either side may feel able to engage in LNOs. The United States's stated policy, moreover, threatens the use of nuclear weapons in response to conventional aggression. And hanging over all discussions of LNOs is the paradox of deterrence: weapons and doctrines constructed to deter LNOs by demonstrating the capability to engage in them may increase the risk that both sides will view LNOs as 'thinkable' options.

Some remarks on the US threat of nuclear use to deter conventional war, the policy of extended deterrence or flexible response and the LNOs designed to support it, will be made below. Here we are concerned with deterring limited *nuclear* strikes once war is underway.

The potential to discourage limited employment of nuclear weapons becomes more apparent when we recognise that our task is to *deter* such use rather than *prevail* in it. Deterrence, as we have seen, requires more than the mere existence of nuclear weapons, yet less than a true war-fighting capacity. What must be done is to establish countervailing assured destruction as an operative concept at the level of LNOs and thereby make clear that a limited nuclear first-use could never achieve military or political ends because limited nuclear responses would impose reciprocal costs.

The United States must therefore possess the capacity to engage in credible LNOs. This requires flexible forces capable of discriminating attacks, such as the Midgetman. It also demands C3 systems able to withstand a very limited nuclear environment, and perhaps survivable US-Soviet communications as well. US officials could then declare their readiness to respond to Soviet limited use in a number of ways. This is not at all to argue for true war-fighting capabilities; the United States need not, indeed ought not, have anything approaching a counterforce capability versus Soviet nuclear forces. It need not deploy a fully survivable C3I system, nor any active strategic defence or civil defence. The requirement is merely to display a capability to match selective strikes, to possess a capacity for co-operative reciprocal deterrence.

For these reasons, deterrence of LNOs can be acquired without significant danger to stability, without running afoul of the paradox. Indeed, a weapon like the Midgetman achieves both pre-war and intrawar deterrence; its survivability deters war and its flexibility is useful for limited strikes.[30] The primary explanation for this is that the threat of assured destruction, not the promise of denial of war aims, is used to deter nuclear use.

This analysis therefore denies the need for escalation dominance. Since the phenomenon of assured destruction obviates the potential for meaningful military victory in a nuclear exchange of whatever sort, limited or complete, neither side need threaten the other with *defeat* to deter it. Promising *mutual symmetrical destruction* at each level of conflict can achieve that goal, with far less danger to pre-war deterrence. It is as unnecessary to deter by denial at the level of LNOs as it is at the strategic level. Escalation *dominance* is not necessary – only escalation *matching*.

The counterpower or countermilitary targeting doctrine described above, under which a retaliation falls not on an aggressor's nuclear reserve but on all other military assets, would also assist in escalation control. By leaving aside threats against an opponent's nuclear forces, one reduces the incentive to 'use them or lose them' during a crisis or war that had not yet advanced to the strategic nuclear level. At the same time, by destroying an opponent's non-nuclear military assets – and his ability to build more nuclear bombs and the delivery vehicles to carry them – one creates enormous incentives to hold the bulk of his remaining nuclear forces as the last line of deterrence. This addresses *doctrinally* the paradox of deterrence: the same doctrine that deters war from occurring helps avoid resort to nuclear use once some sort of crisis or non-strategic war begins. Chapter 4 will elaborate on this point.

What we are left with is this. Deterrence of nuclear use under normal circumstances, or even in mild crises or during a low-level conventional war, is indeed reasonably easy, and existential deterrence can serve this function adequately. However, circumstances could arise under which nuclear weapons would be perceived as being useful, either at the strategic or the theatre/tactical level; indeed, it is worth pointing out that the *only* situations calling for nuclear use would be extraordinary ones. In such an environment, minimum or near-minimum deterrence relying on partially credible, poorly enunciated responses might not suffice. To deter use in those circumstances, to the extent possible given emotional pressures, requires a more robust deterrent posture, one that provides specific evidence of how a response would occur. Deterrence is, after all, a more complex problem than just building nuclear weapons and letting the word out that they exist.

CO-OPERATIVE RECIPROCAL DETERRENCE AND 'DYNAMIC STABILITY'

It may be helpful in further refining the definition of co-operative reciprocal deterrence to measure it against another recently-proposed notion of deterrence. Lt. Col. Fred Reule of the United States Air Force has suggested the idea of 'dynamic stability'. 'Dynamically stable deterrence', in Reule's conception, or 'DSD', is a doctrine for 'using deception and mobility in the deployment modes of offensive forces so that these forces will no longer constitute locatable targets'; its proponents therefore favour the deployment of such systems as Midgetman and additional SSBNs. The doctrine's 'fundamental premise' is that 'it is advantageous to deny our enemy the targets he needs for his counterforce strategy'. The strategy thus emphasises *passive* rather than *active* defence against strategic nuclear attacks. Reule uses language that would suggest that DSD is amendable to the lessons of the paradox: DSD is intended to 'both make a failure of deterrence less likely and greatly increase the chances of preventing total destruction if deterrence does fail'.[31]

DSD ostensibly carries a number of implications for US nuclear strategy. First, counterforce targeting must be given up since the targets will become untargetable. Second, limitations on numbers of weapons are irrelevent, since stability comes through basing, not arms limitation. Third, the United States can move toward a more slow-paced response and should prepare to fight an extended, slow nuclear exchange. Fourth, Reule and his co-authors contend that DSD would reaffirm extended deterrence by offering up a new group of non-nuclear force targets and imposing escalation control.

This volume is very sympathetic to a number of those arguments. Its general portrait of future deterrent stability is the same as Reule's: stability through mobility and concealability, of both land-and sea-based systems. This volume too argues that counterforce should be given up, and one of Reule's co-authors explicitly endorses the counterpower strategy advocated in chapter 4. His picture of mobility closely mirrors one aspect of the co-operative nature of co-operative reciprocal deterrence. Finally, as will be suggested in the next chapter, this volume also suggests a delayed retaliation strategy, though of a more limited nature than Reule's notion. Reule echoes several of the themes outlined in chapter 1, namely the importance of public opinion, the risks of nuclear winter, and the trend toward accurate and discriminating warheads. Finally, Reule agrees with the argument of chapter 7 against the necessity or desirability of large-scale strategic defences.

While the parameters of DSD are insightful, persuasive and very similar to the strategy advocated here, it is in examining the few ill-defined concepts and contradictions in DSD that we can flesh out the notion of co-operative reciprocal deterrence. Reule contends that DSD will increase the credibility of retaliatory threats. This is not necessarily true: it can increase their certainty and scope by decreasing the vulnerability of nuclear deterrents, but it will not necessarily suggest that a given defender would be more willing to respond to a limited attack. Reule contends that DSD is 'escalation neutral', that survivable forces discourage use-them-or-lose-them mentalities and encourage retaliation by reducing the danger of escalation. That may be true, but DSD also would appear to increase the incentive to engage in LNOs in the first place precisely for the same reason; escalation is unlikely. Reule also proposes that 'the prospect of a protracted version' of assured destruction 'is in many ways more terrifying than the spasmodic version'; that is not at all true, in fact, since escalation control and war termination offer ways to reduce the damage of a war, and hence violate the paradox.

These shortcomings are also manifest in the fact that DSD strategies are much too sanguine about the prospects for extended exchanges, exactly the sort of war-fighting emphasis in counterforce which this volume's strategy is directed against. Reule's difficulty with this subject is manifest in a contradiction regarding the need for C3I: at one point he contends that suggested improvements in C3I need not be performed, that 'dynamically stable forces can be adequately supported by a C3I system that cannot be disconnected from those forces long enough for an attacker to destroy them'; yet another author calls for further C3I spending, and extended war plans require survivable C3I. Reule's means of obtaining that goal is reconstitutable systems, but there is no certainty that protracted Soviet strikes would allow reconstitution. That doubt might impair deterrence.

Extremely survivable forces capable of engaging in slow-protracted nuclear conflict without much risk of escalation therefore clearly violate the paradox and increase the risk of limited war. Co-operative reciprocal deterrence avoids that result in several ways. It does not call for the establishment of C3I capable of sustaining large-scale, extended nuclear operations. It also denies (as the next chapter will explain) that slow retaliation is advisable for a *general* response; delayed response is only appropriate for very limited attacks. Beyond that, it can deter LNOs in much the same way as a DSD strategy would, through the pledge of symmetrical response to divest any attack of military or political value.

This volume also places much more emphasis on arms limitation than DSD strategies. Reule suggests that 'Dynamically stable systems would not depend on bilateral arms limitation agreements to achieve their benefits'. As the following chapter will argue, they do indeed; no system is completely invulnerable, and barrage attacks can destroy mobile missiles. Reule contends that barrage attacks 'make little practical sense', which may well be true, but the mere fact that the opportunity to engage in such attacks would exist, and the ease with which arms limitation could rule them out, argue strongly for deep cuts on the START model.

The outlines of co-operative reciprocal deterrence should be somewhat clearer. It rejects extended nuclear conflicts, holds that arms control is critical for overall stability, and above all attempts to design forces responsive to the demands of the paradox. Otherwise its basic notion of stability parallels very closely that of 'dynamically stable deterrence'.

THE DANGER OF DISCRIMINATE OPTIONS

Yet so far we have considered nuclear weapons as extraordinarily destructive, inflexible weapons of substantially different destructive power than conventional weapons. As suggested in chapter 1, however, the trend of nuclear weapons technology seems to be toward lower-yield, more precise weapons closer in destructive force to conventional weapons that are themselves becoming more powerful all the time.

The potential for discriminating nuclear and non-nuclear use would seem to threaten deterrence. Psychological barriers to the use of very low-yield nuclear weapons of pinpoint accuracy could be far less robust than those proscribing the employment of bigger, more muscular nuclear weapons. This would be especially true if very powerful conventional munitions approached the low-yield nuclear weapons in destructive power. Once nuclear weapons of whatever type were used, of course, escalation control might collapse.

Such trends are apparently underway already. Chapter 8 will detail the prospects for conventional arms that have begun to assume some of the targeting tasks previously assigned to nuclear weapons. The superpowers already possess low-yield nuclear bombs and, increasingly, super-accurate delivery systems to place them accurately on target. The literature on deterrence also displays a trend toward the discriminating application of force, ideas that are far from original: Bernard Brodie himself learned to doubt the veracity of his argument that nuclear weapons did not 'lend themselves to discriminate use'.[32] Albert Wohlstetter has argued that 'improved accuracies make feasible greater discrimination as well as effectiveness in the use of nuclear weapons, and they also make possible more extensive replacement of nuclear with conventional weapons'.[33] Elsewhere Wohlstetter has suggested that these advances might make feasible 'radical reductions in collateral damage'.[34] More recently, others have returned to the same themes: the 1988 *Discriminate Deterrence* report, of which Fred Iklé was the primary analyst, called for more discriminate forms of conventional and, to a degree, nuclear conflict.

In general, as the names in the preceding paragraphs would suggest, advocates of counterforce and war-fighting options have led the drive for discriminating options. Their efforts represent attempts to render nuclear weapons usable by divesting them of some of their destructive power. As such, discriminate options have been condemned by more liberal analysts who bemoan the fading firebreak between nuclear and conventional weapons.[35] And indeed, the bureaucratic pressures issuing from within both sides' militaries may point in the same direction. No matter how self-evident the reality of MAD may be, pure deterrence is a task unfamiliar to militaries unaccustomed to the paradox of deterrence; **primarily because** it is their job, military leaders on both sides have tried to find ways to fight and win wars.

Assuming that increasingly discriminate applications of nuclear weapons continue to evolve, then, and that extremely powerful conventional weapons approach low-yield nuclear weapons in power, will deterrence suffer? Will the reasonably sanguine portrait of co-operative reciprocal deterrence painted above be ruined? Theoretically, yes. Any development that renders nuclear or strategic war more thinkable or fightable would seem to undermine the very real psychological barriers to conflict in the nuclear age.

A number of corresponding facts and developments, however, will undercut to a degree the implications of these weapons. First and most important would be numerical limits on strategic delivery vehicles – primarily ballistic and cruise missiles and bombers. No matter how discriminating a warhead might be, if it is not attached to a delivery vehicle it holds little significance. Combined with the increasing survivability of strategic forces and the numerous uncertainties attaching to the employment of nuclear weapons at strategic range, limits on delivery vehicles will prevent low-yield nuclear or non-nuclear strategic weapons from threatening either side's secure deterrent. The potential for counterforce strikes will therefore not grow, and crisis stability should not suffer.

If counterforce applications are what is intended, moreover, there is no reason to deploy lower-yield warheads. Once one side decides to attack the nuclear forces of the other, many, if not all, bets are off. In such a situation large nuclear warheads would have a higher kill probability and do little to undermine escalation control, which would be sacrificed in any case. Chapter 8 examines these ideas in detail.

But disturbing the overall balance may not be the primary threat represented by discriminate nuclear weapons; eroding the firebreak between nuclear and conventional war is. Even here, however, their potential to disrupt the peace is limited.

Initially it should be recognised that the effect of discriminate options might be the opposite of that feared: the more the conventional-nuclear firebreak appears to have weakened, the greater might be the security of deterrence. This refers, of course, to the paradox of deterrence, recognising that the lesser the apparent ability to limit a war, the greater will be the disincentive to start one. As will be noted below in regard to flexible response, however, this sort of suicidal deterrence is a bankrupt way to ensure peace insofar as it writes off the world once a war begins.

But supposing that the leaders of great powers do come to believe that discriminate options have made limited nuclear war more feasible. Would this destroy deterrence by suggesting that a 'nuclear' war might not be as destructive as previously thought? Probably not. Initially, a nuclear weapon is still a nuclear weapon whether small or large, and the psychological deterrent to its use would remain in force at least to a degree, bolstered by the risk that the use of little nuclear bombs would lead inexorably to the use of big ones.

It is unlikely, moreover, that the advent of discriminate options would provide any additional incentives to go to war, even in a crisis. Even today each superpower, if their official statements and military writings are any indication, harbours some hope that a major war could be confined to conventional conflict. A desperate state could cling to that notion to justify going to war if its leadership determined that such a course was its only remaining option. In such a case, the mutual possession of discriminating options would do little to alter that calculus; indeed, as noted, if anything the further integration of nuclear and conventional weapons might reinforce the deterrent to war by discouraging the notion that a firm intrawar firebreak would be built between the two types of weapons.

These comments refer to the notion that war is a *political* action carried out by military means. Thus, individual weapons systems will not cause war unless they degrade crisis stability; a state must have some overriding political reason to initiate hostilities in the first place. The argument that discriminate options are dangerous suggests that they remove some of the disincentive to war by reducing its potential destructiveness, and thus make that political decision easier. The argument here, however, is that there are already reasons to believe that war could be limited, but there are also enormous risks that it could not. Any state desperate enough to risk the current danger of nuclear escalation would certainly do so with discriminate options; but there are very few cases, it seems, where a state would be desperate enough to risk war with discriminate nuclear strikes but not desperate enough to convince itself a conventional-only war could be fought.[36]

Discriminate options, moreover, may merely hasten the day when the notion of assured destruction becomes relevant to virtually all forms of major conventional and nuclear warfare. As we have seen, limited nuclear options do not of themselves increase the risk of war; the capability of both sides to engage in them merely indicates that neither has an incentive to do so – limited nuclear options could destroy all conventional forces on both sides. At the conventional level, moreover, increasingly destructive high-technology conventional munitions may one day ensure conventional deterrence by guaranteeing the destruction of most forces on both sides within hours of the outbreak of hostilities. Discriminate options may lay like an assured destruction blanket over all major potential hostilities, suggesting that no military move could be made without retaliation in kind and the frustration of its objectives. There is therefore no pressing reason why discriminate options need increase the chances of war.

REQUIREMENTS OF CONVENTIONAL DETERRENCE

How do these reflections relate to the deterrence of conventional war? Can we continue to count on nuclear weapons to deter conventional war? Probably not. While credible scenarios for nuclear use exist, deterring conventional adventurism is not necessarily one of them.

US policy-makers could never credibly threaten nuclear responses to the most common form of conventional conflicts – low-or mid-intensity warfare between developing or smaller developed states. The United States tried for a time under Eisenhower in the New Look doctrine and failed miserably. Subsequently, US reluctance to use nuclear weapons in Korea and Vietnam reinforced the notion that such weapons are not suited for deterring less than full-scale warfare. The risks involved are simply too severe.

Indeed, it is today an open question whether nuclear weapons can adequately deter large-scale conventional warfare, in Europe or elsewhere. The notion that the United States would sacrifice New York for Paris or Bonn when there were other options (preparing for a drawn-out conventional war, for example) has always been somewhat suspect. The growing incredibility of such pledges was manifest in the movement of US nuclear strategy away from them and toward advocacy of limited options. Especially as tensions with NATO allies increase, the United States will probably be seen as less and less willing to risk its own destruction to forestall Soviet occupation of the Continent.

Luckily for the alliance, however, as chapter 5 will explain, trends in East-West relations and European politics offer the long-term prospect of solving these dilemmas by reducing at once NATO's ability and need to rely upon that aspect of flexible response (as manifest in extended deterrence) commonly questioned (that is, US escalation) while at the same time improving NATO's capacity to fulfill its more credible deterrent pledges. In short, conventional arms control and NATO conventional improvements will reduce NATO's vulnerability at that level, and European defence co-operation will encourage that trend; both will make flexible response less necessary. Meanwhile, public opposition in Europe to nuclear weapons and in America to European defence commitments will render it less necessary. The end result will probably be that extended deterrence will fade away, relieving US deterrence doctrine of its most difficult requirements.

It seems, then, that the only way to deter lower-level conflicts without relying on nuclear first use is to do so on their own terms and in the same fashion – co-operative reciprocal deterrence – which operates at the nuclear level. That is to say, an aggressor must know that, no matter where he begins a conflict, he will lose. This, of course, is the rationale behind the American theory of 'escalation dominance', that the ability to win *at every level* is necessary for deterrence. Yet as we have seen, the escalation dominance argument misconstrued the requirements of deterrence: the West need not be able to *win* at every level; it must only be able to punish the Soviets so badly as to make victory by any plausible definition an impossibility. The same rationale will probably become operative at the conventional level as well.

This is the real significance of modern conventional weapons. They are so destructive as to render *any* use of force either inutilitous or disutilitous *on its own terms*, and in the background there hangs the threat of unintended escalation. High-technology missiles, precision-guided munitions and the like will someday develop to the point that any battlefield would, within minutes of the outset of hostilities, be transformed into a burnt-out wasteland. Concepts such as Competitive Strategies, Deep Attack and AirLand Battle promise to place at risk all enemy conventional forces, not merely those at the battle-front. As noted, the Soviets clearly recognise the potential for advanced conventional munitions such as tactical ballistic missiles and laser weapons; it is therefore no wonder that they are so desperate to stop US technical progress in SDI and to bolster their own through *perestroika*. Victory might well therefore become impossible at all levels of warfare because neither side would possess any surviving forces.

Certainly, these claims require a good many more qualifications than traditional analyses of the effect of assured destruction at the nuclear level. After all, conventional weapons, no matter how accurate or destructive, will never have the power of nuclear weapons. The psychological stigma attached to nuclear first use may never apply to conventional weapons. No matter how advanced they become, they will never promise absolute destruction; witness the present complaints that advanced technologies have so many inherent flaws that they do not provide much hope for NATO.

Still, the argument here is that the emergence of assured destruction at the conventional level will come slowly, and only in a limited fashion. It will emerge only after another decade or more of development and deployment of high-technology weapons, and will be relevant only for major military showdowns. But the European theatre is the geographic area in question, and it seems probable that by the beginning of the next century both sides in that dispute will have acquired enough advanced munitions to annihilate the standing forces on both sides within minutes of the outset of war.

THE REQUIREMENTS OF DETERRENCE

Deterrence is thus a fourfold problem: pre-war nuclear deterrence, intrawar nuclear deterrence, chemical/biological deterrence, and conventional deterrence. Until today, assured destruction worked only at the nuclear and, arguably, the chemical/biological levels. In the future, however, all conflict may be deterred by the threat of mutual annihilation. What must the United States do to adapt to such a world? The requirements for deterrence are spelled out below.

(1) *Pre-War Nuclear Deterrence.* The United States and the Soviet Union must deploy survivable nuclear forces not subject to first strike; neither side must possess a real or perceived pre-emptive capability. Societies must remain vulnerable. Ideally, all three legs of the mutual triads would be secure. Arms control treaties should limit, control, and in selected areas reverse the arms competition. Command, control and communications must be secure to ensure retaliation and forestall 'decapitation' attacks. Targeting policy should de-emphasise counterforce to reduce fear of pre-emption. For crisis situations, credible nuclear options must be preserved.

(2) *Intrawar Nuclear Deterrence and War Termination.* Both sides must possess the ability to launch discriminating, limited *responses* to attacks by the other side with the goal, not of winning the exchange, but of providing for assured destruction at each level of conflict. Once again partly survivable C3I is required to allow such missions. Wartime communication between the United States and the USSR may be required to terminate a conflict. Targeting policy should de-emphasise counterforce to remove the incentive to use weapons before they are destroyed.

(3) *Chemical/Biological Deterrence.* Both sides must maintain stocks of sufficient size and flexibility to threaten appropriate responses to any cases of first use. Arms control agreements could reduce the prevalence of material.

(4) *Conventional Deterrence.* For deterrence in Europe, robust conventional forces must be maintained, subject to conventional arms agreements. Increasing numbers of high-technology weapons – precision-guided munitions, anti-tank guided missiles, tactical ballistic missiles, and the like – should be deployed. Eventually, their numbers could allow reductions of standing armies. Confidence-building measures, to reduce the fear of and potential for pre-emptive strikes, should continue. To deter elsewhere, traditional low-and mid-intensity conflict strategies such as security assistance and employment of strategically mobile deployment forces must be continued; the interests involved will generally be less than vital.

This chapter has painted a reasonably sanguine portrait of the future of deterrence. The details of its ideas and arguments will be fleshed out in the chapters to follow. They will contend that the paradox of deterrence can be resolved through resort to survivable yet flexible forces, and that assured destruction will continue to be operative at the strategic level and will be increasingly relevant to limited nuclear and conventional warfare. Over a decade ago, Fred Iklé asked whether there could be a 'happy ending' to deterrence; this volume contends that there can and will be as happy an ending as we could hope for. All it will take is a little foresight, a little expense, and – as always – a little luck.

3 Stability

As the analysis in chapter 2 hopefully made clear, undoubtedly the single most critical requirement for deterrence is a stable nuclear balance. A START treaty, combined with strategic modernisation, could provide the context in which just such a balance is constructed: by placing ceilings on the number of deployed warheads allowed, it should institutionalise stability by preventing either side from gaining a usable nuclear advantage. This chapter will examine the nature of and requirements for a stable balance in the context of a theory of co-operative reciprocal deterrence.

A VALID CONCEPT?

Initially, however, we must determine if the very concept of stability, as defined in Western nuclear analysis, is valid. In brief, many analysts of deterrence suggest that a stable balance exists when neither side feels tempted or required, under any circumstances, to strike first. This in turn requires secure nuclear forces and C3I.[1]

The definition of stability can perhaps be uncovered by examining the potential balance under START. If both sides have 6000 warheads and deploy survivable nuclear forces – mobile missiles requiring perhaps 10 000 or more warheads to attack, defended silo-based missiles requiring a few hundred more, bombers capable of launching stand-off ALCMs, and virtually invulnerable submarines – the requirements for an attack would dwarf the warhead totals on both sides. This then would be a stable nuclear balance, since neither side would be vulnerable, and the basic conditions of co-operative reciprocal deterrence would have been established.

Obviously, instability generated by force vulnerability would not be very dangerous on a day-to-day basis. But deterrence must be designed to work under even the most extreme circumstances, such as a state of very high tension. An unstable balance may not pose much risk during normal times, since even a 'winner' in a nuclear exchange would be devastated. But during a crisis the calculus of interests on both sides could change and the option of war could be discussed if one or both sides are vulnerable.

This general theory of stability has been subjected to two basic sets of criticisms, one from the right and one from the left. The right has argued that deterrence based on stable mutual vulnerability is bankrupt, that national security requires an ability to protect a country from any sort of attack. Yet this argument bypasses the central lesson of the nuclear age, that war is no longer a rational instrument of policy. Attempting to protect oneself from its effects, moreover, as the paradox of deterrence recognises, makes war more likely; it is precisely in its huge destructive power that modern war has found a way to render itself improbable. The single most important supporting element for a truly defensive strategy, moreover, is strategic defence, but this, as we shall see in chapter 7, is potentially destabilising. The critique of assured destruction from the Right, in short, simply fails to recognise that in the nuclear age, war is a different phenomenon than it has been in the past.[2]

Perhaps the best example of such criticisms can be found in an essay by Fred Iklé. Iklé argues that 'a two-sided equilibrium of mutual vulnerability is a relationship that cannot remain stable'. Stability and assured destruction, he also contends, are 'like oil and water'; 'the accord on a stable equilibrium of mutual restraint is psychologically incompatible with the constant threat of reciprocal annihilation', and believers 'in the dogma of a stable, mutually agreed vulnerability fail to appreciate the dynamic of this incompatibility'.[3]

There is no reason, however, why this need be true. Simultaneous faith in assured destruction and co-operative restraint are not only compatible, they are mutually dependent, a fact which the whole history of the post-war era confirms. This volume's basic argument, moreover, is that nuclear deterrence is moving (through START and stable weapons) into a new era of co-operative deterrence, and all its evidence regarding the stability of the balance (much of which is presented later in this chapter) argues against Iklé's ideas. Nor are assured destruction and peace incompatible from a public relations standpoint; most Americans favour modernisation of the US arsenal to ensure deterrence.

Iklé then argues that the Soviet Union would be unlikely to accept as stability indefinitely 'a future where any American president, or (in their eyes) perhaps even "some American general", could unleash the engines that would destroy the Soviet Union'. It is perhaps true that the Soviets would like something besides that relationship; as chapter 6 will argue, the *maximal* Soviet goal in deterrence may be a war-fighting capacity. But, as Raymond Garthoff has repeatedly pointed out, the Soviets accept the fact of deterrence even though they may disagree with its nature. In short, even if the Soviets despise the assured destruction relationship, they are unlikely to challenge it.

Iklé also suggests that the balance of terror 'cannot favor the defense of a democratic alliance. Sooner or later, it will favor those most at ease with, those most experienced in, the systematic use of terror'. To argue that small-scale terrorism parallels the use of nuclear weapons to deter war, however, is to over-generalise the phenomenon of terrorism to the point of meaninglessness. Western democracies have demonstrated an uncanny ability to employ fantastic amounts of terror when defending against an aggressor; witness the countervalue raids against Germany and Japan in World War II, including the fire-bombings of German and Japanese cities. To pledge that one will retaliate in kind if one is attacked is not to engage in 'terror', but merely reasoned and proportionate deterrence, an entirely different matter from assassinations or hijackings or the like.

Taking his argument one step further, Iklé argues that distinctions between democratic and totalitarian states serve to render long-term pursuit of assured destruction debilitating for the former and useful for the latter.

> The danger of demoralization by relying on a strategic order of consensual vulnerability goes further and deeper. Upon an alliance of democracies, such a policy imposes a passive, almost cynical, resignation toward the possibility of an atrocity unsurpassed in human history. It offers a prospect of anxiety without relief, an intellectual legacy crippling the outlook of each new generation, a theme of desolate sadness.

Once again, the primary theme of this book denies Iklé's assertions most forcefully: deterrence based on co-operative reciprocal deterrence does not impose a grim, hopeless nuclear future on humanity, for trends in the nuclear balance (especially START) will lead the superpowers to a much more stable environment. Public opinion polls suggest, moreover, that the public rejects such gloom-and-doom scenarios; majorities of 80 to 90 per cent now agree that nuclear war is highly unlikely either in the foreseeable future or ever. Those majorities have been growing, and they should grow even larger as the trends outlined in this volume become increasingly evident.

Finally, the solutions of Iklé and others dissatisfied with assured destruction promise to increase, not decrease, instability. 'We need to accomplish a long-term transformation of our nuclear strategy', he argues, 'the armaments serving it, and our arms control policy'. He argues for such systems as missile defences and counterforce weapons to begin to allow us to get 'beyond' deterrence. Yet such systems violate the paradox and risk, and make war more likely; they argue, as Richard Betts has phrased it, for the nonsensical 'stability of instability'.[4] Moreover, the hope that missile defences will somehow allow us to overcome mutual vulnerability is naive, a point investigated in chapter 7.

More broadly, such critiques of assured destruction-based stability from the Right at once ignore and exaggerate the implications of the nuclear revolution. They underestimate the revolution to the degree that they fail to recognise the unique nature of nuclear weapons: unfortunately, there is no escape from their destructive power precisely because it is so great. Drawing up schemes aimed at reaffirming national security by abandoning assured destruction are bound to fail, as Robert Jervis has eloquently emphasised in his writings. In the nuclear age, the risk of devastation is so clear that wars are much more likely to arise from fear of attack than from aggressive intent; this fact renders the sorts of systems and doctrines advocated by war-fighters absolutely counterproductive.

At the same time, such analysts overestimate the meaning of nuclear weapons since they fail to recognise that some form of assured destruction has always been the heart of deterrence. Nations in the past by and large did not attempt to deter attacks upon themselves with kindly references to their ability to defend themselves; much more often, they promised to find the aggressor and destroy him. The nuclear age is different in only one respect: as long as assured destruction holds up, the defender can promise inevitably and absolutely to devastate the aggressor, rendering moot any thoughts of nuclear adventurism.

Analysts on the Left subject deterrence to a multifaceted critique. Some point to the paradox as an insoluble dilemma of the nuclear age; as chapter 2 argued, however, trends in the strategic environment are leading to its resolution. Others argue that deterrence theories support the arms race by providing justifications for new armaments. Michael MccGwire has argued that deterrence provides an incentive for arms racing 'that leads to heightened world antagonisms and that in the event of war would magnify the level of devastation'.[5]

This argument fails on several counts. First, deterrence theory itself does not demand an arms race; a minimum deterrent, for example, would not require one. Only certain *forms* of deterrence require counterforce capabilities, and those should indeed be given up. It seems as if MccGwire and some other critics of deterrence on the Left have confused the notion of deterrence with the manner in which recent US administrations have chosen to pursue it: deterrence itself is merely the practice of keeping another party from doing something one does not wish that party to do, and in that sense it cannot be 'good' or 'bad'. MccGwire's alternatives to deterrence would themselves presumably have as their goal the prevention of Soviet nuclear attack, and therefore could themselves be called 'deterrent' strategies. Second, the imminent START treaty itself denies that deterrence requires an arms race. Quite the contrary, as we shall see below, arms control and reduction are integral aspects of secure deterrence.

MccGwire also makes another common case against deterrence: it fosters, he writes, the 'insidious' delusion that 'war itself is not the primary danger'. We must recognise that 'the concept of deterrence is part of the problem and not the solution, and that the primary threat is war and not Soviet military aggression'. The solution is therefore 'not in different military force postures, although undoubtedly such adjustments will have to play a part', but in 'restructuring our assumptions'.[6]

This critique of deterrence is also flawed. First, deterrence itself does not presume any intentions; it is a demonstrated fact that the United States and the Soviet Union are adversaries. Even if neither side *wants* war, in a crisis both may feel they *must go to war* for various reasons. Deterrence aims to make that choice unnecessary. Second, and in a related sense, if history is any guide, it is accidents and misunderstandings and misperceptions that will cause war, not pure intention; but if deterrence is robust it can withstand even those pressures. Third, there are ways, as this volume will argue, to construct a strong deterrent force without provoking the other side, and to that extent deterrence does not carry a significant price. Fourth and finally, once again there is no good alternative to deterrence; what precisely 'changing our assumptions' would entail is left conveniently up the the reader to discern. As before, for the foreseeable future deterrence will be the best of a number of imperfect alternatives for dealing with the existence of nuclear weapons and the risk of conflict between opposing systems.

A STABLE BALANCE

Given the need for stability, then, what are its essential components? The most critical one is a secure nuclear balance, and the START treaty opens the door to virtually indefinite security. The strategic nuclear balance before START is summed up in Table 3.1; stability in this balance tends to come from the enormous redundancy found in huge number of weapons, not from survivability of systems, apart from submarines.[7]

Most analysts recognise that the deterrent has been relatively secure.[8] The durability of the American triad, the invulnerability of SLBMs, and the uncertainties inherent in conducting a nuclear strike prevent any Soviet or American planner from possessing confidence in a first strike. There is no reason to assume, however, that this happy state of affairs will continue indefinitely. Several trends in the strategic balance suggest that a future absence of arms control could offer more dangers. This fact is the most basic justification for the pursuit of arms reduction.

Initially, there is the danger inherent in the arms race itself. The accumulation of larger numbers of increasingly accurate and powerful counterforce-capable weapons augurs ill for crisis stability.[9] Some weapons systems are by their nature inherently destabilising, and vulnerable; first-strike capable, heavily MIRVed ICBMs such as the SS-18 and the MX certainly fall into this category. Deployments of missile defences, limited or general, by either or both sides could also upset the strategic balance. A mutual defensive arms race could raise dangers of thinkability and create incentives for a first strike: when both sides possess partially-effective defences better at defeating a ragged retaliation than a full attack, the incentive to strike first is magnified. These arguments are developed further in chapter 7.

Another danger lies in future Soviet strategic deployments. By the mid-1990s, most of the current generation of Soviet nuclear systems will have been supplemented with more modern weapons. The ten-warhead SS-24 and single-warhead, truck-mobile SS-25 will be in service in large numbers. Soviet planners could have in their arsenal between 16 000 and 21 000 warheads, a higher percentage of which would be counterforce-capable than is the case today. And these numbers do not even assume a full effort, which the CIA and others estimate could bring the Soviet total near 30 000.

Given continued modernisation of US forces, the nuclear balance might remain stable. The calculations of a recent Congressional

TABLE 3.1   *The Nuclear Balance, 1987*

System	Launchers	Warheads per Launcher	Total Warheads
United States			
ICBMs			
Minuteman II	450	1	450
Minuteman III	523	3	1569
MX	27	10	270
Subtotal	1000		2289
SlBMs			
Poseidon (C-3)	256	10	2560
Poseidon (C-4)	192	8	1536
Trident (C-4)	192	8	1536
Subtotal	640		5632
Bombers			
B-52G	69	8	552
B-52G (With cruise missiles)	98	12	1568
B-52H	49	10	490
B-52H (With cruise missiles)	49	12	784
B-1B	64	16	1024
Subtotal	329		4418[a]
TOTAL	1969		12339
Soviet Union			
ICBMs			
SS-11	440	1	440
SS-13	60	1	60
SS-17	150	4	600
SS-18	308	10	3080
SS-19	360	6	2160
SS-X-25	100	1	100
Subtotal	1418		6440
SLBMs			
SS-N-6	272	1	272
SS-N-8	292	1	292
SS-N-18	224	3	672
SS-N-20	80	6-9	720
SS-N-23	64	10	640
Subtotal	932		2596
Bombers			
Bear	100	4	400
Bear H	50	8	400
Bison	15	4	60
Subtotal	165		860
TOTAL	2515		9896

SOURCE   Congressional Budget office estimates and Research Service

NOTE   Reflects total inventories. Does not include US FB-111 and Soviet Backfire bombers.

[a] Notional weapons carriage parameters, based on estimates of total inventories of bomber weapons. May slightly overstate inventories.

Budget Office (CBO) study contend persuasively that if both sides carry out modernisation, neither would become vulnerable.[10] The US force mix of the 1990s – including Midgetman, mobile MX, and Trident – would retaliate relatively well against a Soviet attack, indeed even better than the current force. The CBO Study, however, makes the crucial assumption that US modernisation plans go through, though it is looking increasingly likely that they will not; future budget troubles make it exceedingly unlikely that anything like the Reagan administration's planned modernisation will be completed. And even with modernisation, a full-scale Soviet build-up could overwhelm the US effort.

In short, the current nuclear balance is stable. It could remain so if neither side deploys defensive systems and if the United States and the Soviet Union both continue with their strategic modernisation programmes. It seems increasingly unlikely, however, that the United States will follow that course. Unless it wishes to consign itself to perpetual nuclear inferiority, another option must be sought. Even with modernisation, moreover, the Soviet Union could keep much of the US arsenal vulnerable (as we will see below), and the super-powers would have by-passed an opportunity to control and channel the arms race in important, predictable and therefore more stable ways. A START treaty offers an opportunity to address both problems. From the perspective of deterrence, the stability of the balance under START is the crucial equation; as the analysis below will make clear, the willingness of the United States to modernise its forces is the key variable on which the robustness of a START regime will depend.

WEAPONS AND STABILITY

To many analysts it is the type of nuclear deterrent systems chosen by each side that determine the stability of the balance. Hence analyst David Hendrickson would have the United States 'build up those nuclear systems that are good for retaliation but not for initial attack, that can survive a first strike by the Soviet Union but are poor instruments for a disarming first strike against it'.[11]

That certain weapons are less stabilising than others is certainly true. Arguments relating to the dangerous quality of certain weapons rest on the notion that counterforce weapons are bad, because by placing at risk the other side's arsenal they degrade crisis stability.

Weapons like the MX are currently decreasing crisis stability, and systems like stratgic defence could do so. The argument here is merely that to surrender unilaterally all counterforce capability would be sheer folly, especially given that certain C3I targets are hard enough to require hard-target capable weapons. It also seems unlikely that, lacking an arms accord, the USSR would join the United States in a voluntary effort to acquire inaccurate missiles and weak bombs.

Indeed, the idea that weapons *alone* are responsible for instability is simplistic for a variety of reasons. Initially, certain weapons, such as the Midgetman, are both survivable *and* first-strike capable; should we purchase them? Would Hendrickson or others deny that a world of single-warhead mobiles would be stable? More importantly, other weapons Hendrickson assumes to be stabilising might not be so benign: he calls for a manned penetrating bomber and cruise missiles, but if the former is stealthy it could sneak up on the Soviets, and fast, accurate, first-strike capable versions of the latter are probably inevitable. Placing faith in what today are 'stable' weapons is fruitless to the extent that the natural evolution of military technology, intensified on those weapons left to US planners, will eventually render them dangerous.

Hendrickson, as with most such analysts, justifies his position with a short paean to the impossibility of nuclear war given the destructiveness of the weapons involved; he advocates a form of minimum deterrence. Yet as chapter 2 hopefully made clear, a pure minimum deterrent operating along assured destruction lines is insufficient insofar as it fails to recognise the need for limited counterforce responses and coercive strikes. In particular, the lack of flexible nuclear options would rob US planners of any leverage in crises and any ability to threaten various attack scenarios after war has begun, in order to terminate the conflict. [12]

In an era of deep cuts, moreover, it will be critical not to sacrifice any of the deterrent value inherent in the guarantee of a rapid, devastating response to a first strike. In the future, as arsenals become smaller and more survivable, the primary risk may no longer be crisis instability; it may be thinkability, the notion that nuclear war has indeed slipped down into the realm of a survivable conflict. That sort of impression could be encouraged by certain weapons systems favoured by the Right, including counterforce and strategic defences. But thinkability could also grow as a result of policies more generally ascribed to the Left, including the deployment of slower, more vulnerable weapons systems. We must remember that in the end we are dealing with a deterrent that rests fundamentally on assured destruction for its strength, and, ironic as it may seem, measures to restrict the potential effects of a *general* exchange work to increase its probability. That is a law dictated by the paradox of deterrence.

If at all possible, the United States should strive to construct a nuclear balance that is, by its nature, stable regardless of the weapons either side deploys. It should acquire survivable counterforce weapons such as the Midgetman and the mobile MX that impose a highly favourable cost/exchange ratio on the opponent. In this fashion it can preserve a survivable land-based deterrent that would bolster crisis stability, assuming the Soviets deploy similar weapons (which they have already begun to do). The question then becomes, can such a balance be constructed under the general framework of the current START accord?

NUMBERS AND STABILITY

Initially, let us examine the force the Soviets would possess to target against the US arsenal. At the outset of the agreement, the Soviets will deploy a mix of current and developing forces. Because their strategic arsenal is so flexible, they can expect to field a survivable deterrent under a START regime. The table below outlines a potential Soviet force under START.

A similar assessment was made by a recent Center for Strategic and International Studies panel report.[13]

If the United States did not modernise its forces significantly, its deterrent under START might look something like the force outlined

TABLE 3.2   *Soviet Force Mix Under START*

System	Delivery Vehicles	Warheads
SS-18	150	1500
SS-24 (mobile)	100	1000
SS-25 (mobile)	500	500
SS-N-20 (Typhoon)	100	1000
SS-N-23 (Delta IV, V)	224	896
Bombers (Blackjack)	variable	1100
Totals	1000+	6000

Source   Author's estimates.

in Table 3.3. As that table suggests, a non-modernised US force would face severe threats. Just over 2000 warheads would wipe out the entire US land-based deterrent and many of the bombers not on alert; the Soviets would have about 4000 counterforce weapons in reserve, more if they had cheated at the margin. The smaller number of targets eases planning problems, and the Soviets could also be more confident of the effectiveness of a partial, partially clandestine BMD system and of their considerable passive defences.[14] The resulting vulnerability of the US deterrent raises a number of questions.[15]

TABLE 3.3   *US Force Mix Under START: No Modernisation*

System	Delivery Vehicles	Warheads	Warheads Required to Attack
MX	50	500	100
Minuteman II	450	450	900
Minuteman III	500	1500	1000
Trident	306	2448	invulnerable
B-52/B-1B	variable	1100	partly invulnerable
Totals:	1300+	6000	2000+

Sources   Michael M. May *et al.*, *Strategic Arms Reductions* (Washington, DC: The Brookings Institution, 1988); Hans Binnendijk, 'START: A Preliminary Assessment', *The Washington Quarterly* 11 (Autumn 1988), 11–16; Panel on the Future of Strategic Systems, *Securing Strategic Stability* (Washington, DC: Center for Strategic and International Studies, December 1988); author's estimates.

Initially, what sort of retaliation is necessary to preserve deterrence? Some have argued that the United States must be able to retaliate against hard targets, and with regard to Soviet C3I assets, this is certainly the case. But what about silos and other nuclear assets? Should the United States plan to retaliate against Soviet forces?

In fact a START-like accord would make it extremely difficult for US planners to maintain their current policy of damaging-limiting counterforce strikes. Under a deep-cuts regime, and with further Soviet modernisation, such damage-limiting counterforce retaliation would be impossible; this notion will be fully examined in the next chapter. The implication of this fact for US deterrent policy would seem clear enough: the United States need not, after all, guarantee a very large surviving retaliatory counterforce arsenal. This undercuts the rationale for modernisation, since just such a perfectly effective, if not counterforce-capable, deterrent resides in the invulnerable US submarine force.

A SUBMARINE-ONLY DETERRENT

This is really the crux of the matter. With or without arms control, without modernisation the survivable US deterrent will rest almost entirely in submarines.[16] Without arms control, even modernisation might not change that fact. The question then becomes, are US leaders willing to live with such a situation?[17]

There are severe problems with entrusting the entire survivable US deterrent to submarines. Initially, a sudden technological break-through, in the area of blue-green lasers or another, could render the submarines vulnerable. The US deterrent should obviously be immune to such a unilateral technological advance. As Brent Scow-croft notes, if 'our submarines become vulnerable, and we had failed in the meantime to enhance the capability of the other two legs of the triad, that would be a situation of grave instability'.[18]

Second, submarines are imperfect retaliatory tools. SSBNs suffer from communications problems, and might not receive their launch orders in a timely fashion. They cannot retarget their missiles as readily as ICBM commanders. Nor are SSBNs very flexible weapons; since they cannot launch a portion of their missiles without being located, a US planner thus must launch a large number of warheads at once, and this places severe constraints on US war-fighting and conflict termination abilities.[19] During a nuclear exchange, operating submarines at depths where they are capable of receiving communications renders them vulnerable to attack.[20]

Relying totally on SSBNs for a practical deterrent would also minimise the advantages of the nuclear triad. That organisation has been maintained for very specific reasons – it forces an attacker to deal with targets of different natures, and it is very difficult, for example, to co-ordinate ICBM strikes on silos and SLBM strikes on bomber bases. Consigning ICBMs and bombers to perpetual vulner-ability would mitigate those requirements. Certainly, a Soviet attacker will have to strike at all three legs even if the United States does not modernise its ICBMs or bombers, but the practical threat he would face from retaliation from those weapons would be smaller.

The small numbers of submarines available under a START treaty is also problematic. Estimates of how many boats would remain vary, but range between 16 and 19, of which perhaps only 10–12 would be at sea at any given time. The entire effective US nuclear deterrent would thus rest on less than a dozen submarines, and subsequent arms reductions would lower that number even further.[21]

These facts encourage frightening speculation. Suppose, in a crisis or as part of a long-term plan, that Soviet planners hope to strike at the US force. Suppose that commanders of several of their ships report contact with US SSBNs, and that, because of mechanical failures, one or two more US SSBNs than normal are in port and vulnerable. Suppose also that Soviet research and development of medium-technology BMD systems has been continuing. Soviet planners could thus wipe out the US land-based deterrent and destroy perhaps half the US SSBN force with their ICBMs; destroy a few more SSBNs at sea; and count on air and missile defences to destroy most of the bombers and SLBMs that avoided the strike. For the risk of a few dozen warheads falling on their soil – many of which would be aimed at silos in any case – Soviet planners could disarm the United States at the nuclear level.[22]

Even if it is assumed that the Soviets would never desire to begin a war, crisis stability has a dynamic all of its own; if an unstable balance exists, while the vulnerable side might believe that the other will *probably not* attack, it would nevertheless be tempted to strike first given the risk. And – as the Soviets recognise very well – wars can start for a wide variety of reasons besides rational intent. To assume that a conflict will never occur is foolish. Acquiring weapons that are able to deter war, but not to credibly engage in any conflict scenarios, accomplishes only half the task. Moreover, the political implications of vulnerability are severe: the Soviets would obtain a significant psychological advantage in confrontations, and the United State's extended deterrence pledge would lose all credibility – as it has begun to do already.

In short, as a recent study headed by Harold Brown has concluded, 'To have the security – indeed, the freedom and survival – of the nation rest solely on the viability of one particular weapon system could clearly be an unacceptable risk'.[23]

THE REQUIREMENTS OF STABLE DETERRENCE

Creating a stable deterrent for the United States under START,

TABLE 3.4   *Potential US START Arsenals*

System	Budget cutters	Surprise resilient	Max mod (95 MX RG)	Max mod (20 Trident)	
MMIII, IIIA	442/1326	150/450	0	0	
MX silo	50/500	50/500	0	0	—SNDVs/
MX (RG)	0	0	95/950	50/500	weapons
Small ICBM (HML)	0	300/300	300/300	500/500	
Trident D-5	⑯ 384/3072	⑲ 456/3648	⑲ 456/3648	⑳◄ 480/3840	—Number of SSBNs
B-52 (12 ALCM/ACM)	100/1000	11/110	0	7/70	
B-1 (16 bomb/SRAM/ACM)	99/99	99/990	99/990	99/990	
B-2 (16 bomb/SRAM)	0	0	100/100	100/100	
START count* Total SNDVs/weapons	1075/5997	1066/5998	1050/5988	1236/6000	
Real weapons	7682	6614	8082	8108	

*All bombers with CM count ten under START, penetrating bombers count one
Source   CSIS, *Securing Strategic Stability*.

however, is easy enough in theory, merely requiring modern-isation.[24]

The United States has a number of options for modernisation; several potential US START arsenals are summarised below in Table 3.4; Table 3.5 estimates potential Soviet attack requirements against modernised US forces.

Such a force would meet the Scowcroft Commission's recommenda-tions for having a force 'that will so confound, complicate and frustrate the efforts of Soviet strategic war planners that, even in moments of stress, they could not believe that they could attack our ICBM forces effectively'.[25] It would also establish the sort of mobile, survivable force relying on passive defensive techniques called for in the 'dynamically stable deterrence' strategy outlined in the previous chapter.

The cost of these systems would be considerable, but not crippling. The cost of the Midgetman has been steadily declining due to breakthroughs in technology, and currently stands at between $25 and $35 billion. To place 50 existing MX missiles in rail garrison would cost between $9 and $12 billion. Carry-hard systems for silo-based missiles, in which a single missile is shuttled between several silos to increase the number of targets, vary in cost depending on

TABLE 3.5   *US Force Mix Under START: With Modernisation*

System	Delivery Vehicles	Warheads	Warheads Required to Attack
MX (rail)	100	1000	thousands[1]
Minuteman III	100–200	300–600	600–1200
Midgetman	300–100[2]	300–1000	thousands[3]
Trident D5	316	2508	invulnerable
B-1B/Stealth	variable	1400	partly invulnerable
Totals	1000–1600	6000	tens of thousands

[1] 10000 or more Soviet warheads would be required to barrage an MX force in rail garrison. Russell Dougherty, 'The Value of ICBM Modernization', *International Security* 12 (Autumn 1987), 170, concludes that after 12 hours' warning time even the entire current Soviet force could not achieve a high-confidence barrage effect against the MX, and the Soviets would have far fewer weapons under START. See also 'The Future of US ICBM', *Strategic Survey 1986–87* (London: IISS, 1987), p. 37, and Barry L. Schneider, 'Soviet Uncertainties in Targeting Peacekeeper', in Schneider, Colin S. Gray, and Keith B. Payne, *Missiles for the Nineties: ICBMs and Strategic Policy* (Boulder, CO: Westview Press, 1984), PP. 109–34.

[2] These variations would depend on how many were mobilised at first. 300 mobile Midgetmen could be purchased, or 1000 silo–based missiles. Depending on warning times, the two systems might absorb a similar number of warheads. If the silo-based weapons were procured, eventually several hundred of them would be mobilised. Alternately, a certain number of existing Minuteman missiles could be upgraded to Minuteman IV configurations with single new warheads, and a smaller number of Midgetmen could be procured, to be mobilised later. This proposal is discussed below.

[3] To target 500 mobile Midgetmen on just 10000 square miles of space, a Soviet planner would need 2500 warheads. With just two hours' warning time, that force could disperse over 40000 square miles of land; to barrage that area would require 6000 warheads to kill half the Midgetmen, or 12000 to kill 90 per cent of them. See CBO Study and Peter Claussen *et al.*, *In Search of Stability: An Assessment of New U.S. Nuclear Forces* (Cambridge, MA: Union of Concerned Scientists, 1983).

For an outstanding statement of how such modernisation obviates criticisms of the START accord, see Max Kampelman, 'Letter to the Editor', *Foreign Affairs* 68 (Summer 1989), 160–1.

which missile is under consideration: $40 billion for Midgetman, $24 billion for MX, and $19 billion for Minuteman III.[26]

If Midgetman were initially silo-based, these calculations would be affected somewhat. Silo-basing offers a number of advantages, primary among them far lower cost – only about $3 million per deployed warhead ($3 billion for 1000), as against $30–40 billion for an HML-borne mobile weapon.[27] Alternately, the United States could deploy a Minuteman IV or V with one or two warheads; the Air Force has already begun studying these systems.[28] If the United States superhardened its silos[29] and used a carry-hard system for Minuteman, the cost of an attack could be raised above the usual two warhead-per-silo requirement, to three or more. The US deterrent would be even more stable if complemented by a limited, ground-based BMD system. These systems can commonly raise the price of an attack on a silo to between three and eight warheads.[30] British, French and Chinese nuclear forces would further complicate matters for a Soviet planner; in attacking the United States he would leave himself without a significant reserve and completely vulnerable to those weapons. The overall result would be far more stable than proportionately reduced existing forces.[31]

Important issues involved in the distinction between generated and non-generated forces also call for modernisation. A US nuclear deterrent that is generated in a crisis – bombers flushed, submarines put to sea, mobile missiles deployed widely – retaliates much better than one on regular daily alert, and since the prospects for a Soviet 'bolt from the blue' are miniscule, assuming non-generated forces in various exchange scenarios may be unrealistic. Yet there are enormous political costs associated with generation; even in the midst of a deep crisis, there is no guarantee that an American president would generate his forces, an act which might raise domestic opposition.[32] Generation in a crisis could also heighten tensions between the superpowers and, under some extreme circumstances, cause a first strike by the other side. US nuclear forces ought therefore to be robust on a day-to-day basis, and modernisation – through acquisition of such stable weapons as the Midgetman (as opposed, it is important to note, to the rail MX, which must be generated from garrisons) – would contribute greatly toward this end.[33]

The Soviets, in fact, as suggested by their opposition to a ban on mobile ICBMs, would accept such a regime as stable. Marshal Sergey Akhromeyev said in 1989 that such weapons as the Midgetman and SS-25 are stabilising weapons in the hands of both superpowers.[34] They would presumably therefore have little problem with US modernisation.

POLITICAL FEASIBILITY OF MODERNISATION

As a basic condition of stable deterrence, modernisation of the US nuclear force is therefore critical, and this study assumes that it will occur. There is no guarantee, however, that such modernisation will be funded; indeed Richard Nixon's caution regarding START is based, not on the fact that the United States *could* not field a survivable START force, but on the notion that it *will* not. While the argument that a modernised START force would not be vulnerable 'is theoretically correct', Nixon suggests, 'it is politically unrealistic'. In an era of declining defence budgets and the lack of superpower tensions, and given 'expectation in Congress that arms cuts should produce defense budget cuts, it is unrealistic to expect the massive appropriations necessary to overhaul our sea-based and land-based forces over such a short period'.[35]

Nixon's argument characteristically gets quickly to the heart of the matter and examines political reality rather than strategic theory. On this issue, however, he may have exaggerated the dangers. First, the United States would not have to approve 'massive appropriations' to ensure a survivable deterrent. The sea-based leg is still invulnerable, and even a smaller number of Tridents would be acceptable given a survivable land-based leg of the triad; an 'overhaul' of the US SSBN force is therefore unnecessary. Similarly, US bombers need not be rapidly replaced given ALCM technologies; indeed the B-2 programme could be slashed without much damage to deterrence. Where the real expenditure is necessary is in the land-based force, whose flexibility, robustness and striking power can provide a muscular capability that would help cover slight flaws in the other two legs of the deterrent. Procurement of Midgetman is critical to that goal; procurement of rail-MX and carry-hard Minuteman would assist it significantly. And as noted above, the total cost of all three systems is roughly that of the B-2.

Still, the political winds in Washington are not blowing favourable winds on the Midgetman, or indeed on the future of land-based modernisation in general. If Midgetman were cancelled, serious damage would have been done to the sanguine image of stable deterrence outlined above, and indeed some of the basic theses of this volume would have been called into some question. This author, however, continues to believe that the objective rationale for the Midgetman, and the clear facts of its declining and relatively modest cost, will eventually prevail over more emotional opposition, and that the Midgetman or something like it will eventually be deployed. And this is more than hopeful theorising: many leaders on defence in the US Senate have already made it clear that they would not ratify a START treaty without a guarantee of modernisation; this chapter will later take up the issue of how a guarantee of such modernisation can be achieved as the price of START.

THE VALUE OF ARMS CONTROL

Thus, with modernisation, the United States can acquire a highly survivable deterrent. This analysis, stressing as it does the need for continued spending and modernisation, is not meant to deny the value of arms control. Indeed, the specific advantages of a START treaty are clear.

Some doubt the efficacy of arms control. R. James Woolsey argues that mobile missiles, by imposing a huge attack price, undercut 'an important part of the rationale for the military importance of arms reductions'. 'If the United States moves forward with a properly designed and developed small mobile ICBM', Woolsey writes, 'its strategic forces do not require control or reduction of Soviet nuclear arms for survivability'. SLBMs and bombers will remain invulnerable, he suggests, and ICBMs will become more so as they become mobile. Woolsey concludes that 'strategic offensive arms limitations or even substantial reductions are not likely to be particularly important in the future in preserving the survivability of U.S. strategic forces, as long as we move forward' with the SICBM.[36]

As the main theses of this volume attest, Woolsey could not be more wrong. Initially, a treaty is necessary to preserve the survivability of the US force because it would place a cap on the number of weapons the Soviets could deploy. Midgetman and mobile MX are no good if the Soviets obtain 30 000 warheads – such huge forces could overwhelm almost any US arsenal. As the tables above suggest, the requirements for striking mobile missiles are far from infinite, especially given probable public relations-based constraints on SICBM basing areas. By constraining the Soviets to 6000 warheads, a START treaty would cement a favourable cost/exchange ratio for the modernised US force.

Nor will bombers be invulnerable forever, a point that the Scowcroft Commission recognised. The only factor that keeps bombers safe is a problem of timing: the Soviets cannot strike missile fields without giving US bombers tactical warning of an attack, and if they hit the bombers first (with SLBMs from submarines lying close off US coasts) the United States could launch its ICBMs. As the Soviets deploy increasingly accurate and powerful low-trajectory SLBMs, however, they will become more and more able to strike US missiles and bombers simultaneously. New Soviet weapons could undermine the 'synergism' between the US bombers and ICBM forces.[37]

Bombers are also imperfect deterrent tools insofar as they are vulnerable to Soviet air defences. This is true of both penetrating bombers, which can be targeted and tracked, stealthy or not, and ALCM carriers. Soviet advances in look-down, shoot-down radars and other air defence technologies strongly suggest that 'at some time, the cruise missile will cease to be as effective as it is now'.[38] While they are considered stable weapons today, moreover, that image may not be sustained; as one proponent of 'dynamically stable deterrence' has pointed out, long-range combat aircraft (LRCAs)

do rely on tactical warning for survival and . . . once launched, they must be used fairly quickly or returned to very vulnerable airfields. In comparison to currently existing nuclear forces they seem stabilizing due to their slow response capability and their ability to at least partially escape destruction; but . . . LRCAs do not lend themselves to the sort of more controllable, slow-paced conflict envisioned by the dynamic stability concept . . . Thus, in contrast to current perceptions, LRCAs will become a relatively more vulnerable use-or-lose system unless we manage to develop manned LRCA systems that are not as dependent on large airfields and that can be dispersed far more widely than they now can (much like mobile ICBMs).[39]

The problems with relying entirely on submarines for deterrence were highlighted above, and it should also be mentioned that a Soviet planner with 30 000 or more warheads could afford to use several thousand in barrage attacks against potential US submarine and bomber deployment areas.[40] Only arms control can preserve the survivability of US forces.[41]

Arms control offers a number of other advantages. One is predictability: by channelling the arms race into stable patterns, a START accord could allay fears on both sides of sudden technological advances or other developments that would disrupt the balance.[42] Treaties also improve superpower relations, both in fact and in the perception of third parties.[43] And while it was always questionable whether superiority at the nuclear margin had much relevance,[44] a perpetually equal balance, when combined with highly survivable forces, would eliminate fears of inferiority.

Most important, though, is the fact that all alternatives to arms control are both politically infeasible and increasingly unstable. Neither the American public nor European or Third World governments or peoples would be willing to tolerate a perpetual arms race; the Reagan administration discovered to its early dismay that it had at least to give the appearance of arms control to placate popular opinion. A continuation of present trends would also be worse than arms control in terms of cost and stability considerations. As many detractors have pointed out, START offers few opportunities for immediate budget savings, but does hold out the hope of significant savings at some point, which is better than nothing. And as noted, Soviet strategic deployments will preserve and exacerbate the present vulnerability of two legs of the US triad, and for that and other reasons the nuclear balance will continue to erode. Dismissing arms control as an illusion, then, and calling instead for reliance on the 'stable' status quo, is at best a questionable policy. As one observer concludes, START as it stands '*would* promote U.S. goals by putting the United States in a stronger position to maintain the survivability of its retaliatory force than it would be without an agreement'.[45]

OTHER ISSUES: REQUIREMENTS FOR STABILITY

But a secure nuclear balance is not the only requirement for stability. It also requires secure C3I, survivable superpower communications, and other factors. These requirements are examined below.

Command, Control, Communications and Intelligence (C3I)

We have seen that the United States and the Soviet Union will in all probability field survivable nuclear forces; and we have seen that both sides could take operational and doctrinal steps to further bolster stability. But stable nuclear forces are not all that is required for security. Both sides must also possess survivable C3I[46] lest either side come to believe it could disarm the other merely by destroying its C3I and thereby protecting, or at least disrupting, a retaliation.

The most ardent chronicler of this idea has been Bruce Blair, a former Minuteman launch control officer. He argues that the US nuclear arsenal has never been truly secure; indeed, during the days of imputed US nuclear superiority during the 1950s and 1960s, 'In all likelihood Soviet strikes against C3I systems would have severely impaired and possibly blocked U.S. retaliation'. Indeed, an attack on C3I would have been preferable to an attack on missile silos, since 'the expected damage exceeded by a wide margin the damage that could have been expected from an attack on missile silos'.[47]

C3I improvements have altered this situation, but not completely. Key US command posts, such as Washington, DC and Cheyenne Mountain, remain vulnerable to nuclear strikes,[48] and the only partly survivable US command posts remain airborne systems such as NEACP. Even those are vulnerable to various forms of attack. The implications of these facts are serious; Blair argues that C3I vulnerabilities 'have been so severe for so long that developments in the size and technical composition of the superpower's arsenals have been practically irrelevent to the nuclear confrontation'.[49] US C3I facilities remain old and poorly equipped, moreover.[50] Improvements are under way – including a $1.3 billion effort for Cheyenne Mountain alone – but more efforts are obviously required.

One particular danger of C3I vulnerability is the decapitation scenario. Some analysts argue that the Soviet Union could launch a surprise attack, probably with sea-launched cruise missiles (SLCMs), against US command elements. Their hope would be that such an attack would so disrupt an American response that retaliatory damage would be smaller than if the Soviets launched an all-out strike against US missile forces alone; and as Blair notes, historical evidence exists to support such a strategy. A decapitation attack would be an incredible gamble, but to the extent vulnerable C3I encourages resort to it that vulnerability is destabilising.

Another risk of C3I vulnerability is that it places both sides' forces on a hair-trigger. Not knowing whether their command and control systems would survive an attack, both sides must plan very rapid retaliation (in the case of the Soviets, even *pre-emptive* retaliation). The result is instability caused by the risk of accidental launches based on computer errors. Blair argues that 'command vulnerability has virtually dictated a philosophy of early use, and it is this broad instability rather than the narrow one resulting from Minuteman vulnerability' that underlies crisis instability.[51]

What is to be done? The United States must fund and deploy a much more survivable C3I network. Like the present system, it would consist of two parts: warning (intelligence) and command and control. The United States must both recognise that an attack is underway and possess the means to respond to that attack, either before, during or after it has occurred. Reagan administration programmes made some inroads in this direction, particularly in the area of warning, but the core of the US command system remains vulnerable and will become more so; for example, Soviet ASAT advances could allow them to shoot down US MILSTAR satellites, a critical new component of the US C3I network.

Several specific reforms could be pursued. Existing aircraft and command and control sites must be hardened and modernised; Blair estimates the cost of a truly significant C3I modernisation programme at $30 to $50 billion. Arms control accords can reduce C3I vulnerability – an anti-satellite ban would protect space-based assets; bans on stationing weapons (sea- or ground-based) close to the other side's borders would reduce the potential for decapitation attacks; and a ban on low-trajectory SLBM tests would impair both sides' ability to deploy those weapons, which are particularly suited for command attacks. Chapter 9 examines those proposals in more depth.

This discussion leaves decisions on which specific systems to be procured (such as deep underground command posts, alternate National Command Authorities [NCAs], short-takeoff-and-landing airborne command posts, cheap satellites to reconstitute post-attack communications) to subsequent study. But whatever the systems chosen, C3I improvements may become more possible than ever in the wake of a START treaty, which will eventually liberate resources by reducing the need for further nuclear force modernisation.[52]

Improved US-Soviet Communications Systems

The need for superpower communications in a crisis is obvious, and has resulted in the development of a fairly reliable network of superpower communications, which includes embassy channels, the Hotline and new Nuclear Risk Reduction Centers. On a day-to-day basis, or even during a crisis, the superpowers therefore possess significant communications capabilities.

Yet the need for superpower communications *capable of surviving in a limited nuclear environment* has so far been overlooked. Existing means of interaction are not survivable and have no prospect of being so; planned improvements in the Hotline do not include hardening. Superpower comlinks (communications links) are vulnerable to direct attack, sabotage, or even indirect destruction through EMP (electro-magnetic pulse) effects. The United States and the Soviet Union must address this shortcoming to ensure adequate crisis management and war termination.

The vulnerabilities of superpower comlinks could become evident in a number of circumstances, not all assuming any superpower desire for crisis or war. During the early stage of superpower war, Hotline links might be destroyed by direct attack, collateral damage from attacks on nearby targets, or simply EMP effects. A third party attack on either or both superpowers could destroy comlinks, as could accidental or unauthorised launches, by either superpowers or third parties.

These possibilities point to a number of specific dangers. If at the beginning of a superpower conflict the ability to communicate rapidly were lost, opportunities for conflict limitation and termination would be seriously compromised. This would be especially true in an era in which the pace of war has increased very much – life-or-death crisis decisions must today be made in a matter of minutes, and without real-time communications the superpowers might fail to consult effectively.

Superpower communication vulnerability also creates a risk that third-party, accidental or unauthorised launches will lead to all-out war. If both capitals are attacked or damaged by such an attack, surviving leaders might not be able to consult with each other rapidly enough and disaster could ensue.[53]

A number of strategic analysts have recognised the need for survivable wartime US-Soviet communications. Indeed, when describing the conditions that could give rise to the need for the sort of limited war capability he advocated, then-Secretary of Defense James Schlesinger testified in 1974 that '*if we were to maintain continued communications with the Soviet leaders during the war*', and if other conditions were met, then 'in spite of whatever one says historically in advance that everything must go all out, when the existential circumstances arise, political leaders on both sides will be under powerful pressure to continue to be sensible'.[54]

In their study *Beyond the Hotline*, William Ury and Richard Smoke suggested a number of purposes for improved superpower crisis management and communications facilities. Among other tasks, they would help in 'containing' crises, 'coping with nuclear detonations whose source and motive are unclear'. They might also aid in 'halting inadvertently triggered incipient hostilities and return to *status quo ante*'.[55] Survivable communications would serve those ends admirably.

Desmond Ball has recognised the importance of survivable communications for war termination efforts. 'The principal technical system which has officially been identified with facilitating war termination is a direct communications link' between Washington and Moscow, he notes, yet 'despite this system's critical importance to war termination, no special measures have been taken to protect it from the collateral effects of a nuclear exchange'.[56] Ball and a number of other strategic analysts wrote in a joint work on crisis stability that 'It is essential that the superpowers be able to communicate with each other under essentially all conditions'. A survivable comlink, the experts concluded, could 'provide postattack communications that are likely to be indispensable for war termination'.[57]

Survivable superpower communications would thus assist in war termination, which is in turn essential for damage limitation in an era when counterforce capabilities may well decline. RAND analysts Edward Warner and David Ochmanek agree that, excluding missile defences, 'the prospects for meaningful damage limitation in the event of war would turn primarily on intrawar escalation control'. To achieve this goal 'cooperative measures to maintain reliable communications between the sides during a nuclear war could also help to limit and rapidly terminate the conflict'.[58]

Another multiple-author volume on crisis stability agrees, pointing out that

> The current Hot Line links the national command authorities in Washington and Moscow via commercial telecommunications satellites. During wartime such satellites are likely to be used for military purposes, thus creating an incentive for attack. The currently installed backup cable link could also be destroyed unintentionally in attacks on other targets. Furthermore, the satellite link is served by a single ground station in each nation's capital. If the NCA has shifted to an alternate command post, direct Hot Line communication is not possible. Should strategic war have commenced, the terminals could well be destroyed. Survivable links are urgently needed for the Hot Line.[59]

Various means have been suggested to achieve these ends. One proposal has been to dedicate a satellite to the single purpose of superpower communications; presumably, neither side would have any incentive to attack it because it would not serve an, military purpose. As a backup to the satellite, some analysts have suggested dispersed, redundant and hardened High Frequency radio stations.

Apparently it cannot be known in advance which HF frequencies will be usable after nuclear strikes, so a communications system using HF must have the capability to search through a pre-arranged set of frequencies until a usable one is found.[60] Survivable NATO/Warsaw Pact comlinks might also prove extremely useful, helping to prevent conventional warfare in Europe after accidental or third-party nuclear detonations had occurred.[61]

There are, of course, a number of costs and dangers inherent in the creation of such a survivable communications link. These seem clearly to be outweighed by the requirements for and advantages of such an insurance against accidental war, though one particularly troubling critique is the 'thinkability' argument, which suggests that survivable superpower comlinks could indeed encourage the perception that limited nuclear exchanges could occur without escalation.

This argument is not persuasive. The huge dangers that the system might actually fail would discourage nuclear risk-taking. Even if the Hotline works, escalation control is not guaranteed. In short, those circumstances in which the greater confidence in escalation control granted by a survivable Hotline would recommend use of nuclear weapons are so few as to not pose a serious danger. The relative benefits, moreover, are clear; as two analysts have concluded, while there might be some 'minimal risk' of increasing thinkability, 'the greater danger is not knowing how to stop such madness if it happens'.[62]

Speed of Retaliation

Another issue related to stability is the speed with which a defender retaliates against a first strike. In theory, if both sides decided to retaliate more slowly to a nuclear attack, crisis stability would increase. When retaliation is tied to a hair-trigger response system, the chances of war by accident increase, especially in a crisis. Numerous documented cases exist of false warnings partially triggering US nuclear warning systems; during a crisis, such an error could lead to war.

Several analysts have recognised that slower retaliation would augment crisis stability.[63] Stephen Cimbala argues that 'a deterrent less reliant upon immediate retaliation might be a deterrent less dependent upon hair-trigger responses, and thus one that is withheld in a crisis in which out deterrent might otherwise be launched prematurely'.[64] Bruce Blair points out, as was noted above, that vulnerable C3I causes crisis instability by forcing prompt responses on a defender. Blair argues that

> A long-term goal of nuclear modernization should be to adopt a policy that allows for no immediate second use. The basic justification for this policy is that nuclear decision-making should not be reduced to reflexes and brief drills, but should instead be regarded as a careful deliberative exercise of national leadership that could take days or longer ... These matters cannot be given adequate consideration in a matter of minutes or hours.[65]

Scott Sagan agrees that if US planners paid more attention to 'the critical difference between prompt and slow counterforce requirements, the crisis instability problem inherent in counterforce targeting could be significantly reduced'.[66]

If the United States adopted a policy of slower retaliation, that policy would carry a number of implications for US doctrine and force posture. Most importantly, US C3I systems would have to be upgraded to sustain a limited, even relatively large-scale, nuclear attack; otherwise US leaders would be unable to execute retaliation hours or days after the Soviet first strike. Control of nuclear weapons could be tightened, since immediate time-urgent response would no longer be a criterion for nuclear forces. The types of weapons in US inventory could change: fast ICBMs would be devalued while slower bombers and cruise missiles, and arguably also less accurate SLBMs, would be more important. (This would create a situation amenable to Hendrickson's distinction between different forms of weapons discussed earlier.)

Yet there are severe problems with a general strategy of delayed response. Most important, such a strategy might undermine deterrence. Confident in their ability to strike the United States once and have hours or days to reload and shoot second or third salvoes, Soviet leaders might gain significant confidence in their war plans. In this case, the timing of deterrence and its strength trade off.

Sagan recognises this danger. 'Such a lengthy delayed retaliation policy', he writes,

> ... might seriously undermine deterrence. It is not difficult to speculate on the improved effectiveness of an offensive war plan designed by the Soviet General Staff to take advantage of a twenty-four-hour 'no-immediate-second-strike' policy: ICBM and SLBM forces could be launched in prolonged waves and reloaded and

reconstituted with impunity; follow-on ICBMs could be easily retargeted and launched to compensate for any ICBM launch failures,

and so on. In short, 'For a Soviet military planner interested in limiting damage to the USSR in the event of a nuclear war, a twenty-four-hour delay in U.S. retaliation would provide significant opportunities'.[67]

Reliance on bombers and ALCMs also is problematic. So long as general missile defences are not deployed, bombers will remain the most vulnerable type of retaliatory vehicle – just ahead of cruise missiles, against which modern Soviet fighters and look-down, shoot-down radar might be designed. Launching an MX against the USSR virtually guarantees that ten enormously destructive warheads will fall on Soviet soil; sending ten B-1Bs against the USSR, however, is a much more questionable proposition, and deterrence suffers for the difference.

Nor is there any real guarantee that the policy would reduce crisis instability very much. If the United States waited but a few hours to retaliate, it could still end up responding to false warnings or third-party attacks, especially if communications with Moscow had been severed. Yet for US leaders to wait days to retaliate would require degrees of restraint, robustness of C3I, and willingness to absorb follow-on attacks that cannot be assumed.

How are we to resolve this issue? In part, the danger to crisis instability posed by counterforce weapons will be attenuated by START and subsequent modernisation. As noted above, deep cuts in strategic forces combined with increasingly survivable deterrents will improve crisis stability regardless of the types of weapons deployed.

The United States could also address the issue of crisis stability and slower retaliation through doctrine, though not necessarily as broadly as some advocates suggest. The United States should adopt a no-immediate-retaliation policy *for limited attacks* that carry no danger of seriously degrading US retaliatory capabilities. This would virtually eliminate the danger of accidental war based on false warning or an unauthorised launch; it is worth remembering that most publicly-discussed examples of false alerts have involved detections of small groups of planes or missiles, not massive attacks. Even if ten or a dozen nuclear warheads detonated on US soil, general – or even symmetrical – retaliation might be unwise, and a no-immediate-retaliation policy in this regard would allow US command authorities to determine proper responses.

Nor would the doctrine impinge on deterrence. A large-scale Soviet attack would produce a response as immediate as US planners wanted to make it; US authorities would respond slowly only to a very limited attack. The scenarios under which the Soviets could achieve an advantage from feigning an accident and launching several missiles at the United States are implausible, *provided* US C3I assets are capable of withstanding such an attack. US authorities could fire a similar response at Soviet conventional forces (as suggested in chapter 4), a step that might not trigger general war. Or they could do nothing. In any case, it seems clear that the danger of accidental war in a crisis from false warning is greater than the danger of an extremely limited Soviet nuclear strike (to which the United States *could* respond in due time), making a no-immediate-retaliation policy for limited attacks beneficial on balance. The doctrine also contains a healthy recognition of the demands of the paradox of deterrence, responding to a difference in deterrence requirements between limited and general wars.

What implications does this doctrine hold for US policy? Initially, it requires C3I assets able to survive a limited nuclear war; probably the only realistic scenario under which the Soviets could gain a significant advantage from a limited first strike is the well-known decapitation scenario, and improving C3I would reduce the potential for such a strike. The doctrine also demands survivable superpower communications, for if nuclear bombs went off in the United States and US authorities were waiting to determine a response, their most critical requirement would be communications with Moscow. The survivable Hotline suggested above would respond to that need. Finally, the doctrine requires early-warning capabilities sufficient to provide unambiguous, redundant, foolproof warning against an all-out Soviet attack, which is required to prevent accidental war arising from false warnings of the sort of assault to which the United States would still react immediately.

As chapter 8 will explain, non-nuclear strategic weapons (NNSW) might have some effect on the notion of speed of retaliation. NNSW could provide an ability to retaliate quickly without crossing the nuclear threshold – a potentially important capability in certain circumstances. US planners could also use NNSW to respond quickly or slowly to third-party attacks.

4 Targeting Policy

Deterring a nuclear war requires far more than the possession of a secure nuclear force. It also demands, as Walter Slocombe has recognised, 'a doctrine and plans for the use of our forces (if they are needed) that make clear to the Soviets the hard reality that, by any course leading to nuclear war and any course nuclear war might take, they could never gain anything amounting to a victory on any plausible definition of victory, or gain an advantage that would outweigh the unacceptable price they would have to pay'.[1] In short, one of the crucial aspects of nuclear deterrence is a strategy for targeting a retaliation to achieve the greatest deterrent effect.

Just what is required for adequate deterrence has, of course, been the subject of acrimonious debate both within and outside the government since the outset of the nuclear age. The key question has been just what a 'plausible definition of victory' might be – whether the United States needed to threaten multiple nuclear options to deny the Soviets military advantage in a nuclear war, or whether it merely had to promise a retaliation sufficient to destroy Soviet society. These questions were addressed in chapter 2.

That chapter also spelled out the advantages of the co-operative reciprocal deterrence strategy advocated by this volume. This chapter in turn suggests that a series of political, technological and strategic developments will probably usher in the need for a reassessment of the manner in which US nuclear forces are to be employed. Current US plans for counterforce targeting intended in part to achieve damage limitation will probably fail to withstand the multiple pressures of arms control, Soviet strategic modernisation, the US budget crisis, and growing opposition from within US and European populaces and governments. The days of counterforce targeting and damage limitation, in which US planners aim their retaliation at Soviet nuclear forces, are numbered.[2]

CURRENT US TARGETING STRATEGY

US policy for nuclear war has for some time stressed counterforce targeting, making Soviet nuclear forces the primary target of a retaliation or, under very extreme circumstances, a first strike. The key goal is deterrence. Another has been damage limitation: by hitting Soviet nuclear assets, the United States could prevent their being launched against its territory and thus limit damage to itself.[3] Damage limitation is not a stated goal of US policy but is implicit in the acquisition of counterforce capabilities.[4]

Contrary to popular impression, these strategies have been evident since the early days of US nuclear strategy. The initial US nuclear strategy was, of course, massive retaliation. Earlier doctrines contained only exceedingly primitive nuclear war plans: the vague 1945 plan *Totality* had been followed in October of the same year with *The Strategic Vulnerability of Russia to a Limited Air Attack*, which called for 20 bombs to be dropped on Soviet cities to ruin Soviet war-making potential. Those and other early strategies reflected the American proclivity for strategic bombing. Publicly, however, few analyses of potential doctrine or targeting plans were made, and in fact it was not until 1948 that the military was allowed to form plans for the use of nuclear weapons, and even then President Truman retained personal control of them.[5]

Once given the ability to formulate nuclear war strategies, SAC undertook the task rapidly. In December 1948, during the Berlin airlift crisis, SAC planners developed a war plan calling for strikes against Soviet urban-industrial assets, which were the 'highest priority' targets. They were to be attacked over the course of 30 days with the goal of destroying Soviet war-making capability.[6]

In late 1949 *Dropshot* became the official US targeting strategy. The August 1949 Soviet test of an atomic bomb opened the possibility of Soviet nuclear strikes on the United States. Largely as a result, US planners began to emphasise counterforce strikes against Soviet nuclear weapons; by 1956–57 the Soviet Union was expected to possess up to 250 bombs, the stockpiles, production facilities and bomber delivery vehicles of which became the chief targets of the US nuclear force. Other targets included Soviet political control hubs, Other Military Targets (OMT), and industrial targets.[7]

Publicly, this trend was not evident. John Foster Dulles formally endorsed Massive Retaliation in 1954, partly because the Eisenhower administration sought a way to justify decreased spending on conventional weapons. Public versions of massive retaliation strongly implied countervalue strikes. Yet already counterforce targeting had begun, and the list of target priorities would remain essentially unchanged to the present day. In the August 1950 *Shakedown* plan, 'first priority was given to "the destruction of known targets affecting the Soviet capacity to deliver atomic bombs" '.[8] After counterforce targets came OMT (Other Military Targets), political, and finally industrial targets. The 1950–52 JCS plans BRAVO, DELTA and ROMEO emphasised similar priorities; as Michael Nacht has recognised, 'The principal targets were counterforce (military forces) and urban-industrial (factories), not civilian population centers'.[9]

US planners discussed pre-emptive and even preventive attacks on the Soviet Union. NSC-68 admitted that a US retaliation could be delivered in response to an attack 'on its way or about to be delivered'. In the first year of the Eisenhower administration, 'numerous examinations of the preventive war option' took place, according to Scott Sagan; a JCS study group even suggested that the United States consider 'deliberately precipitating a war with the USSR in the near future' to destroy Soviet nuclear forces before they became a 'real menace' to US security. In December 1954 the NSC rejected preventive, but not pre-emptive, attacks.[10]

By the late 1950s the rush to target the Soviet military was in full force. Influenced by RAND Corporation and US Air Force Studies, the Eisenhower administration targeted nuclear weapons and their industries and communications centres. A number of factors encouraged this trend: as the Soviet stockpile of weapons grew, so did the threat it presented to the United States; the development of the hydrogen bomb provided a weapon to take over targeting of urban-industrial areas and freed atomic bombs for counterforce targeting; and continued US superiority provided the means for a reasonably effective strike. Counterforce targets, at that time Soviet nuclear weapons and strategic airpower, constituted the chief US strike mission and the US Strategic Air Command was configured accordingly.[11]

Before the Kennedy administration assumed power, massive retaliation was institutionalised in the 1960 SIOP plan (called SIOP-62) for the employment of US nuclear weapons.[12] The rapid proliferation of large numbers and a wide variety of nuclear weapons had created the need for a re-evaluation of US targeting strategy. A 1958–59 study by the Net Evaluation Subcommittee of the National Security Council, NESC 2009, called for an 'optimum mix' of counterforce and countervalue targets, the latter primarily composed of the Soviet defence industrial base. The study outlined a Comprehensive Strategic Target List with 2021 targets: 121 ICBM silos, 140 air defence sites (to clear a path for US bombers), 200 bomber bases, 218 military/government control centres, 124 OMT, and the rest industrial targets and some in China. In the event of war, the United States would conduct a spasm launch – all US weapons would be launched at once upon the decision to attack. In December 1960, this list was approved as the basis for the first SIOP.

The implications were revealed publicly by Defense Secretary Thomas Gates:

> What we would actually do depends on the circumstances, but we are adjusting our power to a counterforce theory; or a mixture of a counterforce theory plus attacks on industrial centers and things of that character. We are not basing our requirements on just bombing Russia for retaliatory purposes.[13]

Yet massive retaliation was doomed. For while the trend toward counterforce targeting accelerated in the 1960s, it was soon matched by an increasing reliance on limited nuclear options. The strategic objectives of US nuclear forces were and are twofold: to deter war, and in the event of war, to limit damage to US population and industrial centres (achieved, as chapter 1 noted, through escalation control and war termination). The innovation of the Kennedy/ McNamara era lay in the degree to which it (somewhat secretly) emphasised the latter of these two requirements – an attempt, through flexible strategies of employment and counterforce targeting, to pursue damage limitation; US nuclear plans therefore emphasised multiple options and flexibility.[14] US strategy did retain a significant assured destruction capacity, keeping thousands of urban-industrial targets on the lists.[15]

In its new SIOP, the Kennedy administration institutionalised the concept of flexible employment. Believing an all-out, spasm nuclear response to any communist aggression to be incredible, Kennedy's advisors attempted to construct a variety of potential nuclear attacks and adopted a 'no-cities' deterrence concept that avoided counter-city targeting. The new SIOP, drawing on models already constructed, envisioned a five-stage attack: targets would include, in order, Soviet nuclear forces, OMT not near cities, OMT near cities, communications and control centres, and urban-industrial targets. These plans were approved in January 1962, and Secretary of Defense Robert McNamara publicly enunciated the administration's sophisticated new strategy in his famous 1962 Ann Arbor speech.

As Desmond Ball has recognised, this further reliance on counterforce targeting depended upon two crucial US advantages. First, the United States retained overall nuclear superiority, and hence possessed enough weapons to allocate to Soviet nuclear forces. Second, developments in satellite technology allowed the United States to locate and target Soviet forces better than it had in the past.[16] With the capability to find Soviet forces and enough nuclear weapons to fire at them, then, the United States possessed a reasonable counterforce capability.

The administration was forced very quickly, however, to retreat from public statements of flexible options and no-cities deterrence. The outcry against the new strategy came from domestic and international sources. Some media and observers in the United States viewed a no-cities counterforce strategy as suggestive of an intent to launch a first-strike at the USSR. As might be expected, Moscow condemned the strategy as provocative and dangerous. And America's allies expressed their doubts about a strategy that contemplated fighting limited nuclear wars – and perhaps most pointedly, that attempted to avoid a spasm launch in Europe's defence.[17]

Between 1964 and 1966, then, public US policy shifted back to a modified version of assured destruction. Importantly, however, the concept of damage limitation had been appended to that strategy. As originated in the studies of Lt. Col. Glenn Kent and others, damage limitation had long been (and in many respects remains) an implicit US goal, and in practical terms it meant counterforce strikes to eliminate the Soviet potential to launch a second nuclear strike on America. It is important to note, however, that actual war plans did not revert to spasm-launch policies – they changed little, retaining flexible options of nuclear employment.[18]

Nixon administration policies built upon these notions of flexible employment. Kissenger's National Security Study Memorandum (NSSM) 3, requested the day after inauguration in 1969, was partly designed, as he put it, to 'kill assured destruction' and establish the need for limited nuclear options (LNO's) and escalation control. A series of Nixon administration directives, including National Security Decision Memorandum (NSDM) 242 of January 1974 and the first *Nuclear Weapons Employment Policy* guide (NUWEP-1) of April 1974, reflected these goals.[19]

An example of US targeting is displayed in a declassified US target list from 1969 in Table 4.1. Roughly 60 to 70 per cent of US nuclear assets are dedicated to counterforce targets, but a large number of weapons are still dedicated to urban-industrial, assured destruction-category targets.[20]

The Carter and Reagan administrations left untouched much of the

TABLE 4.1   *US Target List: 1969*

Targets	No. of Targets	ICBMs & SLBMs	Air-to-Surface Missiles[a]	Gravity Bombs[a]
		Weapons Assigned		
Urban Industry and govt. controls	150	533		
Satellites	65	27[b]		
Strategic Nuclear				
Bomber bases	210	309		
ICBM soft	122	179		
ICBM hard	100	147		200
IR/MRBM	125	184		
IR/MRBM-hard	113	166		226
Sub bases	35	51		35
Offensive control	45	66		
Defensive and Other Military				
Air defence fields	115	96	65	
Unco-located SAMs	140		280	
Aircraft disp. bases	110			220
Strat./tac. wpns. storage	240			249
Other mil./interdiction	220			220
Total	1790	1758	345	1150

Source   *Draft Memorandum for the President, Recommended FY 1965– 1969 Strategic Retaliatory Forces*, 6 December 1963, p. 1–37 (McNamara Recommended Forces), OSDL-FOI. Reprinted in Scott D. Sagan, *Moving Targets: Nuclear Strategy and National Security* (Princeton University Press, 1989), p. 35. Reprinted here with permission of Princeton University Press.

[a] The air-to-surface missiles and gravity bombs are associated with the alert bomber force only.

[b] These forces could possibly be augmented by missiles in an emergency combat condition, part of the alert bomber force, and the bomber positive control backup force.

basis of NSDM 242 and NUWEP-1, which were reaffirmed in Carter's Presidential Directive (PD) 18 of August 1977. Carter boldly pushed this trend forward in July 1979 with PD-59, which discussed a variety of scenarios for limited conflict and was quickly condemned by many as a dangerous example of nuclear war-fighting plans.[21] However, the Schlesinger/Brown 'flexible response' or 'flexible employment' strategies, known as the countervailing strategy by 1979, clearly represented merely an evolution of existing counterforce targeting policies, and indeed Secretary Brown pointed this out at the time. While McNamara had concealed the plans from public view, however, the Carter administration enunciated them.[22]

During the Nixon/Schlesinger era, economic recovery targeting also achieved a renewed prominence. Nixon administration planners placed a high priority on destroying Soviet war-making and recovery potential, believing such targeting contributed significantly to deterrence. Assured destruction had once again reasserted a greater relative influence over targeting policy.[23]

The Carter administration's countervailing strategy, which began to approach Soviet war-fighting, war-winning doctrines, altered these priorities significantly. This shift was heavily dependent upon an analysis of Soviet nuclear strategy, from which US planners drew the lesson that they must threaten Soviet leaders with death and defeat, not just destruction, to deter them adequately. The distinction between deterrence by punishment and deterrence by denial was outlined in chapter 2; basically it holds that threatening countervalue retaliation might not be credible. The countervailing strategy thus called for a greater relative emphasis on counterforce and countermilitary targeting, to destroy Soviet nuclear and conventional forces and deny their war aims; on counterleadership targeting, to threaten them with death; and for less of an emphasis on targeting of industrial recovery assets.

By 1983, when the Reagan administration instituted SIOP-6, US planners had identified tens of thousands of Soviet targets worthy of nuclear strikes, and probably dozens of highly classified attack scenarios. Deputy Undersecretary of Defense Fred Iklé studied the problem and helped produce the NSDD-13 of October 1981 and NUWEP-82 of July 1982. These again represented an evolutionary step, building on Carter administration calls for abilities to wage extended nuclear conflict and to target Soviet nuclear forces, economic recovery assets, and others.

Importantly, the emphasis today remains on retaliation against Soviet nuclear forces as well as other military and industrial centres. The US target list, as it is known in unclassified circles, contains a mix of counterforce and countervalue targets. One official study from the late 1970s summarises US retaliation in Table 4.2, organised by target; it is similar to the 1969 target list, in that the general emphasis is on counterforce targeting while a large number of urban industrial targets remains. It could probably be presumed that post-1980 target lists are significantly more skewed to counterforce targets, due to the renewed emphasis on them in the countervailing doctrine.

TABLE 4.2   *US Nuclear Retaliation, Late 1970s*

Target	Generated Situation	Non-Generated Situation
Nuclear	2018	1761
OMT	1603	935
Leadership	736	423
Economic-Industrial	4400 (3572 aim points)	2300 (1793 aim points)
Total	8757	5419[24]

The consensus that the United States continues to pursue some form of counterforce targeting is complete. Carl Builder of RAND has argued that there are some 6000 counterforce targets in the USSR, 3000 of which are hard enough to require the targeting of two warheads; 'these targets', he concludes, 'account for 85 to 90 percent of the current U.S. requirements for nuclear weapons'.[25] Desmond Ball has concluded that 'it can be assumed that "at least one reliable warhead"' is allocated to each of the roughly 2000 Soviet nuclear force targets.[26]

In fact, as has been noted, US target lists still contain many value targets. Indeed Philip Bobbitt has commented that it is 'unhelpful' to characterise US nuclear strategy as countervalue or counterforce 'when every United States war plan has necessarily included important elements of both these target types'.[27] Indeed, as noted, the current US strategy is a *countervailing* one, including both counterforce and countervalue targets in an effort to convince an opponent that the United States could retaliate in kind for any sort of attack. This book advocates such a strategy devoid of counterforce nuclear targets.

FORCES FOR CHANGE

Yet there are forces at work that might spur a sea-change in US targeting policy. Strategic arms control, Soviet strategic modernisation, US budget problems and public opposition to war-fighting policies, if they all occur as expected, will combine to call seriously into question US policies of damage-limiting counterforce. None of the developments in question is guaranteed; they are all contingent conditions. But if they occur, they will force a re-evaluation of the way in which the United States deters nuclear war.

A strategic arms treaty would reduce to between 6000 and 9000 the number of warheads in the US nuclear inventory. Retaliatory warheads might number as few as 2–3000, and not all would be counterforce-capable. Such a force is clearly inadequate for damage-limiting counterforce strikes because a US retaliator would not have enough weapons to target the Soviet START forces.[28]

The specifics of the emerging treaty support these arguments. Under the current framework, both sides would be allowed 6000 warheads on 1600 launchers, not more than roughly 1500 warheads on heavy ICBMs and not more than 4900 on ICBMs and SLBMs combined; bombers possess limited counterforce capabilities, as do all but the most recent SLBMs. Whereas today the ratio of counterforce-capable weapons to nuclear targets might be 6 or 7:1, under START it might be 4:1 or even 3:1, and under future treaties this ratio would close even further. (The effect, of course, is de-MIRVing.)[29] The potential for a counterforce second strike would become incredibly small.[30]

This conclusion becomes especially telling if we consider the potential strike requirements against just a set of mobile missiles. One Congressional Budget Office study indicates that, with only two hours' warning time, Midgetman could disperse over 40 000 square miles of land from a starting point of three Minuteman bases. To destroy just half this force, the Soviets would need to expend 6000 warheads; to kill 95 per cent of the Midgetman would take 12 000 warheads, fully twice what the Soviets would have under START.[31] The problem for the United States is even more severe insofar as the Soviets have few political barriers to the wide deployment of their mobiles. These figures, moreover, do not include strike requirements for rail-mobile missiles (as many as 10 000 warheads) or remaining silo-based missiles (if protected with limited missile defences, several hundred more), not to mention bombers or submarines.

The task becomes even more difficult when it is recognised that a counterforce retaliation is supposed to occur during the unprecedented radioactive fog of a nuclear war. Whatever is theoretically possible, US command and control systems are not now and have little prospect of being up to the task of conducting an extended nuclear war, especially one that requires the precise targeting of enemy nuclear forces.[32]

As the Soviets enhance the survivability of their nuclear assets by making some ICBMs mobile and placing other weapons at sea, it will become increasingly difficult for US planners to retaliate against them – or even target them – effectively.[33] Perhaps the two best examples of this trend are the SS-24 and SS-25, the Soviets' rail and road-mobile missiles. Whether US systems can find and track these weapons with sufficient accuracy to permit their destruction is highly questionable. The B-2, for example, which has been touted for the mission of hitting Soviet strategic relocatable targets (SRTs), does not currently possess the sort of sophisticated tracking gear for it to do its job: the bomber is being built on the *assumption* that such equipment will be developed and the US Air Force recently backed off claims that the B-2 could be used in this manner. Nor is targeting SRTs necessarily a good idea; indeed one of the basis theses of this volume is that it is not – counterforce targeting is neither feasible nor desirable today. Michael Brower agrees with regard to SRT's, arguing that 'On purely technical grounds, the SRT targeting programme's chances of success are quite low, because of the relative ease and low cost of potential Soviet countermeasures'. He also recognises that, because mobile missiles enhance security, 'the SRT effort appears to go far beyond what is necessary, or prudent, to protect U.S. security'.[34] And while only 10 per cent of Soviet targets are mobile today, up to 50 per cent will be by the year 2000.[35]

US defence budget shortfalls will further exacerbate the problems of counterforce planners. Although modernisation of US nuclear forces will undoubtedly occur, the United States may not invest enough in strategic systems to support a war-fighting doctrine. For example, with as much as $300 billion being cut from defence budgets over the next five years, such programmes as hardened command and control, advanced targeting assets and other support systems for counterforce may be cut. Strategic defence and the B-2 bomber, both important for damage limitation, may well also feel the budget knife.

Public disgust with the long-standing risk of nuclear war, in both Europe and the United States, will also severely constrain the options open to Western policy-makers in their search for reliable deterrents. Chapter 1 outlined the general parameters of the public opinion issue; a START accord could easily spur additional calls for US renunciation of all forms of counterforce and war-fighting strategies, which might be seen as inappropriate for a new era of international *glasnost*. To the extent that US declaratory policy reflects any admission of a willingness to engage in nuclear war, public opposition might force a change.

BARRIERS TO A CHANGE IN STRATEGY

Yet the obstacles to any shift from counterforce targeting are significant. In a general sense it must be recognised that those agencies of the US government charged with developing US targeting strategy have for many years displayed a real affinity for counterforce. Military control of nuclear weapons policy has aided this process, but in the last two administrations civilian planners also advocated damage limiting strategies. There is no reason to be sure that US nuclear planners, wedded as they are to damage limitation, will accept change quickly.

Their scepticism might be bolstered by several of the developments outlined above, which could easily be double-edged swords, providing a case for continued counterforce as well as one for change. The issue of public opposition, for example, is an ambiguous one: massive reductions in superpower tensions could just as easily divert attention from nuclear matters as reinvigorate peace movements. Indeed, the experience of the INF Treaty seems to be that arms control serves as a symbol to dampen public protest rather than as a spur to further action.

US defence officials, moreover, could mitigate the effects of public opinion by drawing a line between US operational and declaratory policies. There is a precedent for such a policy – McNamara's public statements withdrew hastily from counterforce when it became apparent that the opposition to such a strategy would be severe. Actual US operational plans, however, did not shift back to assured destruction.

Similarly, modernisation of US forces could have ambiguous results. It seems certain that some significant degree of nuclear modernisation will occur under START; the Bush administration and Congress, especially the Senate, are united in the belief that START could prove destabilising unless appropriate US modernisation occurs. At a minimum this will probably include the Midgetman missile; it may also include rail MX deployments and limited defences of missiles fields, all perhaps purchased at the expense of the B-2. But survivable forces on both sides, even as they discourage counterforce by being harder to find, might encourage it insofar as they promised a more survivable force and thereby a bigger retaliation. That is, with a very survivable START force, a US planner could believe that he would have fully 4000 or more retaliatory warheads, and hence the ability to engage in damage limitation.

Technological developments will also encourage continued reliance on counterforce. Already the Trident D-5 missile promises to revolutionise US targeting by transforming the US SLBM force into a counterforce-capable one. Advanced tracking and guidance systems will provide better real-time targeting data, and hardened and improved command and control might offer the potential to control forces during an extended war.

Finally, there is the ultimate technological development in this regard: strategic defences. Especially as nuclear arsenals shrink, it becomes more and more possible to achieve meaningful damage limitation with limited defensive system. If strategic defenses are indeed here to stay, and are someday deployed on a medium or large scale, planners could achieve the damage limiting effects lost because of the trends outlined above through defences.[36]

A NEW US STRATEGY

The analysis above has demonstrated that a number of *objective factors* will arise to call the efficacy of damage limitation through counterforce into serious question; it also recognised, however, that a number of *bureaucratic and technological factors* will operate to preserve some form of counterforce. The question therefore seems to be, not whether the United States *will* alter its nuclear strategy, for it may or may not; but whether it *ought* to do so. The remainder of this essay, therefore, will make a case for replacing counterforce with an alternative targeting strategy. Its argument is twofold: first, that counterforce is imperfect[37]; and second, that a superior alternative exists.

THE CASE AGAINST COUNTERFORCE

One primary assumption of this essay is that the world has entered an era in which large-scale war has become an anachronism. At first glance this seems quite a bold thing to take for granted, even though a number of detailed studies (examined in chapter 1) have supported the proposition. Nevertheless, it appears that the strategic environment is one that has come not to be characterised by major war, that this will be a continuing phenomenon, and that it is an unambiguously good thing.

It is therefore of primary importance to maintain military doctrines that retain a healthy recognition of the fact that their purpose is to deter and not fight war. Strategies must be judged first by their capacity to deter, and almost equally by their inability to make war thinkable once again in the nuclear era. By this criterion, counterforce strategies fail miserably; they are grounded exactly in the perception that credible war-fighting plans and capacities are required for deterrence, and that war could indeed occur. The first argument against counterforce is therefore that it is unsuited to an era whose leaders are unwilling to admit the advantages of major war.

As the critics of counterforce weapons have pointed out, moreover, such systems degrade crisis stability by rendering both sides more vulnerable. Weapons like the SS-18 and the MX, by being both vulnerable and powerful first-strike weapons, encourage both sides to attack in a crisis because the side that strikes first, when both possess counterforce weapons, gets the better of the exchange. This is not to suggest that all counterforce weapons are bad; the Midgetman is counterforce-capable and stabilising at the same time. But generally those systems that serve to limit damage to one side reduce crisis stability by suggesting that it might be willing to strike; once again, the paradox: 'There is an apparent contradiction between the demands of crisis stability and damage limitation. Weapons capable of damage limitation ... put force survivability at risk', thus hurting crisis stability.[38]

Indeed, surrendering damage limitation will be an essential requirement in an area of smaller arsenals. Analysts of the nuclear balance have long recognised that smaller arsenals on both sides could prove more unstable, since the expected destruction would be smaller and the manageability or thinkability of nuclear war might increase. Damage limitation, pursued through counterforce strikes, erection of extensive active defences, reliance on passive defences including civil defence, use of ASW to attack enemy missile-carrying submarines, would exacerbate such instability, especially during a crisis. Post-START deep cuts, down to 4000 or less weapons on each side, might be viewed as too risky.

Deployment of general strategic defences as part of a damage limiting strategy would also be extremely dangerous. When both sides deploy partially effective defences, as many analysts have pointed out, neither may feel able to absorb a full first strike; yet both may feel that their defences could protect them from a retaliation, which would again encourage first strikes. Strategic defences are also enormously expensive and again unsuited to an age in which military concerns are downplayed.

Then there is the issue of practicability. As noted above, it will become less and less possible in the future for the United States to limit damage to itself in a nuclear war. Counterforce targeting will become probably less feasible than it has ever been.

Finally, and perhaps most importantly, the need for counterforce will decline. This chapter is partly dedicated to proving the point that it will not be necessary for general deterrence, an argument dependent upon chapter 2's critique of 'deterrence by denial' strategies. Chapter 5 contends that extended deterrence in the form of flexible response in Europe is fading rapidly, and counterforce will no longer be necessary in that realm either.

Counterforce strategies and weapons therefore hold a number of dangers. Still, counterforce systems undeniably hold some deterrent power, and they may not be fatal to deterrence on a day-to-day basis. In order to argue against counterforce, damage-limiting strategies, therefore, one must propose a superior alternative.

NON-COUNTERFORCE DETERRENCE

US planners possess a number of options in this regard. One would involve a return to emphasis on countervalue, *urban-industrial and population targets*; after all, the vulnerability of society is the real core of deterrence. Nevertheless, enunciating a public policy of retaliation against cities, industries and other value targets would face enormous public opposition, both within the United States and abroad. It would encounter severe bureaucratic opposition within the government, as the services sought to preserve the counterforce justification for their weapons. It would exacerbate the criticisms of deterrence as being immoral. And in case of a limited Soviet nuclear strike on the United States or its allies or military forces, counter-value would leave the United States with few credible response options.[39]

Unique targeting of Soviet *political and military leadership* also suffers from a number of flaws. It is a potentially huge target base, having grown from a few dozen targets in the 1950s to thousands today.[40] US planners, with precious few warheads to employ in a retaliation, would face grave problems in defining the truly critical control centres – those, for example, to which key Kremlin leaders would flee. Even if US planners managed to find them, such command facilities are incredibly hard, and might not be destroyed even by counterforce strikes. Finally, even if the United States managed to find, target, hit and destroy the Soviet leadership, US planners might have achieved a questionable result: they would have made it impossible for the USSR to order or negotiate an end to hostilities.[41]

US nuclear planners know this, claim defenders of leadership targeting, and intend to use it only in response to a massive attack, at which point escalation control is meaningless. That may be true, but if, in a limited exchange, a US submarine commander fires at leadership targets inadvertently, the result could be disastrous. Moreover, the deterrent effects of leadership targeting are dubious: US counter-leadership strikes might fail, and in any case the notion that we must directly threaten Soviet leaders with death to deter them is suspect.

The United States could also engage in *ethnic targeting*, attempting by nuclear attacks to isolate various non-Soviet Russian republics and thereby to break up the Russian empire, and also to wipe out Slavic Russian urban areas and leave non-Russian areas untouched. This idea, too, betrays severe flaws. It presumes that the republics are ready to revolt, that opposition leadership cadres exist within them, and that Soviet forces would be unable to put down disturbances. Nuclear strikes, in fact, might ruin the chances for opposition to the extent that they subordinated all political demands to a pure desire to stay alive and recover from the shock of a nuclear war.[42] Finally, the United States would incur severe domestic and international political costs from the enunciation and, if necessary, execution of a strategy that called for the assassination of Slavic Russian non-combatants as a US national goal.[43]

THE ADVANTAGES OF COUNTERPOWER TARGETING

Each of those strategies contains particular drawbacks and is insufficient as a unique guide to targeting. There is another alternative, however: counterpower targeting. US planners could establish a prioritised list of some 3000 soft or semi-hard military and industrial targets which excludes Soviet nuclear deployments and senior leadership and command centres. These would include troop deployments and mobilisation areas, bases, military industries, primary transportation centres and other targets of military value. It would emphasise targeting of OMT category points. The result would be a combination of countervalue and counterforce known as counterpower targeting.[44]

Counterpower would combine an overarching deterrent threat of assured destruction with the capability to engage in selected limited nuclear options (LNOs). The purpose is not to fight a war, but merely to deter war and, in the event one begins, to terminate or control it. Its primary recognition is of the fact that counterforce strikes have become virtually impossible, and therefore that an extended counterforce exchange would be an exercise in futility; it is also sympathetic to long-standing contentions that the notion of fighting, or even winning, a nuclear exchange of various stages is ridiculous.

The limited options in counterpower would serve two complementary deterrent purposes, outlined by Robert Jervis in his analysis of LNOs: they show resolve, and they establish the 'threat of unintended as opposed to intended escalation'.[45] The risk that the conflict would eventually end in total societal destruction, even if neither side intended it, would exercise a powerful incentive to terminate it.

COUNTERPOWER AND DETERRENCE

Deterrence requires the ability to threaten unacceptable damage, as McNamara phrased it, to the attacker. Obviously, the problems emerge when one attempts to define what 'unacceptable damage' might be. Counterpower targeting offers opportunities to achieve such damage: a Soviet planner confronted with a counterpower strategy would know that even if his nuclear strikes against the United States were partially effective, the US retaliation would totally annihilate Soviet war-making potential (and probably Soviet society) and leave the USSR devastated and vulnerable to whatever US, European, or Chinese standing armies remained. Under counterpower, the threat of assured destruction remains the centrepiece of deterrence, but it is supplemented by flexible schemes to attack various Soviet military assets. In peacetime, the threat of societal and military annihilation would deter Soviet aggression. If war begins, the threat or limited employment of counterpower strikes could be used as coercive tools to effect escalation control and war termination.

Counterpower targeting would thus maximise the deterrent effect inherent in nuclear weapons. The chief complaint of those who fail to see the necessity of counterforce has probably been that the prospect of even a few hundred nuclear weapons detonating over one's soil ought to be more than enough to deter any adventurism; this notion is sometimes termed minimum deterrence. Counterpower maximises the impact of whatever retaliatory warheads get through by targeting them against forces and industries which are soft and vulnerable to the effects of nuclear weapons. Counterpower thus also creates a deterrent resistant to technological breakthroughs – a substantial residual deterrent would always remain no matter how effective a first strike might be, and that fact would increase the deterrent effect of whatever retaliation was expected.[46]

Some defenders of counterforce have contended that a countersilo capability is necessary for psychological purposes, to demonstrate a counterforce capability equal to that of the USSR and thus prevent Moscow from acquiring a subtle advantage in the superpower competition. Whatever the merits of this argument in the past – and there were not many – trends in the nuclear balance today render it irrelevant. As noted above, both sides are already losing their counterforce capabilities in any case. Moreover, stability demands that this problem be approached from the opposite angle: rather than building up counterforce weapons to hold Soviet silos at risk, the United States should make its own deterrent more survivable to eliminate any perceived Soviet first-strike advantage. This suggestion points to the importance of modernisation to accompany a future arms reduction accord on the START model.

War termination is an often ignored, but crucially important, requirement. Unless the United States is to admit that any nuclear explosions will result in holocaust, it must make provisions for controlling and ending nuclear exchanges at low levels. As Stephen Cimbala and other proponents of war termination strategies have noted, termination policies are more moral and offer more potential of ending conflicts than pure retaliatory plans.[47] War termination is not war-fighting – it demands not the capability for extended nuclear conflict but only the potential to engage in nuclear coercion and the capability to maintain control of nuclear forces through a very limited exchange. The goal is to end the war, not to win it.[48]

Counterpower would also allow stabilising changes in doctrine. Counterforce strategies demand very rapid retaliation, for example; under counterpower, the rate of retaliatory fire could be slowed, especially if the United States acquired more survivable deterrent forces and command and control facilities. A slower retaliation is one less subject to accidental or miscalculated launch, and is more stable since both sides can adopt launch policies that create less crisis instability.[49]

Counterpower targeting would allow the United States to enunciate a form of No First Use (NFU). Traditional NFU proposals have been criticised on the grounds that they undercut the West's nuclear deterrent. To the extent that the Soviets believe nuclear war will not break out, the argument goes, they are tempted to attack Europe. After adopting counterpower targeting, however, US leaders could state that under no circumstances would the United States use nuclear weapons first *against Soviet nuclear weapons systems, senior leadership and command centres, and their associated C3 elements.* The deterrent and coercive effects of counterpower would remain strong, and the United States would achieve significant international political advantages while contributing to a reduction of tensions with the USSR, which would presumably have less fear of a US first strike.

COUNTERPOWER AND VALUE TARGETS

But we have arrived at a dilemma. If counterpower is to have a deterrent effect similar to assured destruction, it must threaten vast societal damage and civilian casualties. But if it does that it is arguably immoral, and certainly constitutes a less bold step away from the nuclear precipice.

Thus Bruce Russett found that early versions of his notion of 'countercombatant' targeting (which included tactical forces, supply depots, militarily significant industry, transportation assets, internal security forces, communications and public utilities) proved too broad. Hitting that set of targets would cause damage 'hardly distinguishable from that wrought by targeting population centers per se'. Any deterrent that intends to inflict such high civilian casualties, Russet argues, constitutes a 'denial of humanity' and obstructs a 'move toward a wider, more comprehensive, and truer peace'.[50]

Yet forfeiting both targeting of nuclear forces and the intent to destroy an opponent's society might seriously undermine deterrence. Russett proposes, for example, targeting Soviet troops on the Chinese border to open the threat of a Chinese invasion. Yet such a strike would have little effect so long as Soviet nuclear forces remained to deter Chinese adventurism and Soviet society was left relatively untouched and capable of at least partially reconstituting the lost troops and equipment.

The solution to this dilemma can be found by examining the purpose of the nuclear strike. A very broad counterpower strike is perfectly acceptable on moral grounds if delivered in retaliation for an opponent's first salvo that caused horrible collateral damage, as any Soviet first strike would. Moral problems, and issues of political sensibility in an era of declining tensions, only arise when nuclear strikes are used to achieve purposes other than deterrence of a similar strike.

The US pledge to employ nuclear weapons in response to Soviet conventional aggression in Europe constitutes just such a potentially immoral and insensitive nuclear threat. It is instructive that Russett indeed recognises that it is in the extended deterrent task of US nuclear weapons that 'most [of the] vexing problems of modern strategic policy' lie.[51] As we have seen, many advocates of counterforce support their case by reference to this goal. The solution to our dilemma thus lies in removing the extended deterrent role for US nuclear weapons.

This can be done in two ways. First, a number of developments – prospective conventional arms treaties, public opposition in Europe to US nuclear weapons, a potential START treaty, and others – might eventually eliminate NATO's need and ability to rely on the US nuclear umbrella. With a more equal conventional balance in Europe and independent European nuclear forces relatively stronger after a START accord reduces the Soviet nuclear arsenal, NATO Europe would be more capable of defending itself with some help from US troops but without the American pledge of escalation; concurrently, pressure to remove all US nuclear weapons from European soil will increase, which if it occurs will fatally undermine the credibility of the US pledge. These developments would relieve US targeting policy of its extended deterrent chores.

Second, until that occurs the United States can partially resolve the dilemma by using Russett's model for a less ambitious counterpower – targeting only Soviet standing conventional forces. Such a threat might not be enough to deter a nuclear attack, but it would certainly encourage Soviet caution regarding conventional adventurism. It is also more credible than current, vague US promises to risk suicide to prevent something (Soviet occupation of Europe) that does not immediately threaten US national survival.

COUNTERPOWER AND WAR-FIGHTING

For basic deterrence, then, counterpower seems adequate. But what strategies might it offer for an extended nuclear conflict? The prospect that the Soviets would be willing to fight one – not spasm launches but controlled, discrete strikes over periods of days, weeks or even months – and that the United States had to have a similar capability for deterrence was central to the Reagan administration's nuclear war plans.[52] A nuclear strategy that surrendered counterforce targeting would not possess the ability to fight such an extended counterforce battle, and hence would presumably sacrifice a certain amount of deterrence.[53]

Initially, if one believes that a nuclear war cannot be controlled, the issue is moot; extended, limited nuclear strikes are impossible. Thus, the notion that nuclear war would inevitably escalate and is inherently uncontrollable constituted the heart of the critique of flexible options, the countervailing strategy, and nuclear 'war-fighting'. Some analysts have stressed the fact that the Soviets seem to reject notions of limited war, and that any US attempt to engage in limited options would be met with an all-out strike.[54]

But presuming, for argument's sake, that a limited, gradual nuclear war could be fought, how would a counterpower strategy fight it?

There are a wide variety of answers to this question. First we must place the analysts in perspective: at issue is whether, in a START-constrained world, counterforce or counterpower is better at deterring the Soviets. We must recognise, too, that counterforce is not necessarily an either/or proposition – US planners could dedicate a smaller number of weapons to counterforce targets to preserve some amount of damage limitation. Another issue is therefore whether targeting a few Soviet nuclear assets would be better than targeting none.

A strong case can be made that, even given Soviet war-fighting proclivities, counterforce capabilities are unnecessary for victory denial. In the nuclear age, deterrence by denial and deterrence by punishment seem to merge: is not the total destruction of an attacker's society the denial of victory? The key for targeting purposes, as deterrence by denial through counterforce becomes increasingly impossible, is to choose a target list that sits most nearly at the apex of the intersection between punishment and denial, and such a list can be found in a counterpower strategy.

Indeed, deterrence by denial strategies always suffered from the logical query of whether the Soviets would consider the explosion of at least several hundred nuclear devices on their territory a 'victory', and counterpower targeting significantly reinforces that basic disincentive by promising that those explosions will fall on crucial military and military-industrial targets. It thus constitutes a halfway point between assured destruction and war-fighting policies. As Michael Howard has noted, the best American response to an imputed Soviet war-winning strategy was not to mimic that strategy but 'to make it clear to the Russians, within their own Clausewitzian framework, that it simply will not work',[55] and counterpower would do exactly that.

The threat of *unintended* escalation to general war would also continue to exercise an enormous deterrent effect. As long as societies remain vulnerable, any war could escalate and destroy them. Thus the reason for not abandoning, in the general deterrent form of counterpower, targeting of military and military-related assets in a manner likely to cause huge collateral damage: the prospect of it achieves a deterrent effect critical given that Soviet leaders are allowed a virtually sacrosanct nuclear reserve.

When assessing the requirements of denying Soviet war aims, we must also assume a START-constrained world. Most analyses of Soviet victory calculations assume existing Soviet and US forces; under START, however, reliable Soviet warhead totals would fall below 6000 while modernised US forces emerged requiring many times that number to strike. Regardless of what US targeting strategy is, then, START combined with US modernisation will seriously degrade Soviet chances in a war. US planners can therefore target their forces with less of an eye toward victory denial.

Even supposing these general deterrents to war are not enough, a counterpower strategy could indeed deny Soviet war aims. As defined by the US Department of Defense, these are: to defeat NATO forces, occupy Europe, and utilise Europe's economy to spur Soviet recovery; neutralise the United States and its allies by disrupting and destroying their military forces; deter China's entry into the war, and if deterrence fails neutralise China; limit damage to vital Soviet political, military and economic structures; and dominate the post-war world and spread socialism.[56]

Counterpower clearly denies these goals. By annihilating Soviet conventional forces it prevents any meaningful victory over NATO or an occupation of Europe, and also renders the Soviet Union vulnerable to Chinese forces. It promises destruction of Soviet military and economic assets. It cannot guarantee that the United States will not be neutralised, but neither can counterforce, and counterpower certainly does guarantee that the Soviet Union will be neutralised.

For a wide variety of reasons, then, even if deterrence requires denying Soviet war aims, counterpower achieves that. But what is wrong with dedicating some US assets to counterforce? Again, counterforce is not a yes-or-no proposition; it can be pursued in a manner that leaves the bulk of US warheads to counterpower targets. The argument here, however, is essentially for targeting no Soviet nuclear forces.

At least, that is, in a general retaliation. Distinctions must be made between *limited* scenarios and *general* retaliation against a massive Soviet strike: targeting appropriate to one might not be to the other. For example, as we have seen, leadership targeting in a general retaliation might have some deterrent effect, but targeting Soviet leadership in a limited exchange might ruin chances for war termination because Washington would no longer have anyone to negotiate with. In the same way, targeting Soviet nuclear forces in limited strikes might be perfectly appropriate, so long as they were used in response to similar Soviet strikes. Counterpower does not rule out the possibility of very limited strikes on Soviet nuclear forces if the Soviets attempt similar attacks.

In terms of a more general deterrent strategy, however, one used to prevent a massive Soviet attack, counterpower is clearly superior. Initially, destroying Soviet conventional forces has its own deterrent power. If the Soviets indeed believe that strategic nuclear war could be conducted without causing mutual suicide, they would presumably recognise the need for standing armies to deter attack while the war was going on. In fact, retaliating against conventional forces may be more effective than nuclear forces: Colin Gray points out that, due to the nature of the Soviet state, destroying Soviet conventional forces would create 'threats to the political integrity of the Soviet Union' and would therefore be 'even more dissuasive than would be the prospect of very large civilian population or industrial damage'.[57]

If the United States continued to follow counterforce, moreover, the Soviets might actually be more confident of their chances in an exchange. A retaliation of just 2000 or so American weapons, aimed at hard-to-target mobile missiles and a few remaining silos, might waste itself and leave the Soviets with some ICBMs and much of their SLBM force, as well as a relatively intact society. American modernisation could alter these ratios for the better, but not eliminate the fact that, if the Soviets were confident an American retaliation would fall exclusively or primarily on their nuclear forces, they might judge the survivability of their reserve to be great enough, and the collateral damage to be small enough, to strike in a desperate situation. Counterpower, on the other hand, keeps alive for an aggressor the real risk of societal annihilation.

Counterpower also sidesteps an important shortcoming of counterforce. If one side decides to first-strike the other, and the side being attacked launches a retaliation, even if the attacker's reserve weapons are vulnerable, he is unlikely to wait for the retaliation to hit before launching them. In other words, while the superpowers may avoid launch-on-warning strategies during peacetime, the attacker in a nuclear war would almost certainly employ it to mitigate the effects of a retaliatory blow. Knowing this – and knowing that the attacker's second strike might well fall on his cities – the victim might be deterred from retaliation.[58] Counterpower avoids this problem by aiming the retaliation at military units and facilities, industrial areas and communication and political control hubs that cannot be launched.

Counterpower would in this sense help preserve what escalation control could be salvaged. George Quester recognises that leaving nuclear forces and political command centres untouched would contribute to escalation control.

> It will be relatively legitimate to go after conventional warfare assets for [sic] the other side, especially large arms dumps, troop concentrations, and so on . . . smaller warships might be fair game. Strategic nuclear forces should be avoided, for fear of panicking the other side into firing them off in anticipation of preemption. But a much more legitimate strategic target, probably having the opposite effect on the other side's inclination to fire off missiles, would be any of the industrial complexes that would be used to generate new missiles or reloads or new SLBM submarines.[59]

By leaving Soviet nuclear forces and command and control facilities untouched, US planners would encourage rationality and deliberate decision-making, essentially guaranteeing a Soviet retaliatory capability to deter adventurism against them, whether conventional or nuclear.[60]

Counterpower therefore also renders a US response more credible. If a US planner suspects that any retaliation against Soviet nuclear forces will lead to an all-out Soviet second blow, he may be restrained from retaliating. 'A lack of countersilo capability', then, 'actually tends to bolster U.S. strategy in this context because it reduces U.S. self-deterrence lest the Soviet Union fear that its control systems are being attacked'.[61]

What of Soviet reloadable and refirable weapons? Some analysts suggest that these constitute an important aspect of Soviet war plans,[62] and counterpower would presumably leave them untouched as an invulnerable reserve. But US planners can reduce this aspect of Soviet confidence in a number of ways. A START agreement will reduce Soviet warheads so much, and US modernisation can increase their strike requirements so much, that even two or three salvoes would be insufficient. START provisions could force the Soviets to destroy many of the reloads. Counterpower forces could be targeted against Soviet nuclear production facilities and reload storage areas, if they are known. Finally, since under START and subsequent agreements the number of Soviet silo-based weapons is likely to shrink, some tiny counterforce application could be allowed back into US doctrine with just two or three hundred warheads aimed at remaining silos, to prevent their being used for refires. US negotiators are also attempting to limit Soviet non-deployed weapons in START.

What of the use of anti-submarine warfare (ASW) as a counterforce tool?[63] Developments in ASW would presumably not be restricted under a START treaty, yet they could have destabilising effects similar to an unconstrained arms race – they could render one leg of either side's deterrent force (in this case, the most survivable leg) vulnerable. There are a number of solutions to this problem, although the risk of it suggests, as noted in chapter 2, that the United States should not rely totally on submarines for its survivable deterrent. First, it is unlikely that breakthroughs would occur to render submarines entirely vulnerable, especially given advances in submarine quieting and other defensive technologies. Second, ASW technologies themselves are likely to be either vulnerable (for instance, satellites using blue-green lasers) or possess inadequate coverage of sea areas (for example, surface ships). Third, operational arms control measures could address this problem by creating submarine sanctuaries.

OTHER PROBLEMS

Counterpower or countermilitary targeting that excludes nuclear forces is also subject to a number of smaller flaws. Initially, there is the problem of what exactly to target. There are over 20 000 reasonably important OMT targets in the USSR, according to some reports; with only 2000 or so warheads to use in a retaliation, where should they be put? US planners would merely decide which targets were most important. Presumably, current target lists are prioritised in some fashion already.

Moreover, the Soviet conventional forces the United States might like to attack might already be in Central Europe by the time the US president got around to approving a nuclear strike. US strategic warheads would in turn be too 'muscular' for accurate strikes in that area.[64] Still this is not an insurmountable problem. Even if a few forces had entered Europe, vast numbers of second-echelon units, reserve units being brought up to strength, and units deployed defensively against other potential foes (for example, China) would offer promising targets, as would naval bases, military schools and training facilities, arms production plans and the like.

Conventional forces also move, and might be difficult to target during a war.[65] However, most units would be in known positions at the outset of hostilities, and could be targeted. If limited nuclear strikes were contemplated, command and control assets should remain effective enough to allow further strikes. And if a general strike became necessary, nuclear weapons are destructive enough to allow area targeting. Moreover, some targets, like marshalling areas for reserve units, military industries, major bases, and others, are fixed.

IMPLICATIONS OF THE STRATEGY

A shift to counterpower targeting would thus call for a three-pronged US nuclear strategy: **Deterrence** through counterpower targeting and a more credible threat of various limited nuclear options; **Stability** through arms control, nuclear modernisation and a modified NFU pledge; and, in the event that these fail, **Damage Limitation** through arms control before a conflict and war termination during a conflict. As we have seen, there are a number of precedents for achieving damage limitation through means other than counterforce retaliation – the countervailing strategy, for example, while emphasising counterforce options, also sought to limit damage through escalation control.[66]

Obviously, none of these suggestions are new. And as noted, counterpower targeting is already partially subsumed in existing US targeting strategy. During a crisis, for example, an American president would undoubtedly have the pre-planned option to strike a few Soviet naval bases instead of Soviet nuclear forces. Still, much of the current and prospective US retaliatory force is earmarked for counterforce targets, and as this analysis has suggested, that is a mistake. There are advantages – in terms of both deterrence and stability – to be gained through the enunciation of a counterpower strategy.

Adoption of a counterpower policy carries a number of clear implications for US and Soviet force posture. In one sense, counterpower calls into question the need for modernisation. Given that SSBNs are currently invulnerable, the only immediate goal of modernisation is to bolster the survivability of the land- and air-based legs of the triad. However, SLBM warheads appear sufficient to strike at counterpower targets. As long as US SSBNs remain secure, they would theoretically fulfill the deterrent requirements of counterpower targeting.

Yet the importance of control and flexibility under a counterpower doctrine suggests that reliance on submarines alone would be unwise. SSBNs are difficult to communicate with and control, and day-to-day C3 problems would be vastly exacerbated during a limited exchange. Moreover, submarines cannot launch merely a portion of their missiles because their positions would be exposed with the first salvo. For these and other reasons, submarines are imperfect war termination tools and consequently modernisation of the other legs of the triad is desirable. Modernisation would also be extremely useful in persuading the Soviets of the inadvisability of offensive damage limitation strategies.

Moreover, modern weapons are required to target Soviet non-nuclear OMT. Until the 1980s the Minutemen were the only US weapons 'with the necessary accuracy, flight time, command and control, and retargeting flexibility to be employed' against such conventional targets as Soviet second-echelon forces.[67] Bombers are similarly too slow for such tasks.[68] The presence of cities near many Soviet military deployments also demands accuracy, and the ability of conventional forces to move demands some degree of promptness.[69]

Counterpower does, however, cast doubt on the need for the B-1B or the B-2 bombers. The primary rationale for a penetrating bomber has been as a platform from which to search for Soviet mobile missiles; if the United States gave up counterforce targeting, however, this would be unnecessary. Both bombers suffer from serious conceptual and design flaws, moreover, and their combined cost is huge – over $450 billion into the next century, representing the most expensive single leg of the triad. Cheaper ALCM carriers could replace the B-2.

Counterpower targeting also places the debate over strategic defences in a slightly new light. General missile defences would be highly destabilising insofar as they degraded the ability of either side to retaliate against the other's military deployments, industry and other assets. However, limited defences of missile fields or other *nuclear* weapons deployments would be unquestionably stabilising, insofar as those weapons would not be the target of retaliation in any case. The defences would protect each side's arsenal from a first strike without protecting a secure reserve for the side that struck first, as they would currently do under counterforce strategies.

Counterpower would also allow, almost force, deep cuts in strategic arms. The key argument against the notion that the superpowers possess a vast amount of overkill is that such redundancy is always useful for damage limitation purposes – the more enemy nuclear forces one side can target, the better. Opting out of the counterforce game would remove the requirements for such huge arsenals, and allow a transition to a world of minimum deterrence and arms reductions. [70]

Counterpower, combined with US strategic modernisation, might also encourage the apparent (if glacially slow) Soviet shift toward more defensive military doctrines. If the United States did not modernise its forces, the Soviets might believe they could hold US land-based assets at risk much as they can today, and might continue to pursue an offensive damage-limitation strategy. This, combined with counterpower's offer of a secure nuclear reserve, might seem to confer advantages on the Soviets (though whether such a situation would be unstable is debatable). With modernisation, however – for example, with the acquisition of 500 Midgetmen and a secure basing mode for the MX – the number of warheads required for a Soviet first strike against the US land-based arsenal alone would be enormous, far more warheads than they would possess under any deep reductions scheme. Unable to seek damage limitation offensively through counterforce, the Soviets might well choose to seek it defensively – through further arms control, through war termination, or eventually through a transition to a defensive-dominant world, though the prospects for and value of the latter are questionable. Counterpower combined with modernisation thus might offer exactly the incentive for which analysts have been searching to urge the Soviets down the defensive path.[71]

Finally, if the United States were to adopt a counterpower strategy, it ought to modify its negotiating positions in the START negotiations in a number of ways. It ought to suggest counting all bombers as multiple-warhead systems, whether they carry ALCMs or bombs or SRAMs; this would reduce the premium on penetrating bombers and make targeting of mobile targets more difficult. It ought to propose banning mobile missiles with more than one warhead, which would encourage the trend toward survivable forces. In fact, it ought to propose general sublimits on missiles with large numbers of warheads, perhaps starting with ten-warhead systems (such as the MX and SS-18) and eventually moving to smaller missiles. It ought to allow larger deployments of ground-based missile defences around missile fields alone. US negotiators ought also to place in the agreement an understanding that further deep cuts would be sought.

CONCLUSIONS

Counterpower targeting thus contains a number of promising ideas for US nuclear strategy under future arms control regimes. As the numbers of nuclear weapons possessed by the superpowers dwindles, traditional doctrines of counterforce retaliation will come to be replaced with more general plans for deterrence. In a sense, counterpower begins the move toward a form of minimum deterrence, under which a finite number of nuclear weapons aimed at a set of mostly immobile, mostly soft targets could threaten enough damage to deter an opponent. Once the principles underlying such a strategy have been hammered out, they can be applied to any number of nuclear balances created by a variety of arms accords. The important task for any administration hoping to achieve significant arms reduction is to take seriously the need for a new targeting doctrine.

As noted, there are two potential models of nuclear strategy: one that demands a capability for war-fighting and escalation dominance to deny military victory, and one that seeks to pledge only assured destruction and attempts to deter by threat of punish. ent, not defeat. Counterpower responds well to both. It is a halfway point that preserves the essence of deterrence – the assured destruction threat –

while retaining many of the advantages of counterforce and an ability to terminate or control wars that have begun.

Even more critical is the increasingly apparent fact that no nation can wage a war because today none can protect themselves from its effects. Counterpower, by giving up the hope of damage limitation in major war, would preserve that fact, and with it the peace; counterforce strategies threaten to undermine it.

5 Extended Deterrence

As noted in chapter 1, current deterrence theory and practice is concerned not just with attacks on the homelands of the superpowers or central deterrence. It also labours under the demands of *extended deterrence*, the attempt to deter nuclear or conventional attack upon the allies of the superpowers through the threat of nuclear first use. Given the relative position of the two superpowers and their proximity to their allies, the problems of extended deterrence are almost unique to the United States. This chapter will examine that aspect of the deterrence debate; its analysis is specific to NATO, but its general conclusions about the infeasibility of extended deterrence are applicable in many ways to other theatres as well.

Analyses of the faults in extended deterrence are uncommon today, however. Many observers and practitioners of NATO defence policy are placing great faith in ongoing talks on Conventional Forces in Europe (CFE) and Strategic Arms Reduction (START), and it is easy to understand why. Soviet leader Mikhail Gorbachev seems to have changed everything – virtually intractable problems that once plagued US and NATO defence policy-makers now appear tantalisingly close to being resolved. Especially given Gorbachev's desperate need to cut military spending, arms control now offers an unprecedented potential to wipe away both Soviet conventional superiority in Europe and some degree of US nuclear vulnerability. One such agreement, of course, is START; others include talks on Conventional Forces in Europe (CFE) and the Conference on Security and Co-operation in Europe (CSCE).

Much more is at stake in the emerging conventional and strategic nuclear arms negotiations, however, than is commonly supposed. A successful agreement that effectively eliminates both sides' capability to wage offensive warfare, combined with other developments in East-West relations, could spur a sea-change in Alliance deterrent strategy. In particular, trends in East-West relations will allow – and force – NATO to move beyond flexible response, causing a diminution of the American role in NATO as manifest in its extended deterrence pledge to defend Europe with nuclear weapons.

In short, the threat of Soviet expansion, long the bedrock of NATO's *raison d'être*, is receding. The result is bound to be vast changes in the way in which the Alliance does business, including the way in which it deters war. The broader danger in all of this is that the Alliance will lose its purpose, and its American support, along with its military doctrine; NATO must reassess all these factors in order to preserve any of them. This chapter therefore examines the implications of a number of trends in East-West relations and European and US politics for the *US pledge to initiate the use of nuclear weapons in response to Soviet conventional aggression in Europe*, the key element of flexible response and hence of NATO's deterrent.[1] Flexible response was the first step away from nuclear use, away from massive retaliation[2]; it is now being superseded by another, further step in the same direction.

INFLEXIBLE RESPONSE?

The debate over flexible response – NATO's threat to use nuclear weapons in its own defence and its reliance on American nuclear assets to achieve that goal – is still lively today. The doctrine has always been suspect in some quarters: given the potential stakes of nuclear war, many have contended that it would not be rational for US officials to risk national destruction for an interest (preventing the potentially temporary occupation of Europe) that did not threaten American territorial integrity.[3]

Another great danger of the extended deterrence pledge, argue its critics, is that it might actually be fulfilled. If war began and NATO did escalate, the probability of general nuclear warfare would be high. Even if a ghost of the extended deterrence pledge were invoked, the result could be absolute catastrophe. Flexible response may therefore provide little opportunity for intra-war deterrence; once a conventional war begins, the nuclear option might hold as little appeal for Western governments as it would for the Soviet Union.[4]

If true, these arguments may also undermine the effectiveness of flexible response as a deterrent. The pledge suffers from the traditional paradox of deterrence: there is no reason to carry it out (and, in this case, annihilate Europe) once it has failed in its purpose. If an adversary comes to appreciate that fact, he will not be deterred by the threat. These comments refer back to the paradox of deterrence outlined in chapter 2; the problem here is not the paradox itself but its flipside.

In part as a product of that paradox, flexible response contains dilemmas of its own. Indeed, rendering the promise credible threatens to undermine its purpose of coupling, a fact recognised by Philip Bobbitt in his recent work *Democracy and Deterrence*. Bobbitt's chief 'theorem' in that book is that

> Any effort to cure decoupling will either (1) fail because it does not provide the President with both a lower threshold of choice or some kind of firebreak . . . or (2) it will "succeed" by confining risks to the theater, and thus it *uncouples* the two theaters of war.[5]

Other observers argue that shortcomings in US C3I systems render flexible response impossible as articulated. As command and control expert Bruce Blair has recognised, US C3I systems have never been robust enough to survive even a limited nuclear war.[6] And Alliance C3I and decision-making assets and procedures may not at all be up to the task of tight escalation control.

The risk of Soviet pre-emption may also be great. The Soviet intent to pre-empt NATO nuclear use is well-known, and some analysts suggest that Soviet penetration of NATO's command structure is so complete that Moscow can predict within minutes NATO's decision to initiate the use of nuclear weapons.[7] Dispersal of NATO's nuclear stockpiles might also give the Soviets tangible evidence of the alliance's potential desire to employ them. One writer has noted that 'Without exception, American exercises have shown that whenever NATO is about to use nuclear weapons, it prompts a Soviet pre-emptive strike'.[8]

Before a pre-emption is required, moreover, the Soviet strategy intends to strip NATO of the choice to escalate. Soviet Operational Manoeuvre Groups (OMGs) are designed to get between NATO forces and win a conventional war quickly, before NATO's political decision-making chain can reach any consensus on nuclear use. Spetznaz teams, tactical ballistic missiles, and tactical air units have as their top priority the destruction of NATO nuclear forces.[9]

Flexible response comes with a number of severe peacetime draw-backs as well, argue its detractors. Opinion polls have shown that 80 per cent of both Americans and Europeans 'oppose the use of nuclear weapons if a conventional invasion of our European allies could not be repelled by non-nuclear means'.[10] As the danger of Warsaw Pact aggression recedes, such questions will become increasingly insistent whenever issues of nuclear doctrine are raised. In this context, flexible response leaves NATO with few persuasive answers to the questions of its increasingly sceptical citizens who fail to understand just why the Alliance threatens to destroy itself in order to protect itself. And as we saw in chapter 1, the American public in particular is increasingly opposed to the use of nuclear weapons to defend Europe.

If war does come, moreover, NATO today possesses no firm idea of how it wishes to manage the nuclear question. Reliance on the panacea of flexible response, as Stephen Cimbala notes, results in a 'looser grasp by policy-makers of the process of escalation control', because 'NATO has not fully sorted out its nuclear escalation logic, to the detriment of coherent policy and credible deterrence'.[11] This confusion could lead to defeat or nuclear war – or both.

Paul Warnke has suggested that flexible response also carries dangerous implications for Alliance cohesion. European faith in American nuclear guarantees is more 'theological' than logical, he argues; the process of finessing deterrence risks undermining alliance unity and provoking the Soviet Union. 'If kidding ourselves only means kidding our potential adversary as well', writes Warnke,

> the fact that our nuclear doctrine may be unrealistic poses no serious threat to NATO's security. But if adherence to nuclear illusions threatens to promote divisiveness within NATO, to afford the Soviets' protracted opportunity for mischief, and to stimulate Soviet consideration of destabilizing strategies such as launch-on-warning, then it is time to get serious and explicit about the role that nuclear weapons can play in the defense of Western Europe.[12]

'SUICIDAL DETERRENCE'

Yet all of these flaws might be irrelevent, and the incredibility of flexible response would not be a problem, if the Soviets believed NATO might escalate anyway. Some analysts therefore contend that the US nuclear pledge is sufficient insofar as it keeps alive some risk of unintended escalation. The implication is that if things go badly for NATO, nuclear warheads would end up falling on Moscow, no matter what NATO decided to do.

Some even contend that this is in fact the operative principle guiding NATO force deployment and command and control procedures, that Alliance leaders may have attempted to create a system promising the Soviets unintended escalation in case of war. What NATO leaders may think they need is not, as Yale analyst Paul

Bracken notes, a rational procedure for escalating to nuclear war, but a 'posture that is so complex that war could be triggered in any of a number of different ways without rational control'. NATO's nuclear command structure, he contends, is built to appear 'so unstable and accident-prone that national leaders would exercise little practical control over it in wartime', thus enforcing deterrence 'by necessitating that any war be nuclear'. Placing tactical nuclear weapons close to the inter-German border underlines the chances for such escalation by creating a 'use them or lose them' syndrome. Bracken calls this 'suicidal deterrence'.[13]

Yet this doctrine may be no better, and indeed in case of war would be far worse, than a mere threat to escalate. It is still incredible; the risk of nuclear annihilation is so great, and the prospect of nuclear weapons detonating on NATO soil so odious, that many analysts and military officers are convinced the Alliance would never release any authority whatsoever to use them. Ordering the dispersal of the weapons from their storage sites and granting release authority would require each NATO nation to transfer control over its destiny and security to mid-level NATO military commanders, something NATO governments would under almost no circumstances approve. Dispersal would also risk Soviet pre-emption. And such a doctrine would only complicate further NATO's public relations problem.

If one views the risk of war as arising from Soviet intentions, moreover, suicidal deterrence would be reassuring insofar as it gave the Kremlin pause. 'But for those who perceive that the greatest risk of war stems from an inadvertent escalation of an unintended political conflict', explains Bruce Russett, 'the risk of losing military control' is unacceptable.[14]

Finally, critics of current NATO strategy point to another danger of flexible response: it creates a requirement for US strategic counterforce weapons. The US pledge to escalate would be at least partly credible if the United States possessed some means of damage limitation to reduce the devastation it would suffer in a major war. US counterforce assets provide just such a capability by offering the potential to hit Soviet nuclear forces before they are launched, and the US acquisition of counterforce weapons has therefore been tied in part to US extended deterrence requirements. As one commentator concluded in 1989, 'The extended deterrent commitment remains an important driving force behind U.S. counterforce capabilities'.[15] The dangers of counterforce weapons are spelled out in limited fashion in chapter 4.

THE BEST OF IMPERFECT ALTERNATIVES?

NATO officials would undoubtedly contend that critics of flexible response have erected a straw man. They are not intent on convincing the Warsaw Pact that NATO nuclear weapons would go off unintentionally by the dozens; flexible response merely serves, they would (and do) argue, to keep alive some risk that NATO officials would indeed decide to escalate. In the heat of battle, argue defenders of NATO policy, when Soviet tanks are churning through NATO's defences, NATO, which is after all pledged in MC 14/3 to consider nuclear use as a last-ditch defence, just might launch some nuclear weapons out of anger or fear. This possibility may serve to deter the Soviets.

There is undoubtedly some truth in that argument. The real question, of course, is whether the cure might not be worse than the disease, whether 'getting serious' about NATO nuclear policy, as Warnke phrases it, would promote more divisiveness within the Alliance and nervousness in Moscow than present policies. In this sense flexible response may be the best of a set of imperfect alternatives.

Initially, it may be possible, despite the significance of the doctrine's shortcomings, to paper them over nevertheless. George Quester has argued persuasively that flexible response 'can be finessed'.[16] Quester contends that a number of steps can be (and have been) taken to render the incredible credible. An American president can feign ignorance about the reasons why he should not escalate. Formal alliances can be established to reinforce deterrent pledges. Conventional defence can be left unattended as a sign that nuclear deterrence is taken seriously. US troops can be left in Europe as tripwires. And tactical nuclear weapons can be deployed in the path of advancing armies to create a real risk of unintended escalation and accidental war. 'If it could be carried off after 1949', Quester points out, 'there is no inherent reason why [extended deterrence] cannot be carried off as well after 1989 . . . This kind of extension of deterrence, with all its worries and all its problems, should be capable of persisting into the next century or two as well'.[17]

Others agree. Richard Betts argues that 'If the doctrine is a Great Lie, it is a Great White Lie – a benign deception – as long as it supports deterrence.' And like any white lie, he notes, 'if repeated often enough and with apparent conviction, it can come to be believed',[18] Philip Bobbitt similarly contends that 'Even if it has become, in some theoretical way, irrational for the U.S. to act out of the pretension that decoupling has not occurred, it is not irrational to maintain the pretence. And what adversary can be wholly confident that the U.S. is only pretending?'[19]

Attempting to alleviate the shortcomings of flexible response, moreover, has for 40 years run foul of dilemmas of NATO policy. One is that the requirements for deterring the Soviets and reassuring the Europeans often conflict. Indeed, dilemmas exist even within the latter task; as the Alliance was reminded during the INF crisis of 1983, reassuring European *leaders* about America's willingness to commit suicide for them may call for policies antithetical to the goal of reassuring European *publics* about the robustness of peace. In terms of the present discussion, improving NATO's conventional defence might help deter the Soviets yet alienate European leaders anxious about making Europe safe for conventional war; keeping US nuclear weapons in Europe might reassure NATO leaders about the US willingness to escalate yet frighten European populaces, while having only a marginal effect on deterrence.[20]

There are other paradoxes. One was alluded to above: Europeans want American nuclear weapons on their soil but do not want them exploded on their soil if a war starts. It may therefore be that the largest numbers of NATO weapons – American tactical and battle-field systems – are the least likely to be used in a war. The nature of the problem is such that 'this paradox of U.S.-West European relations is unavoidable as long as US nuclear weapons remain the cornerstone of NATO's defence policy'.[21]

Finally, from a military standpoint, there are dilemmas within the process of establishing a deterrent. No *conventional* deterrent will ever possess the force of a nuclear one. Richard Betts has argued that 'If Soviet tanks are stopped by an effective NATO defense, Moscow would be disappointed, but if the tanks break through and NATO escalates, it could be devastated'. Yet an alleged *nuclear* response to conventional aggression will always suffer from problems of credibility. The distinction is between deterrence and defence – nuclear deterrence adequately prevents war but is incredible as a defensive strategy; conventional forces are suitable for defence but may possess inadequate deterrent power. 'As long as nuclear war is unthinkable', Betts writes, 'what is right for deterrence is wrong for defense', and there is no escape from this dilemma 'short of absolutely credible nuclear threats' or 'absolutely credible conventional defense ... neither of which is attainable'. For this reason Betts suggests that there is 'no way out' of NATO's deterrence dilemmas, and the best policy is something akin to flexible response; 'some wise confusion straddles the dilemma better than does a foolish consistency'.[22]

TRENDS FACING THE ALLIANCE

Regardless of the Alliance's ability to resolve these dilemmas, however – and in the absence of an overwhelming threat, that ability cannot be great – long-term trends in East-West relations and US and European politics offer the prospect of eliminating them. Prospective arms control agreements supplemented with emerging convention defence doctrines and technologies and European and US public opinion on nuclear matters are beginning to remove both NATO's ability and its need to rely on the incredible aspects of flexible response (that is, US escalation) while at the same time improving NATO's capacity to fulfill its credible deterrent pledges. These developments will have a significant effect, not immediately, but over a time frame of perhaps five to 15 years. In short, the circumstances that forced and allowed the United States to threaten nuclear escalation in the defence of Europe are changing. Five trends will be examined below: conventional parity, the loss of ties to the US deterrent, nuclear arms control, closer European defence co-operation, and opinion on NATO within the United States.

Conventional Parity

The most important spur in this direction would be a conventional arms control treaty that would satisfy European leaders about their security. There is no guarantee that Conventional Forces in Europe (CFE) talks will prove to be a panacea. The reduction of NATO and Warsaw Pact forces to smaller, equivalent levels, however, along with defensive restructuring and the provision of tight verification procedures and additional confidence-building measures, might together effectively negate the Warsaw Pact's confidence in its ability to conduct rapid offensive operations. This would achieve the goal previously assigned to NATO conventional improvements.

Already, the unilateral cuts announced by Gorbachev and other Warsaw Pact leaders threaten to virtually eliminate the danger of a quick Soviet victory. Five of the six Soviet tank divisions to be removed are part of Operational Manoeuvre Groups (OMGs) that presented unique threats; the size of the Soviet reduction will be 20 per cent larger than the West's most ambitious Mutual and Balanced Force Reduction (MBFR) proposal and larger than the entire US 7th army in Germany. Phillip Karber has concluded that if Gorbachev follows through on his promises he will be pursuing reductions 'exactly like we would want him to'.[23]

Developments in NATO's conventional defence strategies would help cement this balance. NATO starts, in fact, from reasonably solid ground – a number of studies have already indicated that NATO might actually win a conventional war in Europe, even given existing imbalances.[24] This is not to suggest that NATO has a high probability of victory, only that Soviet leaders must already deal with a significant amount of uncertainty when planning a conventional war.

The deployment of large numbers of high-technology conventional weapons, moreover, may well have revolutionary implications for warfare, a notion to which the Soviets clearly subscribe. Such weapons might one day guarantee that any war in Europe, even one restricted to the conventional level, will result in terrible destruction and, possibly, the total annihilation of forces on both sides. The implications for deterrence can only be salutary. Many doubts have been expressed about these emerging technologies; they are not touted here, however, as solutions to NATO's conventional inferiority, only as weapons that will raise the cost of the future European conventional conflict between two sides at rough parity and hence render such war increasingly unattractive.

Emerging concepts of defensive and territorial, militia-based defences could also help stabilise the resulting conventional balance. Alone, such tactics probably cannot withstand an attack by modern armies. Working in concert with highly-trained, traditional military units and large numbers of high-technology weapons, however, territorial defences can add depth and firmness to NATO's defensive posture.

The economic integration of Europe in 1992 could add further to NATO's ability to defend itself at the conventional level. Some estimates suggest that the economic growth resulting from enhanced intra-European trade will boost GNPs in the region by 4.5 to 7 per cent. 'This enormous windfall', noted Helmut Sonnenfeldt, 'could ease budgetary constraints on defence spending'.[25] Those figures might be optimistic, but to whatever degree the 1992 process spurs European economic growth it will remove pressure on defence budgets.

Operational arms control, such as confidence-building measures in the CSCE framework, also holds great potential. Potential agreements under discussion include a wide range of military observer missions (to monitor permanently such sites as corps-level arms depots), limits on exercises, reforms in the nature of military forces, and others. Operational arms control usually is self-verifying and does not require the sort of exhaustive bean-counting characteristic of numerical accords; CSCE-type agreements could therefore be implemented very quickly and might overtake progress on CFE. Properly implemented, such accords would virtually eliminate either side's ability to launch an offensive without providing the other with weeks of warning time.

These improvements in NATO's ability to defend itself at the conventional level will carry significant implications.[26] Probably the critical factor underlying NATO's reliance on flexible response was Warsaw Pact conventional superiority. Without the ability to deter conventional war, NATO was forced to threaten nuclear escalation in its defence. As the fact of NATO's conventional inferiority is eradicated, the primary rationale for flexible response will go with it.

Loss of Physical Ties to the US Nuclear Deterrent

As the threat of war recedes, moreover, and public pressure increases within Europe to reduce the Alliance's overt military posture, the eventual result may well be a pledge of no first use of nuclear weapons by the NATO Alliance. Such a step still seems politically infeasible. If present trends in the Kremlin continue, however, and if conventional arms control yields significant gains, NATO officials may look more kindly on no first use proposals – though for political, not military, reasons. There may come a time when the risk of war has receded sufficiently so that it seems a reasonable risk to take, especially if it helps preserve other aspects of NATO's deterrence.

Indeed, the shift to lesser emphasis on nuclear weapons is already underway. In the FRG, 'the established political parties, the government, and leading military men agree that raising the nuclear threshold is not only possible but necessary', a position that would have been heretical a few short years ago.[27] Apart from France and with many qualifications and perhaps as-yet incomplete commitment, 'most European governments now officially support the evolution of NATO's strategy toward "conventionalization" and the so-called "no-early-use" '.[28] In part this shift is a product of the long-term fears mentioned above that Europe would become a nuclear battleground, perhaps even for causes over which the Europeans have little control.

An Alliance no-first-use pledge could be bypassed by calls for the removal of all or virtually all nuclear weapons from Europe. Public pressure on that issue is already calling for arms accords eliminating all US-controlled battlefield and tactical nuclear weapons in Europe, leaving only European independent deterrents. The recent changes of government in Eastern Europe must also cast doubt on the need for US nuclear weapons on European soil.

West Germany's understandable difficulty in achieving a consensus on Lance modernisation speaks to the growing public disenchantment with short-range nuclear systems. Indeed Chancellor Helmut Kohl has already been forced to call for arms talks aimed at eliminating them. Yet, as the *Economist* has recognised, many other NATO members oppose such talks 'for fear that the pressure to abandon them altogether would prove irresistible'.[29]

This anti-nuclear political pressure will be fed by growing perceptions that the Warsaw Pact is simply no longer a significant threat to NATO. This view is based on Gorbachev's apparent liberalism, NATO strengths, and Pact weaknesses, and will become more and more generally held as the promised unilateral Pact conventional reductions take place. Already, a survey by the newspaper *Die Welt* found that 70 per cent of Germans thought that the communist threat was 'not very big', 59 per cent thought the FRG was 'not threatened' by the Soviet Union and 58 per cent believed that NATO was as strong or stronger than the Warsaw Pact.[30] And since that time Eastern Europe has become free.

There is always the possibility that once the risk of war, as manifest both in Soviet power and East-West tensions, recedes, European populaces will simply forget about military issues, so long as defence budgets are cut. The peace movements might be overtaken by events, as they were to a degree by the INF Treaty. Still, enough sentiment in Europe, and especially in West Germany, opposes the continued deployment of nuclear weapons in large numbers. This suggests that a continuation of détente will be used as a tool to force some degree of NATO nuclear disarmament. Critically, too, as Philip Bobbitt notes, 'Public opinion surveys do not indicate a shift in public attitudes towards nuclear weapons *per se*', as do US opinion polls. 'What has changed is the attitude of Europeans toward American-controlled nuclear weapons', partly a product of Europe's new desire to equidistance itself from the superpowers.[31]

The INF Treaty has already begun the process of severing the precious coupling ties between the US strategic deterrent and Europe, and that process may well be spurred by the eventual ejection of many US nuclear weapons from Europe. The credibility of the US pledge is at least partly dependent upon the number of nuclear weapons in Europe, and it seems inevitable that it would begin to collapse as their numbers shrink. Without battlefield or tactical weapons, as the *Economist* notes, Europe would be 'dependent on America's long-range weapons, which the Americans might not be as willing to fire' as those in Europe. The result: 'Western Europe would become "de-linked" from its ultimate security guarantee',[32] and another nail would be hammered firmly into the coffin of flexible response.

Nuclear Arms Control

The effect of the START treaty on extended deterrence might well be the most ambiguous of the five factors under consideration, in that such an accord would serve simultaneously to increase and reduce the credibility of the US pledge. In one way, a START regime might actually increase the credibility of the US escalation pledge. The less vulnerable the US nuclear arsenal becomes, the more credible are American pledges to use it to defend Europe or other vital national interests. And as noted, a modernised US START deterrent offers the potential to reduce significantly the vulnerability of the nuclear force. Secure in the knowledge that the Soviets did not possess the warhead count necessary to attack his diverse and defended force, an American president could contemplate limited nuclear options in support of beleaguered US and allied troops in a manner that might be impossible today. Indeed, arms control has already been used in this manner: SALT II was partially intended to bolster extended deterrence by reducing US vulnerability.[33]

Overall, however, strategic arms reductions would seem to affect flexible response negatively. In the first instance this is because, as the last chapter explained, arms reductions combined with strategic modernisation will further inhibit counterforce targeting. And as also noted in chapter 4, the ability to execute a general counterforce strike has been viewed as a critical underpinning of extended deterrence.

Second, deep reductions will reduce the warheads available for theatre missions. Although ICBMs capable of various missions will still exist, as one commentator has suggested, 'Because ICBMs provide a hedge against major failures in the submarine and bomber forces, U.S. leaders may be reluctant to expend weapons needed for major dramatic retaliation on targets that are deemed marginal'.[34] Combined with the ban on INF and likely forthcoming restrictions on short-range nuclear forces, START cuts in strategic warheads will be another trend contributing to the decline of flexible response.

Finally, deployment of limited strategic defences will have a similar effect. By granting each side the ability to knock down limited strikes, thin defensive screens will undercut the credibility of such LNOs in extended deterrence. This phenomenon will be discussed more fully in chapter 7.

Emergence of Closer European Security Ties

Another development that might render flexible response at once less necessary and less feasible would be the gradual emergence of a European security pillar to rival, and perhaps eventually over-shadow, the United States within the Atlantic Alliance. Traditionally, of course, the notion of a European security system has fallen prey to the reality that European states have not been able to agree on much in the security field. Some observers of NATO might concur that conventional arms accords could strip the Warsaw Pact of its superiority; others would admit that public pressure in Europe could force a NATO reassessment of its nuclear weapons policy. But most analysts writing on the question are sceptical of NATO Europe's ability to band together in its common defence, especially if there is no apparent threat to galvanise it.

Many trends, however, suggest that this situation is changing. In the wake of the INF Treaty, SDI and Reykjavik, worried European governments seemed to recognise the need to work together on a number of defence issues. With the advent of Europe 1992, the possibilities for unprecedented defence co-operation will emerge. And the improvements in NATO conventional defence and loss of physical ties to the American nuclear deterrent outlined above will render a more independent European approach to security both more feasible and more necessary. The trend within Europe toward a European pillar is already evident; as Helmut Sonnenfeld has noted,

a revived WEU, Franco-German cooperation, Franco-British co-operation, renewed attention to formerly obscure institutions like the IEPG, EPC and the Eurogroup, nascent EC interest in security issues, particularly armaments procurement; all seem to point to the most serious European interest in working towards a genuine defence identity since 1954.[35]

This is a long-term possibility – the barriers to European co-operation on defence, and particularly to an effective independent European nuclear deterrent, have traditionally been huge. Particularly troubling is the historical lesson than alliances led by a senior partner (for example, NATO with the United States at the helm) are far more robust than alliances of coequals (as NATO with a 'European pillar' might have to be). Furthermore, such an intra-European system would be infeasible today; the power of the United States is still required to counter the conventional and especially the nuclear force superiority of the Soviet Union.[36] As the trends outlined above take hold ever more firmly, however, and as the risk of war in Europe fades, the chances for a successful European pillar of sorts would grow.

It is important to define what kind of 'pillar' might evolve. The system that is contemplated here is not one involving the political integration of Europe or even the evolution of a particularly powerful supranational organisation (like the WEU) with authority over NATO European defence matters. Indeed, what is contemplated here is not even a European pillar as such. Rather, the notion is simply that NATO Europe, *primarily* because of arms control developments but *also* due to increased defence co-operation among its members, will become more capable of defending itself. And while the resulting security system will perhaps not be as strong as the NATO of the past 40 years, the shortcomings of a very embryonic European pillar will not be as relevant in an era of reduced tensions as they might have been in the past.

French writer Pierre Lellouche has summarised the result: an 'American nuclear disengagement from Europe', which will be the product of a number of trends – 'the evolution of the correlation of forces with the USSR, the public mood in the United States, the debate among strategists, the race of new technologies'. For while 'it is perhaps inevitable that the U.S. nuclear deterrent will eventually be squeezed out from Europe', Lellouche concludes,

> The same will not be true for European nuclear forces, simply because the issue of nuclear risk-sharing is not the same when

viewed from California as when viewed from Brittany. On the Continent, the fact of the matter is that all countries bear the same risks, and that is beginning to sink in even in France. Less reliance on U.S. nuclear deterrence does not have to mean necessarily the end of deterrence in Europe ... It is up to the Europeans to reconstitute among themselves the basis of an autonomous deterrent of their own on the basis of the existing and growing European nuclear forces.

While Lellouche recognises that this is an 'awesome challenge', he contends that it is one 'which could be carried out, perhaps when the trends analyzed above have become clearer to all Europeans involved'.[37]

Yet vexing problems lie waiting, like political and military land mines, on the road to creating an independent European nuclear deterrent. Even if NATO Europe reached the point where it could conduct a robust conventional defence, Soviet nuclear power would still be overwhelming. The alliance would have particular difficulty preserving a convincing nuclear umbrella over those European states that do not possess nuclear weapons – including, we must hope (for the Soviets would not have it any other way), the FRG. As Gregory Treverton has recognised, 'All efforts to manage NATO's nuclear dilemma' must reckon with 'how heavily that dilemma bears on the Federal Republic. Simple analytics suggest why. Germany is twice exposed: as the most important state on the front line, it is the most vulnerable; as the largest non-nuclear state in the alliance, it is the most dependent'.[38]

This is a real problem and must be addressed. Although in principle there is no reason why Britain or France would be less willing to escalate in the defence of Germany than would the United States, existing European nuclear forces may be insufficient to make credible threats against the USSR. One scholar, for example, points out that 'It is unimaginable that a small nuclear power would threaten to strike the cities of a superpower to deter attack against a third country'; he continues that, 'In this connection, one should distinguish between nuclear response based on credible deterrence' between two superpowers and 'suicide, which might be a strike by a small nuclear state against a superpower'.[39]

Lawrence Freedman has agreed that a European nuclear deterrent might fail. 'Under any conceivable circumstances', he writes, 'Soviet nuclear power is going to be overwhelming'. The uncertainty created in Moscow by British and French deterrents 'is quite marginal compared with that generated by Washington', he argues, which partially accounts for the fact that West Germany has never been willing to forsake an American nuclear guarantee for British or French ones.[40] Christoph Bertram writes that 'Whatever the answer the alliance gives in the end, there cannot be a non-nuclear NATO doctrine, there can be no notion of limiting the risks of war to Europe, and no alternative, in terms of deterrence, to U.S. nuclear weapons dedicated to the European theater'; Bertram calls for a reaffirmation of flexible response.[41] Gregory Treverton argues similarly that a European nuclear force 'would hardly be credible without a German finger on the button, but will continue to be politically impossible with it'; and if America's extended deterrent pledge is doubtful to the Germans, 'they could hardly believe that Britain or France would commit their much smaller forces'.[42]

These problems are severe, although several facts and potential strategic developments suggest that they are soluble. Initially, a START treaty and subsequent deep cuts in strategic forces would redouble the effectiveness of the independent European deterrents. A START-constrained Soviet force of 6–9000 warheads, and even smaller post-START II and START III arsenals, might be more susceptible than current Soviet forces to the restraining influence of British and French forces. It is critical to remember that the time frame being assumed here is five to 15 years, by which time US and Soviet nuclear arsenals may have been cut down to 4000 total warheads or less – perhaps only three to four times the size of 2010-era European nuclear forces.

Nor is the problem of a 'German finger on the button' impossible to resolve. Germany has never had unique control of any nuclear options[43]; if a pledge from a third party to escalate on Germany's behalf sufficed in the past, there are few reasons why it would not constitute an adequate deterrent in the future. Indeed, the importance of keeping German fingers *off* any nuclear buttons has been constantly stressed by analysts who appreciate the terrible Soviet fear of just such a development. The credibility of French or British extended deterrence over Germany and the Low Countries would not be great today, but could become so after a decade or more of superpower nuclear restructuring and British and French nuclear modernisation.

The argument that it would be 'suicidal' for states with smaller arsenals to escalate, moreover, bypasses the rationale of extended deterrence. Given the destructive power of nuclear weapons and the vulnerability of societies, it seems to many that, without escalation control, it would also be suicidal for the United States to escalate. The limited viability of flexible response resides in the risk that NATO leaders will decide rationally to take an action that many would find irrational. This same reasoning would suggest that European escalation in its own defence might actually occur; indeed, all other things being equal, it should be even more credible than US escalation since European territory would be in question. All other things, of course, are not equal, most pointedly the relative sizes of the US and European nuclear arsenals. But the developments outlined above will help alleviate the intervening factors.

A US nuclear umbrella, moreover, could remain in modified form. The case here is that a number of changes in the strategic environment will doom flexible response as currently enunciated. That is not to say, however, that the United States could not keep in place a pledge to respond merely to Soviet *nuclear* strikes on the Alliance. This would help avoid Soviet nuclear blackmail of NATO, and would be a much more credible pledge than that currently enunciated since the United States is only promising to respond to Soviet first use.[44] The removal of European nuclear systems would not undermine this sort of extended deterrence, moreover, since it relates to strategic nuclear forces.

Nor are European states ignorant of the need to improve their nuclear deterrents and share them in at least some fashion. France has already taken some tentative steps along this road, extending some minimal form of deterrent over West Germany by noting that France's security depends on that of its neighbours. The modernisation of French and British forces will provide them with increasingly survivable, accurate and powerful deterrents; the new French Hades tactical missile, for example, will have improved range and accuracy. By the 1990s European arsenals may include as many as 1500 strategic warheads, many of them based on survivable submarines.[45]

Finally, there is the Europe 1992 process, which holds the potential to transform European economic and political life. A European pillar as such would not come about for some time, and probably in at least two stages – at first emerging as a coequal to the United States, and only later overshadowing it within the alliance. But the emergence of an increasingly unified Europe would change the whole basis of intra-European relations and render most doubts about the efficacy of intra-European security arrangements anachronistic.[46] One result might be that European states would probably pursue ever-increasing amounts of defence co-operation, meaning in turn a declining need for the United States to threaten nuclear escalation in Europe's defence.[47]

What Role for the United States?

If the result of a bolder Europe is an 'American nuclear disengagement from Europe', however, what is the future of the US role in the Alliance? With the continuing improvement in East-West relations, flexible response will be subjected to increasingly close scrutiny as Alliance leaders attempt to root out destabilising remnants of the Cold War. It may well be that the doctrines and forces that undergird the reliance on the US nuclear umbrella would not survive this public vetting. The danger is that the whole American contribution to the collective defence will follow its nuclear umbrella back to the United States.

The last trend to be discussed here, then, is the evolution of opinion on NATO within the United States. Calls for more equitable burden sharing within the Alliance are far from new, but they seem to be reaching unprecedented proportions today, fed by the growing perception in the United States that its European (and Japanese) allies are not doing their fair share in the defence realm. As the American defence budget squeeze tightens over the next few years, intra-Alliance squabbles over spending promise only to get worse. And, as chapter 1 explained, the American public is heavily opposed to the use of nuclear weapons in the defence of Europe.

The importance of this phenomenon lies in part in the fact that the credibility of any US pledges to defend NATO rests on political, rather than military, foundations. Gregory Treverton recognises that 'When Europeans are reasonably confident of American purpose and leadership, nuclear matters will be less salient; when they are not, specific issues, like the SS-20, will emerge as surrogates for concern about the ultimate reliability of the American nuclear guarantee'. As long as the American interest in Europe – 'an awareness of shared stakes backed by the presence of 300,000 American GI's[48] – remains clear and the American recognition of this fact is apparent, the credibility of its pledges will not be questioned. Fred Iklé agrees that 'In the long run, the force of this guarantee depends on its support by the American people'.[49]

But there is no guarantee that the condition of American political support for NATO will be met. Relieved of its burden of promising the incredible, the United States would be free to reassess the danger of war and its security interests in Europe. Plans are already afoot to reduce the numbers of US troops in Europe at the margin, and the developments outlined above – particularly conventional arms control and the outcry of European publics over US nuclear weapons – may add steam to calls within the United States to bring its troops home by offering military justifications for such moves.

There is indeed a real question whether the NATO military alliance can survive in an age when the threat against which it is arrayed declines. NATO was formed in many ways to tie the interests of one superpower to Western Europe in order to counterbalance the influence of another superpower. With the Soviet military threat gone or at least dissipated, that rationale is exploded. Economic squabbles within the Alliance would prove more deadly than at a time when the military need for transatlantic relations seemed clear.[50] This danger is especially apparent today given that 1992 could usher in as much protectionism between the United States and Europe as it eliminates within the European Community.

The result of all of these growing tensions would be further damage to the credibility of the US extended pledge. An America unwilling to commit a few divisions to Europe's defence, while it might come to Europe's defence in case of war, would almost certainly be unwilling to risk nuclear suicide for it. Already public opinion polls show that vast majorities of the American people – between 70 and 90 per cent – oppose the use of nuclear weapons in Europe's defence.[51] A military policy based on support from the rest could probably not be sustained.

EASING THE TRANSITION

There are thus real dangers ahead for the Alliance; moving beyond flexible response will not be an easy task. Already the Alliance is groping for new ways to preserve flexible response: At the May 1989 NATO summit, NATO leaders issued a 'Comprehensive Concept' to guide the employment of nuclear weapons. Recognising that conventional arms parity could be just around the corner, Alliance leaders are now arguing that short-range nuclear forces are necessary, not to counterbalance Soviet conventional superiority, but merely for 'deterrence'. Sources at NATO commented that SNF 'are an essential form of insurance against attack . . . even in an age of East-West parity'.[52] That is a very hollow argument and most probably will not be accepted by European populaces increasingly unhappy about allowing what they view as unnecessary nuclear weapons on their soil.

If that is true, however, if a shift to a post-flexible response European security arrangement is truly underway, NATO must find ways to reduce its dangers. What can the Alliance do to ease the transition? Initially, NATO must redefine its purposes in this era of Soviet *glasnost*. With the Soviet threat waning, many in Europe (and some in the United States as well) are already beginning to question the need for a military alliance. When Gorbachev's unilateral cuts get underway, perhaps followed by ambitious confidence-building measures and eventually conventional arms reductions, these doubts will grow. Coupled with rising transatlantic economic tensions, they could endanger the Alliance as many of its members begin to consider declaring victory and packing off home.

Yet it may well be that NATO, even in weakened form, will prove indispensable over the course of the next decade, and this must be constantly stressed by Alliance leaders. One reason is the great danger of instability inherent in Gorbachev's glorious reforms. During the Brezhnev era, Soviet government, while repressive, seemed stable. Now, however, with established party apparachiks being embarrassed at the polls in the Soviet Union, and with Baltic states declaring independence, there is a serious risk that things could spin out of control. That could spell the end of Gorbachev's rule, and perhaps (as unlikely as it may be) the ascendancy of a neo-Stalinist. As a military alliance, NATO is therefore required, first and foremost, to guard against reversals in the Kremlin; and while this is a relatively common refrain among Western defence officials these days, it is also a very valid justification.[53]

NATO will also prove useful as a joint verification organisation for approaching conventional arms control. Indeed, Phillip Karber has suggested that, in order for the West jointly to verify Conventional Forces in Europe (CFE) in an efficient manner, 'If NATO did not exist, we would have to invent it'.[54]

NATO must also stake out a successor to flexible response, and the trends outlined above suggest some possible contours of a new NATO doctrine. NATO Europe, along with the assistance of a large body of American troops, will promise to wage a spirited if non-provocative conventional defence, using **highly-trained (if smaller)** standing armies, territorial defence tactics, and emerging technologies. This task will be eased by confidence-building measures from CSCE and force reductions from CFE. Within a decade the opportunity for either side to possess any confidence in its ability to launch a successful attack in Europe should have been reduced to miniscule levels.

On the nuclear level, France and Britain will pledge to escalate in their own defence and, increasingly, in the defence of West Germany and other non-nuclear NATO states. These pledges will become more credible as Soviet forces are cut in strategic arms accords and as intra-European defence co-operation increases across the board. The United States, meanwhile, commits its strategic nuclear forces to deter Soviet nuclear blackmail of Europe.

IMPORTANCE OF THE US ROLE

These short comments on strategy make clear the imperative that a significant number of US ground troops remain in Europe. The United States still retains critical national interests in the security of Western Europe; NATO Europe has contributed as much to the common defence as it could reasonably be expected to do; and a full or even partial US withdrawal would accomplish little and risk much.[55] The military and economic cases for large-scale reductions in US European deployments, moreover, are extremely questionable.

US forces in Europe also exercise a critical coupling effect, guaranteeing to the Soviet Union that it will not under any circumstances be able to fight Western Europe alone. Moreover, US troops keep alive an acceptable risk of unintended nuclear escalation by suggesting to the Soviets than an attack on Europe cannot achieve limited territorial gains and will embroil them in a drawn-out war with the United States, a war with the inherent potential to escalate. Lawrence Freedman has perhaps phrased the argument best:

> The critical requirement for deterrence is substantial U.S. forces in Europe, not simply to ensure that there is no pressure to resort to first use because of conventional disaster, but because only participation in a major conventional war on the continent could create the conditions in which U.S. nuclear use would be at all conceivable.[56]

The presence of American troops was always the strongest argument that extended deterrence was credible; US troops raise the prospect of an extended conventional war – no American leader could write off the loss of perhaps half a million of his soldiers, sailors and airmen and sue for peace – which, as we have seen, carries its own risks of nuclear escalation.

Finally, an insightful American participation is essential to manage safely the evolution of a more independent European pillar. A key dilemma with intra-European co-operation, as Helmut Sonnenfeldt has recognised, remains 'how to build the European pillar in such a way that it is supranational enough to stand on its own, and to ensure that all the major states participate, while avoiding damage to what remains a very satisfactory arrangement'.[57] European co-operation can damage NATO in a number of ways – by fostering anti-Americanism within an increasingly bold Europe, for example, and by promoting resentment in the United States as the Europeans go their own way. The key dilemma here is that a strong US role is necessary for greater European defence co-operation, because Europeans may not seriously pursue that goal if they fear that doing so will encourage a diminished US role in the Alliance; yet the US nuclear guarantee provides a convenient justification to avoid co-operation.

The sort of European co-operation outlined here is unquestionably of a sort that would work within existing institutions to strengthen the transatlantic Alliance rather than to supplant it, although the latter development could occur at a later date. But the dilemma of European co-operation points to the need for the United States to redefine its role, admitting (and welcoming) greater European confidence about NATO Europe's ability to defend itself. US officials must attempt to allay European fears that too much European independence will spark an American withdrawal. Eventually, a stronger, more independent Europe will emerge from the shadow of flexible response, a development that will contribute to better Alliance burden sharing; the United States must encourage that trend with a continued active participation in the Alliance.

Close American co-operation, rather than withdrawal, is therefore necessary to spur a European pillar of sorts. Sonnenfeldt argues that 'The challenge to statecraft on both sides is first to beyond short-range thinking, then to manage the transition'. A real European pillar, he concludes, 'with all its uncertainties, may well be a risk worth taking. To achieve it', however, 'will require American engagement, patience and leadership. To bring it about may be the best guarantee of substantial American engagement'.[58]

SEPARATING ECONOMIC AND SECURITY ISSUES

The Alliance must also work to disconnect economic and military issues. Populaces on both sides of the Atlantic must recognise that the value of the NATO Alliance is not directly related to the degree of economic amity among its members. Such a justification for the alliance demands that all members perceive they are making a roughly equal contribution to the common defence, which in turn requires a slightly more equitable sharing of the burden.

In fact, the burden of preserving transatlantic relations is one that will fall more to economic negotiators than defence ministers. If in fact economic competition results from a more 'threatless' era, and if the Europe 1992 process runs its course, then economic tensions within Europe will decline – and disagreements between Europe and the United States might well grow, as Europe leans more heavily on internal markets. The potential for an economic falling-out, spurred in part by growing anti-Americanism in Europe and demagogic protectionism in America, is great.

REDUCE UNNECESSARY NUCLEAR ASSETS

NATO should also remove as many as 1000 battlefield and tactical nuclear weapons once the promised unilateral Warsaw Pact conventional cutbacks have occurred. This move would not impair the Alliance's ability to escalate, yet would win NATO significant political points and might provide Gorbachev with some much-needed evidence for his hard-line opponents of the success of his defensive reforms. It would also send an important signal of Alliance recognition that flexible response and the weapons that undergird it may well be doomed. Promises of further reductions in NATO nuclear weapons could be held hostage to success in CFE.

The best candidates for such a reduction are probably NATO's nuclear artillery shells, which could serve little military purpose and, because of their proximity to the front lines, could encourage rapid, thoughtless escalation in the early stages of conflict. Reserving certain artillery units in combat for nuclear escalation, as is likely to be done, also hurts NATO's conventional capabilities.

IMPROVE CRISIS MANAGEMENT

NATO and the Warsaw Pact must separately and together establish better procedures for crisis management. In a period of high tension, there are some risks that the two alliances' interlocking alert systems could foster an inadvertent escalation from crisis to war, much as occurred in 1914. Once hostilities have begun, moreover, few procedures exist for terminating a conflict. CSCE and CFE accords can address part of the problem by reducing both sides' capability for a successful attack, but further steps are needed. NATO and the Warsaw Pact should investigate joint crisis-management centres (similar to those being pursued by the superpowers) to resolve crises and help terminate hostilities under way.[59]

The shift to a European deterrent and defensive posture relying far less on US pledges to consider escalation, and far more on NATO conventional defences and European nuclear deterrents, is already underway. The signs of such a shift, which will probably take over a decade to run its course, are unmistakable. NATO's task now is to accommodate itself to the emerging security context and to adopt policies aimed at avoiding its dangers and exploiting its opportunities. The process will not be easy, but the Alliance's extraordinary success over the past 40 years speaks volumes about its potential to meet its most difficult challenge ever. And it would solve for American deterrence theory some of its most tricky problems, allowing an easier transition to a strategy along the lines of co-operative reciprocal deterrence.

6 Soviet Nuclear Doctrine

A debate has raged for many years over the true nature of Soviet thinking on nuclear war. Many influential strategic analysts have argued that Soviet nuclear doctrine is aggressive, guided by the central assumption that the USSR could fight and win a nuclear war. As such it is depicted as the tool of an expansionist, revisionist Marxist-Leninist state whose primary goal is the subversion of the West. Naturally, these analysts contend that Soviet nuclear doctrine constitutes a significant threat to Western security.

Others disagree, contending that no matter what the Soviets say, they really subscribe basically to the same assumptions about assured destruction as most officials in the United States. While averring victory in nuclear war for ideological purposes, Soviet leaders know that nuclear war cannot be won in any meaningful sense, and hence basically support a stable nuclear balance.

Striving for a middle ground between these two positions is difficult. Either the Soviets believe they can fight and win a nuclear war and are planning to do so, it seems, or they do not and are not; either the Soviets support strategic stability or they do not. Unfortunately, US nuclear doctrine and policy are held hostage to this debate, insofar as no consensus can be reached on the true nature of Soviet intentions or the proper US response to them. In the context of this volume, it would be difficult to outline with confidence a potential US nuclear strategy without some assurance that Soviet strategy would not work to undermine it.

And the debate continues. Over the past few years, statements by Soviet leader Mikhail Gorbachev and many other top Soviet officials to the effect that nuclear war cannot be won have greatly strengthened the case for the 'softer' version of Soviet nuclear doctrine; at least publicly, Soviet officials have authoritatively rejected the usefulness of nuclear war as an instrument in the struggle against capitalism. These developments have not deterred conservative analysts of Soviet doctrine, who continue to point to current and past Soviet statements on war-fighting, pre-emption and superiority as evidence of an unrestrained Soviet attempt to achieve a usable nuclear advantage. Soviet arms control proposals are thus viewed in the same context and depicted as attempts to slow Western arms acquisition while Soviet deployments continue, covertly if necessary.

Resolution of this debate is possibly more important today than ever. As the United States and the USSR approach an accord on strategic arms, Soviet nuclear doctrine will become a critical issue. Soviet leader Mikhail Gorbachev, moreover, seems to be offering the West the potential for a long-term 'Detente II', if not a permanent resolution of the East-West divide. Conservative arguments about Soviet nuclear doctrine, however, are part of a larger case that would contend that the Soviets cannot be trusted, a case that would firmly reject the viability of a superpower accommodation. In short, as the United States begins to contemplate a new relationship with the Soviet Union, one including strategic arms control, a careful analysis of Soviet ambitions at the strategic nuclear level is required.

The primary contention of this chapter is that even the hawkish, war-fighting model of Soviet nuclear doctrine does not suggest that the leaders of the USSR are willing to fight a nuclear war or that they have any long-range plan or desire to do so. The MAD school – which contends that the Soviets accept mutual deterrence – obviously supports such a conclusion, but the war-fighting school would seem to deny, or at least qualify, it. This chapter aims to demonstrate that merely the hawkish version of Soviet nuclear willingness to engage in nuclear conflict represents a partly aggressive, partly paranoiac insistence on fully accounting for every possible security threat.

That conclusion carries serious implications for US nuclear force doctrine and structure. If the Soviets truly desire and plan to avoid a nuclear conflict, US confidence in the security of the nuclear balance, today and under prospective arms control treaties, can safely be pegged at a very high level. And the analyses of potential co-operative nuclear balances sketched out in preceding and following chapters would be borne out, a point for which this chapter is intended to argue.

The foregoing and following analysis should not be taken as a total rejection of the dangers posed by Soviet doctrine. Certainly, Soviet leaders plan to win future wars if they come. Certainly, Soviet leaders are opportunistic and might move to create vacuums of power or credibility created by the West. Perhaps most clearly, Soviet leadership seeks to maximise the power and security of their state, as often as not at the expense of the West. But the notion that Soviet strategy suggests that Soviet leaders are ready to initiate any sort of nuclear war is a gross and irresponsible exaggeration of the Soviet threat. Soviet nuclear doctrine is in fact the product of a variety of military and political considerations, easily the most important of which is to prevent a nuclear war from occurring at all.

BASIC TENETS OF SOVIET NUCLEAR DOCTRINE: THE CONSERVATIVE VIEW

For the purposes of this chapter, the war-fighting, war winning model of Soviet nuclear doctrine will by and large be used as the 'correct' portrait of that doctrine. The assumption is that, for at least much of the development of Soviet doctrine, these conservative or 'hawkish' beliefs are accurate.

There is, of course, another school of thought on Soviet doctrine, which contends that Soviet planners essentially accept Western notions of assured destruction, and merely conceal them behind ideologically necessary claims of the ability to win a nuclear war. If this view is correct (and as we shall see, recent changes in Soviet military doctrine tend to support that school of thought), the conclusions of this chapter are sustained in any case – the Soviet nuclear arsenal is intended primarily to deter war. By assuming that the war-fighting school of thought is valid, however, this chapter seeks to take the worst-case analysis of Soviet intent and demonstrate that its implications are not as clear as some would suggest. Hence the analysis in this first section, while stated conclusively, should be treated as the outline of an assumed model of Soviet doctrine, and not of the author's view of that doctrine.

Before 1954 Soviet nuclear doctrine lived in the fantasy world of Josef Stalin's personal predispositions toward war. Unwilling to admit his failure to recognise an imminent German attack – or the devastating effectiveness of German *blitzkrieg* tactics – Stalin de-emphasised the role of surprise and pre-emption. Unable as yet to acquire his own nuclear weapons, he rejected the notion that they carried any unique military significance; they were merely another weapon to be used in battle. And believing that World War III would basically be a replay of World War II, Stalin emphasised traditional notions of conventional land warfare.[1]

With Stalin's death in 1953, however, Soviet military doctrine underwent a revolutionary change. His ruthless monopoly of all military thought ended, and Soviet military theorists were free to re-examine their doctrine from the ground up. Conservative analysts see this reassessment as crucial, as it established basic tenets of nuclear doctrine that remain essentially unchanged to this day.

In contrast to Stalin, the new doctrine laid particular stress on the initial period of war, and the advantages of surprise and pre-emption. As a result of this emphasis, Soviet leaders are unwilling to allow themselves to be struck first: despite a 'no first use' pledge they are committed to pre-empting any US nuclear strike, to getting in the first blow. More recent Soviet doctrinal writings tend to conceal this predisposition in such phrases as 'adequately responding to imperialist aggression', but the commitment to pre-emption remains.[2]

Soviet planners also began to see nuclear weapons as the decisive implements of war. Soviet rocket forces were viewed as the key weapons in the struggle against US imperialism, and their employment would be the crucial event of any future conflict. In a sense, though, the nature of war had not changed – it was still, in Clausewitz's and Lenin's formulation, a continuation of politics. And most particularly, it was a continuation of *Marxist-Leninist* politics, just another stage in the unending war against capitalism. No Soviet doctrinal writings advocate a simple first-strike to obliterate the United States, but they recognise the need to fight a nuclear war if that circumstance arises.[3]

This carries two particular implications. The first is that the Soviet Union must acquire nuclear superiority over – not just parity with – its primary capitalist enemies. The huge Soviet nuclear buildup is viewed as a desire to overwhelm the US nuclear arsenal and to acquire a politically and militarily usable measure of nuclear superiority.[4] As Fritz Ermarth has remarked, 'the Soviet elite . . . has clung in the worst of times tenaciously to the belief that nuclear war cannot – indeed, must not – be deprived of strategic meaning'.[5]

Second, and most controversially, the Soviets believe they must be prepared to fight *and win* a nuclear war. Quite simply, then, the Soviets are ready to engage in nuclear war, and believe they can prevail. As we have seen, analysts adhering to this model of Soviet nuclear doctrine see it as extremely threatening.[6]

Hawks in the United States also point to Soviet force posture as indicative of an aggressive *operational* doctrine. The Soviet nuclear force is configured along very specific lines, and its composition indeed provides far more evidence to the war-fighting school of interpretation of Soviet nuclear doctrine than to the mutually assured destruction school. The requirement for a socialist victory has led to the acquisition of a huge, accurate, land-based counterforce set of heavy ICBMs, defences against ballistic missiles, and civil and air defences.[7] In short, it seems that Soviet planners have acquired the capability **both** to destroy much of the American nuclear arsenal and to survive whatever retaliatory blow US leaders can muster. Such strategies clearly point to an operational doctrine that must be offensive, some argue, and that would be inappropriate for a defensive nation seeking stability.[8]

SOVIET DECLARATORY DOCTRINE: GREAT POWER OR MESSIANIC MARXIST?

We have thus arrived at a picture of how conservatives view Soviet nuclear doctrine, and must determine whether it could be the policy of a state whose only goals are to deter nuclear attacks on itself and reserve some hope that it could prevail in a nuclear conflict, rather than one assembling the offensive and defensive forces necessary to make nuclear attacks on others truly feasible. To do this, the chapter will assess each aspect of Soviet nuclear doctrine outlined above. While the general intent is to assume the conservative model as correct, when significant doubts about the continuing validity of a particular hawkish interpretation have arisen, these will be pointed out.

It should become apparent that the whole of these parts is perfectly consonant with the basically defensive goals of the USSR at the nuclear level. The basic framework for this analysis contends that the Soviets view nuclear deterrence and defence as a two-sided requirement. The overall Soviet goal is to avoid war, which would clearly be a calamity. On the other hand, such a war is viewed as a risk inherent in the existing international environment, especially as capitalism edges into its inevitable death throes; and if war comes, Soviet leaders are determined to win it. The same distinction accounts for the 'political' and 'military-technical' aspects of Soviet doctrine. The Soviets do not want war and would not contemplate starting one intentionally, but, guided by an ideology of competing systems, recognise that it might well happen and therefore take the risk much more seriously than do US leaders. Thus, while the overriding political side of doctrine has as its purpose the deterrence of war, the military-technical side is where the Soviets discuss their strategies for war if it comes.[9] Such distinctions are perfectly applicable to the nuclear planning of other states – witness the US SIOP, a detailed plan for fighting a nuclear war which all US strategic policies are designed to avoid. And as Stephen Cimbala has concluded, a doctrine that aims to win a war if it comes is 'eminently sensible'.[10]

The Role of Ideology

The notion of ideology is very relevant to this discussion, as it is to any analysis of Soviet policy. The assumption of most who see Soviet nuclear force posture and doctrine as a significant and immediate threat is that the Soviet Union is an ideological state irrevocably committed to the destruction of the West. Soviet nuclear doctrine is seen as a stepchild of this larger strategy. Hence Harriet Fast Scott and William Scott conclude that 'The Soviet concept of military doctrine, which demands a never-ending military buildup . . . is based on a Marxist-Leninist interpretation of the world and of human relationships'. This *political* aspect of doctrine 'best explains Soviet moves in the international field'.[11] William Lee and Richard Staar concur, noting the tie between political ideology and military doctrine.[12] Richard Pipes laments the inability of Westerners to understand that 'the most influential elements in the Soviet Union indeed hold such [ideological] views'.[13]

The implications are serious. Soviet leaders, concludes Leon Goure, view history 'dialectically', and have 'no thought of resting content with the present situation'. Instead, they intend to 'press for further and ever more decisive shifts in the balance of world forces against the United States and in favour of the USSR'.[14] Fritz Ermarth fears that 'the most dangerous consequence of our misunderstanding of Soviet strategy involves an excessive confidence in strategic stability', with the result that US complacency will encourage Soviet aggression that promises, in turn, to 'increase the probability of a major East-West confrontation'.[15] The assumption seems to be that the USSR is, as one analyst characterises the argument, 'systematically amassing the necessary military capabilities for an eventual "once and for all" military showdown with the West'.[16]

There is nothing, however, in Marxism-Leninism that demands such a policy. Marxism-Leninism never provided a real road-map of policies for leaders in the Kremlin to follow, relentlessly, generation after generation. Nathan Leites's concept of the 'operational code of the Politburo' is particularly instructive here.[17] That code is formed according to Marxist-Leninist guidelines and provides the basics of societal analysis, a worldview that relates to the nature of man and nations but that does not outline a specific master plan for world domination. Soviet planners thus possess a great deal of flexibility in making particular decisions, since Marxism-Leninism establishes the geopolitical *ends* of Soviet policy but not the *means* by which they are to be pursued. One important corollary is that ideology does not, contrary to the assertion of some, compel the Soviet Union to undertake nuclear or conventional hostilities with the West; it does not actually instruct them to do anything besides 'ensuring the victory of socialism', which they can pursue – and indeed interpret – as they see fit.

A good Communist can be perfectly happy merely deterring the West's nuclear weapons, while seeking victory through political harassment, subversion and other means in Eurasia and the Third World. Zbigniew Brzezinski, Max Singer and others have been quite right to point out that the USSR is not essentially either a defensive or offensive power; as Singer concludes, 'the insatiability of their self-perceived defensive requirements takes all the relief out of seeing the Soviet Union as a defensive power'. [18] But it will be argued here that the end goal of Soviet *nuclear* doctrine is indeed defensive, though it merges offensive and defensive tactics to achieve that end. In other words, Soviet military doctrine rejects the offensive/defensive distinction as to the means of deterrence – but not necessarily as to the *end*, which is to deter attacks on the USSR.

Seweryn Bialer concurs. 'Marxist-Leninist doctrine', he writes,

> expresses its 'laws' of continuity and change in highly theoretical, abstract ways, and, partly because of its complex methodology, provides uncertain guidelines for understanding the changing world, let alone for determining the actions necessary to achieve its goals. The doctrine alone cannot explain Soviet international behaviour. The level of its generality can seldom be translated into policies and can be so broadly interpreted as to leave enormous latitude to the policy-maker.

Top policy-makers in the Soviet Union are relatively unfamiliar with Communist doctrine, Bialer continues; it is the role of the theoretician 'to provide a doctrinal justification for the policies adopted by the "practical" policy-makers'. [19] Thus 'the Soviet belief system does not provide a detailed blueprint for the decisionmakers . . . Throughout its history, the Soviet Union has adapted its international behaviour to the changing circumstances of world politics and to its own domestic conditions and requirements'.[20]

Sovietologist Paul Dibb agrees. 'There is, in fact', he points out, 'little in Soviet international behaviour that cannot be understood by reference to political power alone'. Marxism-Leninism does not provide a 'map of international reality'; in fact, 'Soviet foreign and strategic policy is about power and the will to exercise it and ideology is therefore no guide to Soviet actions. Rather, ideology is a stereotyped and bureaucratic ritual in the service of an authoritarian state'.[21] These conclusions are as applicable to Soviet nuclear policy as to its general foreign policy.[22]

This is a product of Marxist beliefs on the political nature of war itself. War will begin, it holds, not by the Soviet Union, but by capitalist nations on the verge of collapse caused by the contradictions within them. Thus it seems hardly surprising that ideology instructs Soviet leaders to prepare for war; not, however, to crush a weak, calm, reasonably healthy yet enfeebled capitalism with a nuclear attack, but to annihilate a collapsing, predatory, desperate capitalism. If the latter condition never arises, the USSR possesses no ideological requirement to go to war. Here again we see a distinction between political requirements – which demand the ability to win the war that political analysis says might arise.

This section has hopefully provided an analytical prism through which the reader can examine the following analysis. Soviet ideology does not imply that Soviet nuclear doctrine is uniquely offensive or dangerous; what about the characteristics of the doctrine itself? When discussed in a relatively objective, unprejudiced manner, the tenets of Soviet nuclear doctrine reveal themselves as merely prudent steps taken by tough, pragmatic men of power.

The Stalin Years

Stalin's explication of nuclear doctrine makes perfect sense for any non-nuclear-capable great power intent on deterring an opponent in possession of nuclear weapons. His doctrine was essentially a bluff, designed to create uncertainty in Western minds until the USSR could acquire a nuclear arsenal. Stalin's own personality, as we have seen, also dictated much of the doctrine – his inability to recognise his errors translated into a policy that ignored them. Indeed, the effect of Stalin's unique personality was so strong that this period of Soviet nuclear doctrine is relatively non-controversial; its guiding principles were clear enough.

Thus Vernon Aspaturian concludes that 'Among the factors which conditioned and often defined the decisionmaking process was Stalin's personality and character. Decisionmaking during the Stalin era was highly idiosyncratic and intensely personal ... The institutional setting of decisionmaking was often ambiguous, ill-defined, or nonexistent'.[23] Nikita Khrushchev certainly agreed with this contention, writing in his memoirs that later in his life 'Stalin did everything in his own name. He refused to discuss military matters with me ... Defense was his exclusive concern and he guarded it fiercely'.[24]

Since 1953, however, Soviet doctrine has taken on a distinctly different cast, and conservative analysts contend that it has remained extremely threatening. Let us now turn to this model to determine if its primary aspects can be explained in the context of defensive motivations.

Pre-emption

Some writers emphasise the danger inherent in the Soviet desire to pre-empt their likely opponents in a future war. This offensive strategy seems to confirm the aggressive intent of the Soviet leadership.

In fact, the Soviets see the adoption of a pre-emptive strategy as simply the learning of a key military lesson. Notwithstanding Stalin's denials, the sudden German blitzkrieg in 1941 convinced many Soviet officers that surprise and striking first were crucial, and they have applied this lesson to nuclear warfare as well. Richard Pipes notes that the Soviets are 'obsessed' with the lessons of World War II,[25] and the importance of pre-emption is just another one of them.

Nor must it be forgotten that Soviet literature only advocates pre-emptive strikes in the face of an imminent enemy attack, in order to deprive the opponent of the initiative. There is absolutely no discussion of Soviet-initiated, 'bolt from the blue' attacks designed to cripple the West. The Soviet pledge that they will not be the first to use nuclear weapons reinforces the idea that they view pre-emption in a defensive light, and have adopted it in response to what they see as threatening Western nuclear policies.

Holding out the possibility of that Western threat, and the possibility of sudden nuclear attack embodied within it, was also useful in justifying the Soviet Union's military build-up, which the

Soviet leadership in turn saw as necessary to maximise and protect its power. In an article on the initial stages of war, Lt. Gen. A. Yavseyev wrote that 'The possibility of a surprise attack by an aggressor using all the available power of its armed forces requires that the army and navy be maintained in a constant state of readiness to repel aggression and inflict powerful retaliatory strikes on the enemy'.[26] Adoption of a strategy of counterforce pre-emption is a logical extension of such threat perceptions.

Pre-emption also makes sense from a purely rational perspective. In the nuclear age any first strike will carry enormous destructive power, and there is no guarantee that the nation absorbing the blow will be able to retaliate effectively. Command systems might fail under the pressure of hundreds of nuclear explosions; submarines might not receive orders to fire. Given these uncertainties, magnified by the USSR's lack of sophistication in C3I technology, a prudent Soviet military planner might well decide to hit first if he believed an enemy attack was imminent.

In this sense the Soviet strategy of pre-emption can be compared with Israel's. Indeed, the USSR and Israel share arguably similar strategic positions, insofar as both are surrounded by potentially hostile powers that, in total population and military power, significantly outnumber them. The Israelis have adopted an offensive strategy of pre-emption, used in wars and in specific operations like the raid on the Iraqi nuclear project.[27] That Soviet planners have developed a similar strategy should hardly come as a surprise. US analysts have also considered the potential for pre-emptive attacks: the doctrine of Massive Retaliation contemplated a first strike against Soviet nuclear assets in response to conventional aggression, and, as chapter 4 noted, during the 1950s the US JCS and other executive departments considered both pre-emptive and preventive wars, and to this day a pre-emptive strike has not been ruled out.

Thus the Soviets are not unique in favouring the offensive. Nuclear analyst Andrew Goldberg recognises that the risk of Soviet offensive orientation 'has been somewhat overstated in the policy literature. Most military establishments, that of the United States not excluded, stress the virtues of offensive over defensive military action at the tactical level'. Even the French army during World War II 'intended to go on the offensive at the earliest possible opportunity'. Goldberg properly concludes that the Soviet military 'is hardly unique in recognizing the advantages of surprise and the potential value of going first to better impose one's will on the enemy'.[28]

War as a Continuation of Politics

Alarmist observers also bemoan the supposedly Clausewitzian notion in Soviet nuclear doctrine that war is merely an extension of politics. The Soviets, presumably, are more likely to use or risk the use of nuclear weapons because military conflict is seen as merely another step on the ladder of confrontation with the capitalist West. Richard Pipes warns that 'as long as the Soviets persist in adhering to the Clausewitzian maxim on the function of war, mutual deterrence does not really exist'.[29]

Of course, the ideological underpinnings of this notion were undercut when Nikita Khrushchev declared that war between the Communist and capitalist camps was no longer inevitable. Thus war as a continuation of political, economic and ideological struggle against capitalism was given up, an action reinforced by Brezhnev's emphasis on the peaceful coexistence of ideological rigidly in Soviet nuclear planning – Paul Dibb has described it as an 'exercise in realpolitik'.[30] and indeed it was, placing the realities of the modern world above strict Marxist-Leninist dogma. Defence Minister Dmitry Yazov has stated flatly that 'It is perfectly obvious to anyone that the old notions of war as a means of achieving political aims are completely outdated'.[31] Marshal Nikolai Ogarkov reaffirmed the flexibility of Marxist-Leninist doctrine when he wrote in 1985 that, in coming to accept the lack of 'the fatal inevitability of war', the Party was guided by the theory of Marxism-Leninism, *'creatively developing and enriching'* the theory *'as it applies to the present situation'*.[32] These shifts reflect the means/ends distinction of Leites's operational code at work.

Even if it were still true, however, that the Soviets considered nuclear war in some cases merely another usable tool in their political arsenal, the implications are not necessarily foreboding. Even if the Soviets believed war was a continuation of the political effort against the West, they would not necessarily start one – unless it were in their interests, which a nuclear conflict clearly is not. Raymond Garthoff says in regard to the notion that nuclear war is a continuation of politics that 'of course it is! . . . [but] it is very clear that authoritative Soviet political and military leaders have rejected the ideas that this truism carries any implications as to the acceptability of war'.[33]

Soviet leaders also admit that war can kill politics.[34] The men in the Kremlin stand to lose power, and perhaps their lives, in a nuclear war, as well as the lives of many of their countrymen. Without an absolutely compelling reason to do so, they would be foolish to risk war. In a political sense, war is unadvisable, and this fact undoubtedly encouraged the enunciation of the doctrine of peaceful coexistence. As George Kennan has recognised, moreover, a nuclear strike at the West would kill off much of the proletariat, and – if the Soviets are truly fanatical Marxists – this must occasion them great ideological heartburn.[35]

The Quest for Superiority

Conservative analysts argue that the Soviet Union is not content with a nuclear balance, that it strives constantly for a usable nuclear superiority with which to cow and defeat the West. The Soviet leadership is portrayed as the primary instigator and perpetrator of the nuclear arms race, acquiring far more weapons than are necessary for simple deterrence.

Initially it must be borne in mind that, publicly at least, the Soviets have given up the quest for superiority. In various arms talks, Soviet negotiators have displayed a willingness to surrender the ability to build up their nuclear forces to the point where they would enjoy clear superiority over the West. *Parity* was always the chief goal, parity that would grant the Soviet Union independence from American nuclear threats (of the sort embodied in the Cuban Missile Crisis, for example) and allow them to operate with impunity at the sub-nuclear level. The resulting 'nuclear détente' would also lessen the capitalist strategic threat to the USSR.[36] Here we see a mixing of offensive and defensive goals – but the goal at the *nuclear* level is clearly defensive.

The notion of superiority is also a relative one. Certainly, it could be credibly argued that the Soviets have achieved superiority over the United States in many categories of weapons; but the United States is not the only threat to Soviet security, and such US-USSR comparisons are inherently misleading. In the nuclear realm, the Soviet Union confronts British, French and Communist Chinese nuclear forces – and perhaps Pakistani, South African and Israeli ones as well – in addition to American ones. The USSR is quite simply ringed with enemies, and to point out that it has acquired military forces in excess of one of its opponents is to stress the irrelevant.

But again, even if the Soviets sought, or had achieved, superiority over *all* their adversaries, what would this tell us about their nuclear plans? Not much. Soviet planners might well feel that the possession of nuclear weapons *at least* equal to that of their combined adversaries is necessary for their security. Certainly, the traditional Soviet emphasis on raw numbers to overcome technological deficiencies could have been applied to nuclear planning – if the Soviets do not have much confidence that two warheads on an American silo could do the job, for example, they might feel compelled to build a force allowing them to put three on each target.

This sort of overcompensation where national security is concerned is not new; it is an integral aspect of traditional Russian security policy. Arthur Alexander has pointed out that

> ... the Russian view of national security and defense ... does not accept the notion of overinsurance. One can never have enough security to protect oneself from the ever-present possibility of annihilation. Indeed, the belief that implacable foes are continually seeking the annihilation of the Russian state and the Bolshevik-Communist system is not inconsistent with history.[37]

Given this historic Russian and Soviet proclivity towards over-preparing, their commitment to parity *at a minimum* with its adversaries seems hardly surprising. Soviet leaders also know that, as a revanchist, not a status-quo, power, they are in for an unusual degree of international confrontation, and perhaps they therefore saw the acquisition of an unusually large military as necessary to defend themselves. Their Marxist-Leninist rhetoric would certainly indicate that this is the case.

From a purely pragmatic military standpoint, the pursuit of superiority makes perfect sense. Such a goal, as the strategic analyst Paul Stockton notes, is 'not surprising' in the Soviet case. 'Given the emphasis in Soviet doctrine on damage limitation, strategic superiority – particularly in weapons capable of destroying the enemy's forces – seems a logical goal.' The greater the superiority, Stockton points out, 'the better prepared the Soviet Union would be for deterring war, as well as for fighting a war should deterrence fail'.[38]

Superiority is a logical goal for the USSR in another sense. As many analysts, particularly Edward Luttwak and Zbigniew Brzezinski, have pointed out, the Soviet Union's power in the international arena has since World War II been concentrated today almost exclusively in the military sphere – its economic and political institutions hold little appeal, except to ambitious dictators or would-be dictators intent on institutionalising their power. For the USSR to attempt to maximise its one area of strength would be perfectly natural.[39]

War Winning

The most controversial, and probably least understood, aspect of Soviet nuclear doctrine is the notion of a war-fighting, war-winning strategy. Certainly, the Soviets do plan to win a nuclear conflict, and have said (until recently) that in a nuclear war only capitalism would be destroyed. Many analysts respond with frightening claims that the Soviets are gearing up to launch a nuclear first strike, or at least to start a conventional war which, if it happens to go nuclear, they are prepared to win. A closer examination reveals that current Soviet war-fighting plans are perfectly consistent with the defensive motivations of a conservative (though not a status-quo) great power.

Initially, there is some reason to doubt that the top Soviet leadership still believes a nuclear war could be won in any meaningful sense.[40] The debate on this point is wide-ranging and sometimes acrimonious, but there is good evidence to suggest that since sometime between 1969 and 1982 top Soviet leaders have discounted the reliability of nuclear war as a usable method of conflict. In 1981, for example, Leonid Brezhnev told the 26th Party Congress that 'to count on victory in nuclear war is dangerous madness'. While parts of the Soviet military appear wedded to war-winning beliefs, top Party leaders seem to believe otherwise.[41] (This will become abundantly apparent during the discussion below of recent Soviet doctrinal developments.)[42]

For Soviet military men, war-fighting is simply a prudent strategy designed to deter war. As Leon Goure has written:

> Soviet military writings and military posture do not specifically distinguish between deterrence and war-fighting nuclear capabilities or postures, but appear to view them as one and the same. The Soviet assumption is that the better the Soviet Armed Forces are prepared to fight and, if possible, to win a nuclear war, the more effective they will also be as a deterrent to an attack on the Soviet Union ...[43]

In other words, the Soviet goal is to prevent an attack on their homeland, and the acquisition of a war-fighting capability is the most absolute way to guarantee this outcome. As Mark Miller has recognised, 'These pragmatic men of power are apparently at a loss to find any disutility in striving for a warwinning capability'.[44] John Van Oudenaren has outlined 'minimal' and 'maximal' goals in Soviet nuclear strategy, the 'minimum' being an assured retaliation, 'maximum' constituting a true war-fighting capability.[45] But all these strategies are aimed at defending the Soviet Union, not attacking others.

Two other reasons why the USSR takes the possibility of war more seriously than the West have been outlined by Stephen Cimbala. One is that Soviet planners are more concerned about the potential for war by accident or miscalculation – a Sarajevo rather than a Munich scenario. If war can come in that fashion, by no one's choice and with little warning, it makes sense to overcompensate on security matters. The other reason is that their ideology teaches them to fear a Western pre-emptive strike as the capitalist system collapses; 'capitalism in its death agonies is the most dangerous and might resist being deterred at any cost'.[46] Again the potential need to fight a war not of the Soviet Union's choosing.

The end goal, however, is clearly *defensive*.[47] Soviet war-fighting strategy does not of itself recommend or make advisable an eventual nuclear attack on the United States or anyone else, but is formulated to convince other nations that the Soviet Union would withstand their blows and prevail. No Soviet doctrinal writing ever admits of the possibility that the Soviet Union would cause a war; of course, this is in large part the result of propaganda ('imperialism is impossible under socialism'), but it must be assumed that at least a few leaders truly believe that starting a war would be against Communist principles.[48]

The Soviets themselves make distinctions between offensive and defensive tactics in an interesting fashion. William Scott suggests, as was explained above, that Soviet military doctrine has 'two sides, the political and the military-technical – and only the political side is "defensive"'.[49] He notes that Soviet attacks on Finland, Czechoslovakia and Afghanistan were all considered defensive wars. The implication is that the West can have no confidence in any defensive aspects of Soviet doctrine, but in fact, as noted above, the political/military-technical distinction supports the analysis in this essay. Once a war has begun, Soviet tactics call for offensive operations, since 'the best defence is a good offense'. But wars are only acceptable when political conditions recommend them and when political leaders approve them – and neither condition is true today, nor are they likely to emerge in the near future. In short, by marking off a boundary between political and military doctrines, Soviet doctrinologists have provided themselves with an ideological justification to renounce conflict. (And in fact, the three invasions mentioned above were defensive operations in many senses – just as were US interventions in the Dominican Republic in 1965 and Grenada in 1983.)[50]

Then there is the Soviet notion of the just war, from a Marxist-Leninist perspective. This doctrine holds that any wars waged for the liberation of the worker are by definition just; as Scott summarises the implication, 'the only type of wars in which the "peaceloving" Soviet Union would engage, by definition must be defensive wars'.[51] But again this means little in practical terms. Just because Soviet leaders have created a doctrine that justifies warfare in Marxist-Leninist terms does not mean they desire any sort of large-scale conflict. Leites's analysis explains this practice perfectly: the Soviet state needs to intervene in various places to protect its security, but its ideology seems to forbid such violations of self-determination. It therefore evolves a just war doctrine to justify actions it deems necessary. But those small-scale interventions do not in any fashion speak of a willingness to engage in nuclear or large-scale conventional conflict, any more than the US invasion of Mexico in the 1840s or of Cuba in 1898 suggested that the United States was prepared to invade Europe.[52]

Soviet preparations for war may seem unnecessary to Western observers well aware that their governments have no plans to attack the Soviet Union. But the effects of Soviet paranoia – which may or may not be the primary motivations for Soviet actions – should not be overlooked. There is strong reason to believe that, on several occasions since World War II, the leadership of the USSR actually did expect an American attack.[53] Even if war is not an immediate fear, moreover, the historical experience of two bloody world wars taught Soviet leaders to be on perpetual guard, and the evolution of a war-winning strategy is the ultimate extension of this principle.[54]

The Reagan administration's adoption of its own form of war-winning strategy also helps place Soviet strategy in perspective. While US nuclear doctrine still officially accepts MAD, it has evolved closer and closer to a form of war-fighting with the simple contention that the better prepared a nation is to fight a conflict, the better equipped it is to deter it. Certainly at the conventional level the notion of war-winning is as old as warfare itself; it is the nature of strategy. In short, the United States plans and hopes to win the next war, in whatever form, and while American leaders and planners might (though this may not be true today) lean more to the view that there can be no winners in a nuclear war, they nevertheless adhere to the same basic notion that to deter a war entails preparing to win one.

Michael MccGwire has outlined the primary goals of Soviet leadership in difficult-to-dispute fashion. Soviet leaders attempt to promote the well-being of the Soviet state; ensure retention of power by the Communist party; avoid world war; retain independence of action; and if war comes to win it.[55] In some contexts, such as the intervention in Afghanistan or provision of support to worldwide insurgencies, expansion and creation of instability can serve those purposes. It is against these tactics that the West must guard.

The initiation of large-scale nuclear war, however, would obviously not serve those purposes. The Soviet homeland would inevitably sustain massive damage, and the Party might well be destroyed – certainly, its primary mechanisms of control, including the armed forces, would be annihilated. Even Marxist-Leninists would not risk a nuclear war without reason. A nuclear conflict is simply not in the Soviets' interests, and their recognition of this fact seems clear.

Given these qualifications, the fact that the Soviets plan to fight and win a nuclear war is largely irrelevant to Western security – unless a nuclear war were to occur through miscalculation or accident, in which case, if the West had not adequately prepared, it might – just might – lose the conflict in a definable sense. But the desire to win a war at any level could be expected as much from a state whose primary concern was to defend itself as it could from a state attempting to achieve a usable conventional or nuclear military superiority.

Thresholds in Soviet Military Thought

One important aspect of Soviet policy not paralleling US doctrine carries specific implications for US nuclear strategy: the issue of nuclear thresholds. It has generally been agreed that historically the Soviets have placed less emphasis on finely-tuned thresholds between various forms of warfare. The decision to go to war in the first place was seen as the critical decision, not the manner in which that war would be conducted. More recently, a rough consensus seems to have emerged on the point that the Soviet Union wishes to create the opportunity for a conventional-only phase to a war in Europe, thereby establishing at least one 'threshold'.

What is important for this analysis is not the Soviet view of theatre war, however. Western analysts could never predict with real accuracy just how the Soviets might react to a given situation, and in any case the limited nuclear options suggested in chapter 2 would provide flexible means of deterring limited Soviet use within Europe. The question here is this: once the Soviets have decided to employ strategic nuclear weapons, how will they do so – in one all-out spasm, or in gradual, selective strikes? Once again, either could be possible. But there is strong evidence for favouring the former proposition, that a general Soviet nuclear strike would be more all-out than limited in character. Much of the Soviet literature on pre-emption and war-fighting stresses the need to deliver a crippling initial blow. Andrew Goldberg recognises that the Soviets 'likely will try to implement as much of their targeting missions [sic] as possible on the very first strike'.[56] This point was also made in the critique of counterforce targeting in chapter 4.

The implications for US nuclear planning are reasonably clear. The United States must, to be sure, possess the capability to respond in kind to limited nuclear options of various kinds. But there is a very strong chance that, should the Soviet side consider nuclear conflict, they would have as their primary option an all-out attack. This means both that deterrence of such an attack (through the acquisition of survivable forces and other methods) is a primary requirement for US strategy, and that doctrines (such as existing countervailing strategies) based on a need to respond to Soviet extended-war strategies have misplaced their emphasis.

DECLARATORY VERSUS OPERATIONAL DOCTRINE

Some conservative analysts, not content to outline the provocative aspects of Soviet nuclear doctrine, extend their analysis (somewhat confusingly and apparently contradictorily) to conclude that, in fact, we cannot base any conclusions on what the Soviets say their doctrine is, either publicly or in their military journals. Soviet declaratory doctrine, these observers contend, is merely propaganda, designed to deceive the West about true Soviet intentions. Thus, Albert Weeks concludes – and the emphasis is his own – that 'when one makes the distinction, *as the Soviets themselves explicitly do*, between *declaratory* strategy and *operational* strategy (or doctrine)', then the motivation for more peaceful pronunciations becomes clear.[57]

This position, of course, makes the open Soviet discussion of pre-emption, superiority and war-fighting totally inexplicable – why would they make such hard-line statements, bound to worry the West, if all they were up to was an extended deception? Such a strategy is perhaps understandable through the mid-1960s, when Soviet statements on nuclear weapons were meant to influence the strategically superior United States; but similar statements in the later 1960s or 1970s, and those that are still made today, are unjustifiable by this standard. Dan and Rebecca Strode make essentially the same point. They contend that

> the notion that all incongruities between the USSR's word and deed can be attributed to a systematic propaganda campaign to deceive the West suffers from a major theoretical shortcoming. Specifically, proponents of the disinformation thesis have provided no criteria by which we can distinguish authoritative Soviet pronouncements from efforts intended to mislead Western analysts. Yet ironically *the disinformation thesis has been propounded most avidly by the very analysts who in previous Western debates over Soviet strategy have been most insistent upon the validity of using Soviet open-source publications as guides to understanding Soviet military doctrine.*[58]

That the Soviets would spend so much time and effort producing a series of technical military journals filled with lies also seems unlikely. One wonders where the true discussion of Soviet doctrine goes on; the notion of a group of Soviet officers studiously filing the latest issue of *Military Thought* in the trash, having a laugh about American gullibility, then marching off to engage in unanimous backroom planning for the West's destruction in nuclear war is, to say the least, unpersuasive. Strode and Strode note that 'if the West is being "disinformed," so too are Soviet armed forces personnel and the Soviet public as a whole'.[59]

The truth about the usefulness of Soviet statements on nuclear war is, of course, far more complex. It may indeed be true that there is an inverse relationship between a statement's honesty and the degree to which it is made in a public forum; hence pledges at summits or even Party Congresses to adhere to treaties and accept MAD may be less valuable as indicators of true Soviet thought than the more complex debates in Soviet military journals. Or it could be that the difference – and more public statements do tend, of course, to be far less polemical and aggressive – reflects a divergence of thinking between

Party and military. As we have seen, too, there may be a whole host of reasons for a given position or statement besides a real belief in its truth. But simply to dismiss all Soviet statements on the nuclear issue as propaganda is as unprofitable as taking them all at face value. The analysis above has hopefully suggested a few motives for the aggressive nature of Soviet military doctrine besides the desire to make nuclear war fightable and winnable.

OPERATIONAL DOCTRINE

Even if Soviet declaratory doctrine does not prove any aggressive or revisionist intent, however, Soviet force posture, and the operational doctrine for nuclear war to which it refers, certainly does, contend those who see the Soviet nuclear threat as immediate and significant. Analysts who portray declaratory doctrine as irrelevant, of course, contend that the only valid evidence about Soviet intentions is to be found in their force posture. Soviet acquisition of an offensive and defensive force mix arguably capable of striking at the West and absorbing the retaliation is seen as destabilising and indicative of expansionist intent. Thus, two writers conclude that the 'principal evidence' against the notion that the Soviets believe in MAD can be found in 'Soviet military hardware'.[60] On closer examination, however, Soviet force posture appears consistent with solely defensive aspirations.

Offensive Nuclear Forces

Initially, examine the heavy ICBM force. Some view its acquisition as provocative, but even in its present guise it is not sufficient to guarantee a high-confidence strike against the US nuclear arsenal.[61] Soviet leaders can destroy American fixed ICBMs, but certainly not the entire triad – they possess barely enough prompt, hard-target-capable warheads to attack all the crucial targets, and the success of the attack would assume that everything functioned perfectly.

One must also remember that Soviet military planners contend with British SSBNs – four older Polaris boats and, soon, newer *Tridents*; French SSBNs, IRBMs, MRBMs, in addition to a few SSBs and SSBNs that are beginning to become operational in the PRC's inventory.[62] The British and French weapons are modern and accurate, and the Chinese ones are close to Soviet borders if nothing else. Taken together, they further degrade the capacity of Soviet forces to fulfill their operational requirements. Were the Soviets truly seeking a first-strike capability, they should have built a far more impressive force than the one they have.

Though this may be the case, some would still maintain that the nature of the Soviet force – biased toward the best counterforce weapons (heavy, accurate ICBMs such as the SS-18) – indicates a desire to be able to strike at the West. While the ability to hit Western targets reliably and hard is certainly a consideration for the Soviets, however (just as hitting Soviet targets is for Western planners), other motives were probably just as important in dictating a concentration on ICBMs.

One such motivation might have been technology. Soviet naval technology was relatively primitive for many years – the missiles on early Soviet strategic submarines sat in casings that protruded upward in ungainly appendages above the hull of the submarine, and those missiles possessed only the most dubious accuracy. Building relatively obsolescent bombers that would have great difficulty reaching the United States – let alone hitting anything when they got there – would have made little sense when faster and more reliable ICBMs were available. From the perspective of purely rational military planning, under the tight constraints of a very poor defence technology base, the Soviet concentration on fixed ICBMs makes perfect sense. Indeed, given the Soviet technological weaknesses through the mid-1960s, it is a wonder they built anything but ICBMs.[63]

Political considerations may also have played a role in the Soviet commitment to ICBMs. Soviet leaders have for many years been obsessed with control of their subordinates, and the image of a rogue submarine or bomber commander deciding to strike against New York – or Moscow – must be a disquieting one for them. Fixed ICBM deployments are more susceptible to tight control, and this may have influenced the emphasis on such weapons.

Geography also dictated a concentration of ICBMs. Without access to convenient warm-water ports and lacking the extensive net of worldwide basing characteristic of the US military, Soviet planners would be hard-pressed to reliably conduct bomber or submarine operations far from their own borders during wartime. This is still true to an extent today, and it represented a crippling constraint in the 1950s, when Soviet leaders began to develop their nuclear force.

Given this analysis, as Soviet technology and basing facilities improved, and as the confidence of Soviet military men in their subordinates grew, one would expect a decreasing emphasis on fixed ICBMs, and this is exactly what has happened, although the trend is as yet quite slow and indicates a shift to mobile ICBMs more than SLBMs or bombers.[64] Nevertheless, the transition to less accurate but more survivable SLBMs and mobile ICBMs is evidence of a desire to place deterrence of a strike against the USSR above acquisition of the ability to strike the West.[65]

Thus, the Soviet acquisition of a force of accurate, counterforce-capable ICBMs could easily have been dictated by a combination of military prudence and economic, technological, political and geographic factors inherent in the Soviet state. This force does not necessarily connote any aggressive intent.[66]

Soviet Defensive Deployments

If the Soviets did not intend to acquire a nuclear war-winning capability, conservative analysts query, why would they acquire huge defences against nuclear attack? If they accepted MAD, as the West presumably does, they would recognise that mutual *vulnerability* is the key to stability, and that the construction of defences is inherently destabilising. Notwithstanding the fact that hawkish American analysts themselves are now arguing for stability based on defence, the fact that the Soviets do seem to place far more emphasis on air, civil and strategic defence than the United States is indeed troublesome.

These defensive deployments, however, are simply not as significant as some maintain. For example, the Soviets have engaged in large amounts of research on defensive technologies since the signing of the ABM treaty. But thoughts that this research is designed to allow a breakout to support nuclear blackmail of the West are very probably misguided. The Soviets have not stretched the treaty to its absolute limits – until very recently they had not deployed anything close to the 100 interceptor launchers it allows. Further, since one of the primary motivations for the Soviet signing of the ABM Treaty in 1972 was to slow the progress of far more advanced US technology, a vigorous research programme designed to narrow this gap simply represents a prudent hedge against an existing inferiority.[67]

Similar responses could be made to the March/April 1988 claims of a Soviet ABM breakout, in which accelerated production of anti-missile-capable SAMs and radars was begun. The Defense Department denied the validity of that conclusion, but in any case it could be seen as a simple response to US SDI progress, and hedge against American deployments. The true indication of Soviet intentions would come after the ABM Treaty was reaffirmed and the US SDI programme scaled back – if they continued fast-paced ABM work, a possible offensive inclination would be uncovered. But as this analysis suggests, such a development is highly unlikely.

Moreover, strategic defences – even had the Soviets deployed them – merely fit into the larger strategy of damage-limitation and war-fighting that the Soviets pursue. As we have seen, this is a defensive strategy whose goal is to convince enemies of the USSR that they could not prevail in nuclear conflict with it and so to deter them. In fact, some Soviet analysts see the *lack* of strategic defences as provocative; nations with totally vulnerable forces, they argue, may well be planning to use those forces in a surprise attack, when defences would be unnecessary.[68]

Soviet leaders possess many motives for constructing a partially-effective ABM system besides the desire to engage in war-fighting. As many experts contend, the Moscow system might have been deployed to counter the Chinese minimum deterrent, whose use the Soviets, always fearful of the Chinese, could not rule out. Such a defence might also defeat accidental launches or third-party attacks on Moscow.[69]

Similarly, the Soviet *civil* defence programme is not particularly impressive.[70] It is simply not capable of protecting the Soviet population from the immediate or lasting effects of a nuclear war, and many analysts view it as merely a doctrinaire programme – one designed to fulfill pledges that the Soviet people will be safe in a nuclear war, but one whose operational utility is known by the Kremlin to be minimal. Since most civil defence will protect only leadership cadres, it can be seen as another programme designed to achieve the Soviet leadership's key goal: their own maintenance of power. But it does not contribute very significantly to a true ability to wage a nuclear war.

In any case, the simple provision of protection for one's own population in the event of nuclear hostilities is not particularly provocative; the Swiss, for example, are probably the world's greatest practitioners of civil defence, yet no one would point to any Swiss expansionist designs on slices of Austria or France.[71] Once again Soviet leaders seem to take the possibility of war much more seriously than their American counterparts, but this does not mean they would be any more inclined to start one. And the Soviet enthusiasm for protecting their population is again bound up in complex cultural and ideological factors that have demanded a high degree of societal militarism.[72]

Soviet air defences are simpler to explain. A land power ringed with potential adversaries would be foolish not to acquire a significant air defence capability. Soviet paranoia and obsession with control of their country – and in this case its airspace – reinforce this desire. And early US concentration on a strategic bomber force created immediate incentives for the Soviets to establish such a system.

NEW DEVELOPMENTS IN SOVIET NUCLEAR DOCTRINE

Trends in Soviet thinking on security suggestive of a possible understanding with the West – the decline of ideological rigidity, loss of military influence on decision-making, a more overt emphasis on defensive doctrines – have reached their apex during Mikhail Gorbachev's tenure. This chapter has to this point assumed the validity of the conservative model of Soviet nuclear doctrine, and has attempted to explain how even a worst-case analysis of Soviet planning does not prove Soviet leaders are willing to engage in nuclear conflict. Recent developments in Soviet military doctrine, however, question more seriously than ever the appropriateness of that hawkish model of Soviet doctrine; the practical aspects of Gorbachev's very real peace offensive, at the nuclear level, point to what may be another revolution in military affairs as perceived by Soviet planners. If this is indeed the case, the conservative case for the existence of a dangerous Soviet nuclear doctrine has become outdated.

Basis of the New Doctrine

At the core of this doctrinal shift are several strategic judgements by Soviet leaders. One concerns the nature of the imperialist threat. Though Western governments, and in particular the United States, are still portrayed as expansionist and dangerous, the image of an 'unappeasable opponent' has faded.[73] In part this may have been dictated by the need to downplay the threat to justify a decreasing emphasis on military spending. Perhaps the reality that the United States and its allies really had no desire to attack the Soviet Union finally became apparent to the men in the Kremlin.

Other influences recommended a less provocative military stance.

Soviet leaders may have recognised that their own unceasing military build-up has caused a distinctively undesirable reaction in the West; in Mark Miller's phraseology, the prudent military men in the Kremlin may indeed now have found some 'disutility in the pursuit of superiority' – the West's own military build-up. Jack Snyder adds the important notion that it was changes in the political situation in the USSR that finally allowed a shift to take place; 'the military-industrial complex, the orthodox ideologies, and autarkic interests', he concludes, 'are in decline'.[74] Those sort of political changes also reflect the desire within the Kremlin to reinvigorate the USSR's civilian economy, a process that will require lower military budgets.[75]

The Infeasibility of Nuclear War

One important result and corollary of these changes in Soviet thinking, and the aspect of them most relevant to a discussion of nuclear doctrine, is the growing Soviet consensus on the uselessness of nuclear weapons. Again, the cause-effect relationship is hard to gauge; Soviet policy-makers might honestly have come to the conclusion that a nuclear war could no longer be won, and shaped their statements and plans accordingly; or the pragmatic needs to uphold ideological consistency and shift funds to the civilian economy might have dictated the public posture that wars could not be fought. Either way, the result is a growing body of Soviet literature that is refreshingly candid on the point that in a nuclear war there can be no winners, a view tending, of course, to dispute the war-fighting model of Soviet doctrine outlined earlier.

This shift, in the eyes of some experts, is far from new. As was noted, analysts adhering to the MAD model of Soviet doctrine always denied that Soviet leaders believed they could fight and win a nuclear war. Raymond Garthoff, for example, dates the shift to 1969. It could well be that the change is still going on; major doctrinal shifts, as with all political change in the Soviet Union, occur at a glacial pace. But whenever it occurred, it is now indisputable that Soviet political and military leaders alike claim that in a nuclear war, there will – and can – be no winners.

The Soviet rejection of nuclear means of conflict was occasioned in part by their recognition that nuclear war was so messy and unpredictable that it ceased to be a reliable instrument of policy. Hence General Vitaly Shabonev argued in 1986 that 'more and more leaders, politicians and scientists the world over, including the United

States, are becoming aware that a nuclear war cannot be won'.[76] Lt. Gen. D. Volgkonov, a Deputy Chief in the Main Political Administration (MPA) – and a man thus in a good position to be aware of the current Soviet ideological line – concurred in 1985, expressing the view that the huge build-up of nuclear weapons has rendered nuclear war unfightable. 'Nuclear war can no longer be used by the aggressor as a means of attaining political objectives', he argued, because a 'point, a limit, a borderline' had been reached beyond which 'it is no longer a question of victory or defeat, but rather of destruction or existence'. He refers to this as a 'qualitative change ... in the means of waging war'.[77]

Similarly, an article in *Communist of the Armed Forces* by Rear Admiral G. Kostev concludes that the 1980s version of Soviet doctrine was formulated in a period when 'the two leading powers – the USSR and the United States – had accumulated an enormous nuclear might', and when several other states had acquired smaller stocks of nuclear weapons. 'This is the principal peculiarity of the present epoch', Kostev explains, 'which gives rise to new views in the socialist countries about the character of a future war and which differs fundamentally from those held in the 1940s and 1950s'.[78]

Gorbachev himself agrees. In 1986, at the 27th Party Congress, he stated that 'not only nuclear war itself but also the preparations for it ... can ... bring no political gain to anybody'. At another time he explicitly rejected the Clausewitzian notion when he stated that 'after Hiroshima and Nagasaki, world war ceased to be a continuation of politics by other means ...' In his book *Towards a Better World*, he concludes that in a nuclear war, 'neither the Kremlin nor the White House; neither man nor beast will survive. There will be no living thing left!'[79]

Soviet Defence Minister Dmitry Yaszov has expressed similar sentiments. As noted earlier he, too, rejects the war-politics connection. Parity, he admits, has rendered war fruitless; 'the approximately equal correlation of the two alliances' military forces, given the tremendous destructive power of modern weapons, both nuclear and conventional, makes war between them senseless'.[80] In John Van Oudenaren's equation, it could be said that the Soviets have opted for the 'minimum' requirements of deterrence over the 'maximum' aspirations for war-winning capabilities.

Practical Expression: The New Doctrine

These general ideas were officially sanctioned by a statement issuing from a conference of Warsaw Pact member states on 28 and 29 May 1987. It was signed by the General or First Secretaries of seven Warsaw Pact states, including Gorbachev. It restates what are viewed as the traditionally defensive outlines of Soviet military doctrine, and as such addresses issues broader than merely nuclear doctrine.

The doctrine outlined in the statement is 'purely defensive'. It recycles old Soviet promises not to use nuclear weapons first or to violate the territory of other European nations. But the phrasing of these pledges is perhaps less ambiguous than ever before, and their practical implications, as has been shown since that time, extend also to Eastern Europe, where Gorbachev's promises have been interpreted as pledges not again to invade other Warsaw Pact countries.[81]

The statement also outlined a notion of 'sufficiency', which really was a formalised renunciation of the drive for military superiority over adversaries. What exactly 'sufficiency' means, especially to a nation so concerned with not falling behind its adversaries, is unclear, however.

Still, the language of the statement is impressive: 'the Warsaw Treaty member states will never, under any circumstances, start hostilities against any country or alliance of countries unless they become the target of an armed attack themselves. They will never be the first to use nuclear weapons. They have no territorial claims to any other state either in Europe or outside it. They do not view any state or people as their enemy'. It went on to call for six specific actions: a test-ban treaty, a ban on chemical weapons, conventional arms control, verification of arms control, creation of nuclear and chemical-free zones, and (interestingly) the dissolution of NATO and the Warsaw Pact 'as the first step in the liquidation of their military forces and, ultimately, in [the creation of] an all-embracing system of international security'.[82] The overall thrust of this doctrine would seem clearly to reinforce all the notions of defensive thinking and the priority of deterring the West outlined in the preceding analysis.

Critiques

Immediately, a number of Western analysts dismissed the new Soviet doctrine as a propaganda ploy. Albert Weeks stressed the difference between operational and declaratory doctrine, and argued that the latter was designed simply to deceive and sedate the West.[83] The 'totalitarian predispositions', he writes, include 'the exploitation of peace propaganda'. The journal *Disinformation* began its article on the new doctrine by stating simply that 'The Soviet Union is waging a strategic deception campaign designed to affect the global balance of power' by persuading Western audiences of the inadvisability of nuclear war, while 'Soviet military doctrine, as well as Soviet offensive and defensive systems, still demonstrate that Moscow believes nuclear war can be fought and won'.[84]

Significance of the Doctrine

As Soviet emigré Lev Yudovich, currently a Soviet analyst with the US army, has noted, however, whereas some in the West dismiss the new doctrine as propaganda, 'the Soviets and their Warsaw Pact allies have taken the public disclosure of their military doctrine more seriously. Soviet political officers in the Main Political Administration (MPA) have rushed into print articles intended to explain to the rank and file that this new doctrine is not an abandonment of the traditional Marxist-Leninist principles on war and the army'. As he notes, 'the new military doctrine ... more than ever implies that the struggle between capitalism will shift into the political arena'.[85]

The new doctrine thus demonstrates that the Soviets are taking seriously the implications of peaceful coexistence, which renounced large-scale conflict but admitted, indeed very specifically warned, that Soviet leaders still viewed history as a clash of opposing classes. They still see the Third World as an arena in which they can sometimes safely use their military power, or more commonly that of their surrogates, to undermine the influence of capitalism. Yet ideology does not demand specific actions, and nuclear war could be given up as an instrument of policy.

It is important, of course, not to overestimate the changes wrought by the new doctrine. Claims by left-wing analysts such as the late I. F. Stone that the Chernobyl disaster shocked the Soviets into pacifism are as misguided as they are dangerous. As noted, too, most of what the 'new' doctrine asserts has been said, in one form or another, at some time in the past, a fact underscored by Yazov's subsequent insistence that Soviet doctrine had always been defensive and there was no need to alter it.[86] Nor has the Soviet military necessarily stomached the full scope of the changes: many military writings have preferred the term 'defense sufficiency' to 'reasonable sufficiency', and some have suggested that the former implies larger military budgets than the latter. A number of Soviet analysts have claimed that both the political and the military-technical sides of doctrine are already completely defensive, and there is no need for change.[87]

In a sense, too, those analysts are exactly right. Soviet nuclear doctrine had since Brezhnev's time already begun to show signs of a 'defensive' cast. As noted above, the Soviet intent with their nuclear build-up was never to achieve the capability to launch a first strike – merely to pin down the West's nuclear forces. The change wrought by the 'new' military doctrine on nuclear affairs is therefore less significant than on conventional strategy.

Most important is the simple fact that Soviet leaders have chosen this path, not out of some ethereal concern for 'peace', but simply and purely because they feel it is the best way to maximise their power. As such it may represent the recognition that a constant arms race does not serve the Soviet Union's interests. But the shift, as a logical extension of the principle of peaceful coexistence, does offer significant advantages for the West. In short, if the Soviets wish to redirect the worldwide competition between capitalism and communism from the macro-military level into political and economic fields, the West should welcome the shift – it is clearly superior in two of those three categories and arguably superior in the third. The United States and its allies must be careful to arrange a stable, ordered transition to a less-armed world, but given such caution there is no reason not to welcome the enunciation of a new Soviet military doctrine and the implications that flow from it.

THE NATURE OF SOVIET NUCLEAR DOCTRINE

What, then, is Soviet nuclear doctrine? When examined in an objective framework, keeping in mind the nature and requirements of the Soviet state, Soviet declaratory and operational doctrine emerges as merely a pragmatic strategy well-suited to the perceptions and requirements of such a state. Ideology is still relevant to the Soviets, but in the sense of a worldview, not a step-by-step plan for the annihilation of the West. The implication is clear: ideology will not cause the USSR to attack the West, because Soviet leaders do not believe that such a course is advisable and their ideology allows them total flexibility in choosing means to the end of victory. And so it is with Soviet nuclear doctrine, which provides no clear evidence that the Soviet Union is bent on expansion; that it contemplates an inevitable military showdown with the West; or even that it actually believes it could fight and win a nuclear war. Soviet nuclear posture rather most closely resembles that which an internationally outnumbered, revanchist, authoritarian state might adopt for itself.

Interestingly, the analysis outlined above suggests that the polar differences between the two schools of Western interpretation of Soviet nuclear doctrine can be at least partially resolved. The Soviets do prepare and plan to fight and win a nuclear war, and their resulting force posture can appear enormously provocative to a peace-minded Western audience. But these policies and weapons are adopted to deter a Western attack and render the Soviet Union free of Western nuclear intimidation.

The implications of all of this for American nuclear strategy are clear enough. Washington can pursue arms accord with Moscow with reasonable confidence that the latter, given its primarily defensive goals, has more of an interest in abiding by treaties than in violating them. And as suggested in chapter 4, the United States must attempt to disabuse the Soviets of any confidence that they could actually fight and win a nuclear war, but do so through defensive measures such as the deployment of mobile missiles.

So much of the debate over Soviet strategy and arms control revolves around the question of 'whether we can trust them'. Hopefully, the analysis in this volume has suggested that we can indeed trust them *to do what is in their interests*, given the primary goal of defending the Motherland. As long as the nuclear balance remains one of relative parity, it will not be in the Soviets' interests to risk war. And since the United States has no intention of beginning one, it can reach some mutually beneficial compromise, at the nuclear level at least, whose effect would be to end the arms race and reduce the risk of war.

These conclusions are informed in important ways by the military analyst John Collins' notion of the distinction between capability and threat. Certainly, the Soviets possess frightening capabilities, but without an active intention to use them they constitute only a minor threat. Conservative analysts tend to merge these two notions; John Dziak, for example, former head of the US Defense Intelligence Agency's political-military affairs department, has concluded that 'The reality of Soviet military power ... simply does not square with the softer signals emanating from trendy Soviet spokesmen'.[88] That may be true, but neither does 'the reality of Soviet military power' *necessarily* imply any desire to use that power.

The time when the chief Soviet military threat was embodied in the nuclear arsenal, whose aggressive uses were spelled out in Soviet nuclear doctrine, have come and gone. If the West fails to recognise this, it will both miss an historic opportunity for arms control and truly jeopardise its credibility. The whole argument of this chapter could be summed up in a quote from John Collins: 'The probability that the Soviets are going to launch a nuclear attack against the United States as a deliberate act of national policy is somewhere between zero and about minus eight million. They are not going to execute any of these cockamamie scenarios that are so prevalent right here in Washington ... The answer [to those who warn of a Soviet first strike] is "forget it"'.[89] Soviet nuclear doctrine provides no evidence to dispute this conclusion.

Changes in US doctrine, moreover, can encourage a continued belief in such principles. As Andrew Goldberg has recognised, Soviet doctrine is subject to influence; 'the more the United States is viewed by Soviet decision makers as reluctant to use nuclear weaponry', he writes, 'the greater is the Soviet reliance on non-nuclear means of combat for war in Europe'.[90] In a direct sense, then, the decline of flexible response outlined in the previous chapter should serve to reduce Soviet reliance on nuclear options, which should in turn raise the nuclear threshold and reduce the risk of escalation.

More broadly, moreover, a START treaty, combined with counter-power targeting and US modernisation, would encourage the Soviet shift toward defensive military doctrine for nuclear weapons. The Soviets today emphasise offensive damage limitation more than the United States. A modernised US START force, however, would as we have seen create attack requirements far greater than the sum of Soviet forces. Unable to seek damage limitation offensively through counterforce, and prohibited from seeking superiority through a continued build-up, the Soviets might well choose to seek it defensively, through passive defences, further arms control, war termination strategies, or eventually through transition to a defence-dominant environment (although the risks of the latter notion will be outlined in the following chapter).

7 Other Issues: The Mechanics of the Nuclear Deterrent

Discussions of the stability of a START regime also involve a number of issues besides straight comparisons of numbers. The superpowers have not fully evolved positions on a number of issues within START, in particular strategic defences, verification and sea-launched cruise missiles (SLCMs). If not properly constrained, any of these weapons systems or issues could emerge to undermine the stability so carefully crafted in an accord. These issues are considered below.

STRATEGIC DEFENCES

Chapter 3 has already suggested that modest point defences deployed strictly around missile silos would be stabilising. Presumably, ICBMs would be the first weapons used in an initial strike, and thus silo defences, unless they have wide coverage, would be useless in knocking down a retaliatory blow because they would only be defending empty silos. This argument is especially strong if the United States adopts counterpower targeting; in that case silo (or missile field) defences would not affect a retaliation at all, because they would not protect a secure reserve for either side – neither would plan retaliation at the other's forces. Very limited defences of that sort would also help defeat accidental or third-party attacks on either superpower.

General Strategic Defence

What of the value of more ambitious, if still limited, defences? Most proponents of strategic defences have given up Ronald Reagan's original vision of a virtually leak-proof shield, and focus instead on partially-effective defences intended to augment deterrence. A good example of such a system is provided by the one outlined as a minimum deployable requirement for the Bush administration:

defences must be effective against 50 per cent of the Soviet SS-18 force and 30 per cent of an imputed first-wave attack of 4700 warheads to be considered for deployment by the Joint Chiefs of Staff.[1]

Yet such partial defences have the potential to be highly destabilising. Contrary to Reagan administration assertions, as the number of nuclear weapons shrinks, the instability caused by partially effective defences grows. With only a few thousand warheads to target, either side could feel that its defences are robust enough to knock down most of an opponent's 'ragged retaliation'. Even if neither side desired to start a nuclear war, moreover, the instability thus created would impel both sides to do so during a crisis.[2] Unless the development and deployment of defences were perfectly symmetrical, too, the transition to a defensive world would be dangerous.

As these arguments suggest, strategic defences are destabilising precisely because they run afoul of the paradox of deterrence. Some contend that limited defences are advisable or even required to limit damage in the event of a war; by doing so, however, defences threaten to undermine to a degree the consequences of nuclear war and hence its deterrent effect.

Strategic defences are, moreover, clearly unnecessary for deterrence. The analysis above, and especially that in chapter 2, has suggested that co-operative reciprocal deterrence will adequately preserve the peace. Arguing that defences are required to deter the Soviets assumes that the Soviets would in some circumstances have a motive for striking first, yet, as we have seen, there are no national interests significant enough to call for nuclear war in their protection. The only threat of sufficient magnitude to demand a nuclear strike would be the degradation of one's deterrent, which would hold open the possibility that an opponent could launch a nuclear strike. And ironically, defences have the possibility to do exactly that – to call into question the reliability of both side's deterrents.

The cost of even limited defences, moreover, would be enormous. Given the need to modernise US retaliatory capabilities, the costs of defensive systems simply could not be borne. The money would be better spent on Midgetman or other modernised systems.

Nor is it in the US interest to allow large-scale competition in defensive systems. As former US Defense Secretary Harold Brown has written, an abrogation of the ABM Treaty 'would allow the Soviets to indulge in their historic proclivity toward defensive systems', which 'budgetary constraints and congressional limits' would prevent the United States from matching.[3]

The best course, then, would be a general reaffirmation of the narrow ABM Treaty, perhaps with a new exemption for protection of missile fields and bomber bases. Such an outcome is not entirely unlikely; before being nominated as George Bush's national security adviser, Brent Scowcroft had argued that a commitment to respect the ABM treaty for an additional decade would not seriously constrain US research in the SDI programme. It seems therefore probable that either no or extremely modest strategic defences will be deployed under START, a result that would respect the arguments made above against broader defences.

A 'Defence Dominant Environment'?

Proponents of strategic defence, however, make another, broader claim than the fact that defences will augment deterrence. Many argue that they will herald a transition to a 'defence-dominant environment' in which the United States (and presumably the Soviet Union) deter war, not by threat of retaliation, but by the ability to defend themselves. Thus strategic defence is held out as a means to transcend deterrence by mutual vulnerability.

It is simply not true, however, that defences will cause such a revolution in deterrence. The reasons are simple. First, it is now generally accepted that nothing even approaching a leak-proof shield can be constructed. Vast numbers of countermeasures exist, and it is not at all clear that space-based systems can be made survivable enough to withstand dedicated attacks. Defences can therefore create some ability for a country to defend itself against nuclear attack, but not a complete ability. In this sense they are like defences of all sorts – against sea, air, land or space attacks; no nation in history has been able to promise a foolproof defence of its borders. All merely establish some ability to defend themselves, combined with a clear pledge to retaliate, to seek out the aggressor and destroy him.

That is the same manner in which deterrence would work if strategic defences were deployed. The heart of deterrence would remain, not the ability to knock down half or more of an attack, but the capacity and willingness to retaliate and cause devastation in the aggressor's country. Mutual vulnerability would remain. To the degree that that vulnerability is circumscribed, however, stability declines because both sides must worry about the security of their deterrent.

It must be admitted that strategic defences would complicate an

attacker's planning, another common argument for their deployment. But they also risk destabilising the balance, as suggested
above. Many other means exist to create such complications, such as
developing mobile ICBMs. And point defences of critical military
targets can serve the same functions without impinging on the mutual
hostage relationship.

On balance, therefore, general strategic defence is not justified. It
would not allow the superpowers to transcend deterrence; it is not a
necessary augmentation to deterrence, especially given the START
treaty (which will work the same 50 per cent cut on Soviet SS-18
forces as proponents have claimed for strategic defence). Defences
do, however, create crisis instability, are hugely costly, and promise
to establish a new avenue for the arms competition when the primary
one is beginning to run into a dead end.

Very Limited Defences and Limited Nuclear War

We have seen that more general strategic defences could prove
destabilising and not at all in the US interest, but that point defences
of certain targets related to nuclear deterrents would be stabilising.
Such limited defences could also have profound and critical implications for limited nuclear war.

Initially it is important to note that even defences designed to have
limited scope would be able to knock down missiles aimed at targets
besides those precisely defended. This collateral coverage must have
limits, lest point defences intrude into the unstable realm of general
population defence. (Even defences of counterpower category
targets would be destabilising insofar as they would guard against a
retaliation.) Nevertheless, it might be fair to claim that point defences deployed in certain regions might have the capability to
destroy a few missiles, or perhaps 20 to 50 warheads, no matter what
their targets. Thus point defences could not protect a country against
a general retaliation, be it counterpower or countervalue; but it
perhaps could protect against a very limited strike, that is, an attack
of several missiles or, at most, two or three dozen warheads.

One result of the deployment of extremely limited defences would
be, as we were reminded above, the augmentation of deterrence
through the provision of additional security to both sides' deterrents.
As nuclear analyst Andrew Goldberg has suggested, another result
could be 'to reduce the ability of central strategic forces to conduct
limited nuclear operations'. Because of START, the force will be

smaller, and 'light ballistic missile defence screens will hinder any attacks involving relatively small numbers of warheads'.[4]

This seems to have two immediate implications. First, limited defences can serve a barrier against limited nuclear warfare. Chapter 2 explained how co-operative reciprocal deterrence can deter LNOs by convincing a potential nuclear aggressor that no strikes could achieve military or political goals. Limited strategic defences provide additional disincentives to LNOs by raising the potential that the attacks might be shot down. A defence-dominant environment could therefore arise at the level of LNOs.

Very limited defences would also deter limited options by raising the threshold for an attack. Currently, one of the superpowers might believe it could achieve military or political purposes through the firing of a handful of ballistic missiles against the other. Such an attack could be used, for example, to destroy particularly critical military facilities, to cripple command and control, or to show resolve. Limited defences would offer the possibility that such an attack would fail. A potential nuclear aggressor would have two options: give up the partial attack plan, or expand it significantly to ensure that some warheads arrived on target. The latter course, however, is rife with dangers of escalation and asymmetrical, or at least symmetrical, retaliation. Given the requirement to make a very limited nuclear strike less limited, the option of not attacking at all might appear more attractive.

It was argued above that such defence dominance would prove dangerous insofar as general strategic defences would cause crisis instability. This would not be true, however, for defence dominance at a more limited level; since the defences would not be capable of defeating a full retaliatory blow, neither side would need to fear being disarmed. Both would continue to possess a reliable deterrent, and symmetrical mutual vulnerability would continue to prevail. All that would be lost was the ability indiscriminately to launch limited attacks, at least by ballistic missiles.

Second, limited defences might undercut flexible response. Goldberg argues that 'What could be compromised seriously is the U.S. ability to threaten a limited nuclear response to Soviet conventional attacks in key regional theaters'; in other words, 'what the United States may gain in "simple deterrence"' through missile defences 'may be lost in the ability to extend deterrence to its allies'.[5] Goldberg suggests a number of alternatives to ballistic missile escalation, such as medium-range sea- or air-based systems. Still, with cuts in SNF and strategic forces, dedicating such systems to theatre missions will detract ever more seriously from central deterrence. As was noted in chapter 5, limited missile defences will further undermine extended deterrence.

Arms accords might have to be reached to augment the capability of limited defences. Both sides could, and most probably would, develop countermeasures to help their warheads penetrate even the most limited defences.[6] It might be feasible, should both sides agree to the value of very limited strategic defences protecting retaliatory assets, to agree to a ban on certain countermeasures, such as the inclusion of decoys or chaff in missiles. These could be verified by national technical means and on-site inspections at missile production facilities.

VERIFICATION

Perhaps the most vehement claim of arms control sceptics is that the Soviets cheat on arms agreements. The USSR has allegedly violated SALT II, the ABM Treaty and numerous other accords, and they can be expected to do the same with START, these pundits argue. In fact, they view the primary Soviet motive in arms control, not as seeking stability, but as freezing Western armies acquisition while the Soviets clandestinely continue their own build-up. Those charges are all hotly disputed, but even assuming the Soviets would like to use a START accord to increase their nuclear leverage over the West – could they do it by cheating?

The common answer to this question involves complicated references to the various surveillance systems available to the West and how well they could detect Soviet cheating. And indeed, the requirement to upgrade US monitoring systems seem clear.[7] But, aside from whether they *could* do it, two important lines of analysis suggest that the Soviets *would not* cheat significantly on a START accord. As the military analyst John Collins has recognised, a *capability* does not necessarily equal a *threat* – it is only when that capability is wedded to certain political or military intentions that it becomes dangerous.[8] The argument here is that, even if the Soviets had the ability to violate START (which they probably do not), they would not.

The first reason relates to the potential benefits of cheating. Could the Soviets achieve a usable advantage by secreting away several hundred, or even a few thousand, missiles? Provided the United States deploys the modernised systems described above, the answer is no. The Soviets would have 6000 'legal' warheads; to target the US land-based force they would need tens of thousands, and again the US submarines remain relatively invulnerable. In short, the Soviets would have to construct about *four times as many weapons as they are allowed* under the treaty to possess a reliable first-strike potential against *just the US land-based deterrent*. After launching that strike, the Soviets would be vulnerable to US SLBMs and the British, French and Chinese deterrents.

It is ludicrous to suppose that the Soviets would be able to build and hide that many illegal missiles. Even assuming that the estimates of Soviet needs are high – assuming shorter warning times, smaller Midgetman bases, a Soviet strike before the full US modernisation programme is complete – a Soviet planner would still need more than twice as many warheads as he is supposed to have to strike the US land-based arsenal. And one can expect the Soviets to make worst-case calculations, which would balloon their warhead requirements. Given these prospects, it would take a truly lunatic planner in the Kremlin to begin a large-scale cheating programme – if he were caught, which the huge scale of cheating makes probable, the international repercussions would be enormous. The risks of such a course far outweigh the benefits.

On the point that the United States could detect the cheating necessary to attack a *modernised* US force, the consensus is impressive. Former defence official Richard DeLauer has written that 'We could easily detect the massive cheating the Soviets would have to undertake to erode the much higher survivability and mobile missiles'.[9] R. James Woolsey, John Deutch, and Brent Scowcroft agree that 'If the United States had a survivable mobile ICBM, the Soviets would need so much throwweight to attack it ... that any cheating they could do by covertly deploying mobile ICBMs themselves would be strategically insignificant'.[10] The Center for Strategic and International Studies Discussion Group on Strategic Policy, which included, among others, Les Aspin, Sam Nunn, Harold Brown, Robert McFarlane and (up to his appointment as national security adviser) Brent Scowcroft, contended that 'If the Soviets decide to cheat, it would be virtually impossible for them to deploy enough illegal forces to substantially improve their ability to attack a mobile U.S. system successfully'.[11]

Nor would such cheating be cost-effective. The CSIS Discussion Group pointed out that even if the Soviets attempted to cheat against a modernised force, the United States 'would be in a position to expand [its mobile missiles'] deployment area much more economically than they could add the warheads necessary to attack it'. [12]

Supposed Soviet arms control cheating to date has been on a scale dwarfed by these requirements. Critics sometimes suggest that the Soviets have a few dozen more delivery vehicles than allowed under SALT II, or that they have a questionable ABM radar, or a few dozen more SS-20s than our intelligence had thought. Certainly, cheating of that magnitude would do absolutely nothing to disturb a START regime.

The second reason why Soviet leaders would not cheat on START involves their reasons for signing it, and is hence debatable. But it seems undeniably true that, whatever the merits or seriousness of Mikhail Gorbachev's *perestroika* camapaign, the current Soviet leadership would like to save money on the military if they can. This derives, not from any soft-headed desire for peace, but from a simple intention to maximise Soviet power. Nevertheless, it establishes some crucial non-military priorities.

For the Soviets to construct thousands upon thousands of illegal nuclear weapons and conceal and maintain them throughout the USSR would take an investment of funds, manpower and resources that boggles the mind. START verification procedures could ensure that Western inspectors are on hand to witness the destruction of currently existing missiles; Soviet leaders would then have to start from scratch to violate the new treaty. That would involve essentially re-building an entire nuclear force. Even if his reform is is just a 'front', spending on that scale would break Gorbachev's bank.

The United States can also prepare in a number of ways to offer a tough response to any proven Soviet cheating. Perhaps a production line for the Midgetman, or some other inexpensive and relatively survivable weapon, could be kept open. Certain missiles could be down-loaded, that is, not loaded with their full warhead complements; the counting rules agreed to at the Washington Summit make this possible. If Soviet cheating is detected, Trident missiles could be upgraded from eight warheads to 12. These and other similar measures could help convince the Soviets in advance that any cheating on START would have counterproductive results.

In summary, then, verification concerns should not stand in the way of a strategic accord. Variants of the tight on-sight inspection procedures established in the INF Treaty, made even more stringent and supplemented by new satellites and by traditional intelligence sources, would make cheating very difficult. But most crucially, a

TABLE 7.1 *US Tomahawk Programme*

	IOC*	Length (Feet)	Diameter (Inches)	Speed (Mach)	Range (Kilometers)	Accuracy	Warhead
Tomahawk Land Attack Missile—Nuclear (TLAM-N)	June 1984	20.3	20.4	0.5–0.75 (400–570 mph)	2500+	250 ft C.E.P.†	W80-0 5–150 kiloton
Tomahawk Land Attack Missile—Conventional (TLAM-C)	March 1986	20.3	20.4	0.5–0.75	1300 (ship) 920 (sub)	circa 30 ft C.E.P.	100 pound high explosive or submunition dispenser
Tomahawk Anti-Ship Missile (TASM)	Nov 1983	20.3	20.4	0.5–0.75	460	active & passive radar seeker**	1000 pound high explosive

* IOC (Initial operational capability) refers to date system declared operational.

† C.E.P. (Circular Error Probable) is a common measure of missile accuracy. It refers to the radius of a circle within which 50 percent of the missiles will land.

** Traditional measures of accuracy are not applicable because TASM is not pre-programmed to strike a given target, but rather the missile will seek out a moving target through active and passive radar. One DOD spokesman has called TASM "the most accurate anti-ship missile system in the world".

Source: James P. Rubin, 'Sea-Launched Cruise Missiles: Facing Up to the Arms Control Challenge', *Arms Control Today* 16 (April 1986), 5–9. Reprinted with permission of the Arms Control Association.

TABLE 7.2   Existing and Potential US SLCM Programmes

Type of Vessel[1]	# of Vessels	Launcher Type[2]	# of Planned Slcms per vessel[3]	Total Planned SLCM Deployments (estimated)	# of Potential SLCMs per vessel[4]	Total Potential SLCM Deployments by mid 1990s
Battleships BB-63 (Iowa-class)	4	8ABLs	32	128	40	160
Destroyers DD-963 (Spruance-class)	7	2 ABLs	8	56	12	84
Destroyers DD-963	24	VLS	45	1080	61	1464
Guided Missile Destroyers DDG-51 (Burke-class)	29	VLS	28	812	90	2610
Guided Missile Cruiser CG-47 (Ticonderoga)	22	VLS	26	572	122	2684
Guided Missile Cruiser-Nuclear (California)	5	ABL	8	40	12	60
Submarines SSN-688 (Los Angeles)	36	VLS and torpedo tubes	20	720	32	1152
Submarines SSN-688 (Los Angeles)	31	torpedo tubes	8	248	20	620
Submarines SSN-637 (Sturgeon-class)	39	torpedo tubes	8	312	20	780
Total	197			3968 (estimated)		9614 (estimated)

This chart illustrates the number of SLCM deployments estimated to be deployed by the US Navy by mid 1990s. The chart also projects the number of SLCMs the Navy could deploy by 1990 if additional weapon spaces were made available on cruise missile carrying vessels. As the table indicates, the Navy could expand from about 4000 to almost 10000 by modifying its deployment program.

ABL = Armored Box Launcher which carries 4 Tomahawks
VLS = Vertical Launch System

For Cruisers: Two 61-missile magazines installed fore and aft on CGN-class.
For Destroyers: DDG-class will have a 29-missile magazine forward and a 61-missile magazine aft; DD-class will have one 61-missile magazine installed aft.

Los Angeles-class SSN: 36 attack submarines will have a 12-missile magazine installed between their inner and outer pressure hulls.

Notes:

[1] numbers and type of vessels are detailed in Navy testimony; see House Armed Services Committee, *FY 1986 DOD Authorization*, Part II, pp. 503–513.

[2] Information on Tomahawk launcher capabilities supplied by Joint Cruise Missile Project Office.

[3] Estimates of planned Tomahawk loadings for various ships detailed in Naval Testimony; see House Armed Services Committee, *FY 1985 DOD Authorization*, Part II pp. 361–3.

[4] Possible 'weapons spaces' for Tomahawk assume:
    a) Two additional ABL on Battleships
    b) One additional ABL on Destroyers and Cruisers
    c) Full loading of VLS on Destroyers and Cruisers
    d) 12 additional torpedo tube-launched Tomahawk carried by Los Angeles-class and Sturgeon-class SSN.

Source: James P. Rubin, 'Sea-Launched Cruise Missiles: Facing Up to the Armed Control Challenge', *Arms Control Today* 16 (April 1986). 5–9. Reprinted with permission of the Arms Control Association.

modernised US START force would confront Soviet planners with the stark reality that even massive cheating would be useless. By the same token, however, if the United States did not modernise its forces, marginal cheating could be useful, and this fact would create incentives to cheat which would not exist given modernisation. Again, modernisation is the key to a stable START accord.[13]

SEA-LAUNCHED CRUISE MISSILES

The last major roadblock to a START accord is the issue of sea-launched cruise missiles. Ground-launched cruise missiles (GLCMs) with ranges of between 300 and 3000 miles were banned in the INF Treaty; air-launched cruise missiles (ALCMs) are covered in START as outlined in chapter 1. The issue of sea-launched cruise missiles (SLCMs) remains to be resolved, however. Until recently, the formal Soviet offer called for a cap of 1000 SLCMs, 400 nuclear and 600 conventional; subsequently Soviet negotiators suggested a single limit of 1000 covering both nuclear and conventional versions, and most recently they have proposed a total ban on nuclear SLCM.[14] The United States opposes limits on SLCMs, citing verification concerns.

In order to determine what outcome would be best for US interests, it is necessary to examine the nature of SLCMs and determine whether deployment of nuclear or conventional SLCMs

TABLE 7.3   *Soviet SLCM Programmes*

System	(Greater than 300 Kilometers)			
	*Year Deployed**	*Range (kilometers)*	*Speed (mach)*	*Nuclear Warhead Yield (kilotons)*
SS-N-3	1962	450	0.9	350
SS-N-12	1976	550	2.5	350
SS-N-19	1980	550	2.5	500
SS-NX-21	1986	3000	?0.8	?300
SS-NX-24	1986–1988?	?3000 (long-range)	supersonic	n.a.

* Systems deployed prior to 1986 are assumed to be primarily for anti-ship missions, while two new systems will have a land-attack mission.
Source   James P. Rubin, 'Sea-Launched Cruise Missiles: Facing Up to the Arms Control Challenge', *Arms Control Today* 16 (April 1986), 5–9. Reprinted with permission of the Arms Control Association.

TABLE 7.4 *Potential Soviet SLCM Deployments by 1995*

Type of Vessel	SLCM type[1]	# of Vessels[2]	# of SLCMs per vessel (estimated)	Potential SLCM Deployments
Surface Ships				
Kiev	SS-N-12	4	16	64
Kirov	SS-N-19	8	20	160
Slava	SS-N-12	6	16	96
Kresta	SS-N-12	4	4	16
Kynda	SS-N-12	4	8	32
				368
Submarines				
Echo II	SS-N-12	29	8	232
Oscar	SS-N-19	12	24	288
Victor III	SS-NX-21	20	18	360
Akula/Sierra	SS-NX-21	28	18	432
Mike	SS-NX-21	12	18	216
Yankee	SS-NX-21/24	20	24	480
				2008
Total				2376[3]

[1] Assumes production of 50 submarines and 10 major surface combatants (consistent with Defense Intelligence Agency assessments indicating Soviet production of attack submarines averages 6–7 per year and production of major surface combatants averages 9 per year). Also assumes conversion of 10 Echo II to carry SS-N-12 and conversion of 20 Yankee submarines to cruise missile carriers.

[2] Missile totals assume reloads on surface ships but increase of launcher capability on Kiev carriers. Loadings for attack submarines assume similar loading as for US Tomahawk.

[3] Potential Soviet SLCM deployments projected appear consistent with the presentation to Congress of the 1985 C.I.A. National Intelligence Estimate that states: 'Over the next 10 years, we expect them to deploy 2000 to 3000 ALCMs, SLCMs, and GLCMs'.

Source   James P. Rubin, 'Sea-Launched Cruise Missiles: Facing Up to the Arms Control Challenge', *Arms Control Today* 16 (April 1986), 5–9. Reprinted with permission of the Arms Control Association.

would help or hurt US national security. This section makes such an assessment in three parts: first, it examines the potential values and costs of SLCMs for US security; second, it discusses whether some, many, or no SLCMs would be best given those values and costs; and finally it proposes several promising verification schemes for the limits that are suggested.

Types of SLCMs

The history of the SLCM is an interesting one: apart from the US navy, no military services had an interest in the weapon, and the navy's interest was lukewarm. The weapon was pushed primarily for political reasons, by such government officials as Henry Kissinger and Melvin Laird, in part as a bargaining tool in the SALT negotiations.[15] Once they began development of the cruise missile, however, the convergence of a number of technological factors – including terrain-contour guidance and better air-breathing propulsion systems – rendered cruise missiles effective from military and fiscal points of view.

The various types of SLCMs deployed by both superpowers, and some of their characteristics, are summarised in tables 7.1–7.4. As they suggest, each superpower could deploy roughly 10 000 reasonably accurate and powerful SLCMs within a decade.[16] Within the 1990s, for example, fully 200 separate US surface and subsurface ships would be SLCM-capable.

Values and Costs of SLCMs

Potential uses of SLCMs have been suggested primarily in three types of conflict: strategic nuclear, theatre nuclear and conventional, and low-intensity. At each level proponents of SLCMs have outlined their advantages. On closer examination, however, it appears that SLCMs are unnecessary to fulfill any of the missions touted for them, although they would be especially useful as flexible non-nuclear weapons.

In terms of nuclear deterrence, SLCM proponents make a number of arguments. First, they suggest that SLCMs augment deterrence in a basic sense by contributing to the US assured destruction capability. This is true because SLCMs are deployed on flexible, mobile, survivable platforms such as attack submarines and cruisers; because they are difficult to detect; and because they provide flexible, highly accurate targeting.[17]

SLCMs are unnecessary for pure assured destruction, however, providing no unique retaliatory capabilities.[18] SLBMs can perform all the same missions SLCMs can, and are just as survivable if not necessarily as flexible.[19] These arguments are especially valid under a START treaty, when (given modernisation) the security of the US deterrent has increased; and virtually undeniable if Midgetman are procured, which are just as flexible and probably more survivable than most proposed SLCM-basing schemes. And calls for SLCM deployments to improve the survivability of the submarine-based deterrent suffer from the obvious flaw that any ASW breakthrough that rendered SLBM carriers vulnerable would do the same to SLCM carriers.

Other analysts contend that SLCMs would be highly useful in US war-fighting schemes (which fall under the broad definition of countervailing strategies discussed in chapters 1 and 2). Specifically, their secure basing mode aboard submarines would allow them to constitute a strategic reserve to be withheld during an extended nuclear conflict, a role which their slow flight time would not impair since they are not relied upon for prompt targeting.[20]

Again, there are severe problems with this justification. First, this volume has rejected the prospect of an extended nuclear war as a planning guide for US nuclear forces; it views such a conflict as unlikely and the preparations to engage in it both unnecessary for deterrence and provocative. Second, given the limited number of survivable platforms on which nuclear SLCM would be deployed, very few would probably be available in any post-war environment, and they thus would have little influence unless 'each side's survivable ballistic missile reserves had been severely or totally depleted'.[21] Such exhaustion of ICBMs, in turn, would be extremely unlikely in a START environment in which each side had fewer weapons for a first strike and more survivable weapons than is the case today, a shift detailed in chapter 4. Finally, if a strategic reserve is required, once again, SLBMs or mobile ICBMs could fulfill the mission.

In terms of nuclear deterrence, then, SLCMs can make at best a small contribution to US security. This is especially true in light of the analysis in the preceding six chapters about the stability of the START regime. As one American analyst has concluded, 'Under plausible and probable conditions . . . the marginal contribution to offensive strike power of adding nuclear SLCMs to the U.S. strategic arsenal is *perhaps* positive in sign but *certainly* small in magnitude'.[22]

Yet SLCMs could impose severe costs on US planners when used by both sides to augment strategic deterrence. It must be presumed that the Soviet Union would develop and deploy SLCMs of similar numbers, if not necessarily technical proficiency, as the United States. As will be argued below, while today the slow speed of such weapons has led many to consider them 'stabilising' systems, eventually they might develop into promising counterforce weapons. Many more critical US targets, moreover, such as naval bases, cities and command and control sites, are close to shore than is the case for the USSR; SLCMs launched from submarines or surface ships would therefore disproportionately impair US security.[23]

Nor will SLCMs necessarily remain cost-effective weapons. One of the cheap attractions of cruise missiles has been that they are relatively inexpensive. However, as cruise missiles become more and more advanced, they will require greater and greater specialisation, and commonality between systems (between the ALCM and the SLCM, for example) has been one of the primary factors keeping costs down. Richard Betts has noted that 'Cost advantages may recede along with commonality, and low cost and high military utility may diverge'.[24]

Finally, deploying attack or ballistic missiles submarines armed with SLCMs to support SIOP missions would detract from their conventional warfare missions. In wartime US attack submarines (SSNs) would have the critical job of escorting US carriers by attacking enemy submarines and surface ships in the vicinity of carrier task forces. Every SSN deployed as a cruise-missile carrier in the 'nuclear reserve' would be unable to fulfill its carrier-protection role.[25]

Another common justification for cruise missiles is that they improve US theatre posture in Europe, a claim that is made for both nuclear and conventional SLCMs. Nuclear SLCMs guarantee flexible response by providing secure escalatory options on submarines, it is argued, and conventional SLCMs can contribute to Follow-On Forces Attack (FOFA) strikes against Soviet second- and third-echelon forces.[26]

Neither nuclear nor conventional SLCMs are necessary for such missions, however. At the nuclear level, as chapter 5 argued, flexible response is fading away, and therefore deploying systems to support it would be a waste of resources. In any case, NATO has plenty of systems capable of escalating, and certainly some would survive even the most ferocious Soviet anti-nuclear pre-emptive attack. Even if none did, SLBMs – especially the increasingly accurate ones such as the D5 missile – could at least fulfill the minimal purpose of escalating the conflict or threatening to do so. And once again deploying SSNs in support of ground forces or other tasks risks upsetting the navy's plans for war and rendering US carriers vulnerable.

Finally, SLCMs aboard SSNs would fail to accomplish what has become the primary aspect of flexible response – its political mean-ing. As noted in chapter 5, doubts were expressed from the beginning about Washington's willingness to escalate for Europe's sake during a war, and many analysts therefore considered flexible response's political implications – its expression of close alliance bonds and willingness to share all risks – paramount. Indeed, NATO recently issued a document arguing that, in the rapidly-approaching era of conventional parity, flexible response is designed, not to counterbalance Soviet conventional superiority, but to bolster deterrence by demonstrating political resolve. SLCMs, however, are inadequate for such purposes; as Terry Terriff has recognised:

> As a symbol of the American nuclear guarantee TLAM/N may not be entirely satisfactory, in that its off-shore basing mode does not provide a high political profile. In addition ... it is not clear that the TLAM/N would provide greater political assurance of coupling to the American strategic deterrent than is ostensibly furnished by the five US SSBN already allocated to NATO's general strike plan. It must also be considered that the TLAM/N is tasked with augmenting the strategic reserve force, and that in the event of war there might be pressures for the US to withhold these missiles to fulfil the strategic mission.

In short, 'The major disadvantage to relying on TLAM/N is that their off-shore basing may not furnish the political visibility or operational availability necessary to reassure the European allies, particularly in a period of crisis'.[27]

Conventional SLCMs possess drawbacks as well for use in Central Europe. Most troubling is the fact that they are simply not cost-effective for striking Soviet ground forces; spending millions to put 1000 pounds of explosive on a target with a single-shot weapon is wasteful. Nor are weapons with pre-programmed targeting data particularly useful for attacking conventional forces, which move rapidly. (The exception to that rule is when nuclear weapons are used, rendering absolute accuracy unnecessary; hence the counter-power targeting policy advocated in chapter 4.)

US planners must also consider the implications of theatre nuclear and conventional SLCMs for US forces. Soviet SLCMs of either sort could wipe the seas clean of US carriers and troop convoys, or could strike at the embarkation or debarkation points of NATO-bound US reinforcements. NATO airfields, military bases, POMCUS sites, and other critical military installations would come under attack. NATO retaliatory blows might be partially defeated by the incredibly thick Soviet tactical air defences over Eastern Europe and the Western

USSR. In short, tactical applications of SLCMs provide neither side any particular advantage.

More promising uses for SLCMs can be found in other areas. In the Third World, the United States could use SLCMs (especially conventional versions) to strike at various regional challenger states such as Libya, Iran and Syria if circumstances called for it. While the weapons are relatively expensive compared to air-deliverable munitions, using SLCMs would help avoid politically unpopular casualties. And SLCMs might be especially useful against states with a sizeable anti-ship capability but poor ASW – US SSNs could slip in close to the shores of such states (if they had shores) and launch SLCMs, where US carriers might be subject to vicious air attacks (as the British navy was in the Falklands conflict).

Yet the appropriateness of SLCMs for even these missions is far from clear.[28] As noted, they are not necessarily cost-effective, and the number of cases where the US navy could not ensure the safety of a carrier against a Third World opponent might be relatively small. Moreover, alternatives exist – tactical aircraft, naval gunfire, or (if cruise missiles are deemed necessary) ALCMs. While conventional – or even nuclear – cruise missiles might augment US capabilities *vis-à-vis* Third World powers, then, the degree to which they would do so is open to serious question.

Some/None/Many SLCMs?

From the preceding analysis of the US interests involved in the deployment of SLCMs, we can make some conclusions about what the United States ought to allow under the START treaty.

Initially it is clear that the unrestrained deployment of nuclear SLCMs would be destabilising insofar as it would undermine the stable numerical balances created under START. While SLCMs are currently considered a stable, second-strike weapon, there is no reason why they must remain so. Their speed could be doubled or tripled, and their accuracy is already extremely precise. Analyst Theodore Postol has in fact concluded that 'U.S. early warning systems have, for all practical purpose, *no* ability to detect the launch, approach, and overflight of SLCMs that might be in the initial stage ... of a comprehensive nuclear attack', and Postol does not believe that a particularly effective means of detection or interception can be found.[29] Partly because of this, large-scale deployments of fast, stealthy SLCMs might encourage resort to launch-on-warning policies by either or both sides.[30]

It was argued in earlier chapters that relying on cruise missiles for deterrence would be insufficient because of the potential vulnerability of the systems. This would seem incompatible with the argument here, namely that cruise missiles are virtually invulnerable weapons. For at least two reasons, however, the conflict is not so great. First, cruise missiles in general and SLCMs in particular might be better for a first strike than a retaliation insofar as their delivery systems are vulnerable. That is, bombers, surface ships and to some degree attack submarines can be destroyed while still in their bases by a well-coordinated first strike.

Second, however, this apparent contradiction uncovers a paradox of cruise missile deployments, and especially SLCMs, that renders them an unpromising addition to the US strategic arsenal. Ballistic missiles are detectable but, so long as deployments of BMD are restrained, unstoppable. SLCMs may well be either undetectable (in which case they are destabilising) or vulnerable (capable of being shot down by Soviet air defence, including interceptors with advanced look-down shoot-down radars). Primarily this dilemma arises because of the nature of Soviet air defences – cruise missiles, as air-breathers, fall into a category against which either side can deploy defences. And efforts to overcome those air defences impair the cost-effectiveness of the SLCMs.[31]

Permitting the deployment of only some *nuclear* SLCMs would also hurt US security. US carrier battle groups provide a target for such weapons whose value is vastly greater than any similar Soviet target. The Soviet navy could cause much more relative damage, therefore, with a few nuclear SLCMs than could the American navy. This accounts for the Soviet negotiating stance, which calls for low ceilings but not a ban on nuclear SLCMs. It seems that nuclear SLCMs ought to be totally banned; as one commentator has concluded, 'The best course for the US would be to negotiate a complete ban on all nuclear-armed SLCM, *whatever their mission and whatever their range*'.[32] Indeed, the Soviet Union recently proposed exactly such a modification to its negotiating stance on SLCMs.[33] Although this step would seem to contradict the previous analysis of costs and benefits about how a few SLCMs would benefit the Soviets more than the United States, one must assume that the Soviets see some other unique value in a total SLCM ban – perhaps advantages from general denuclearisation, or perhaps preventing future US technological advances.

What of conventional SLCMs? This problem is rendered more tricky by the support for such weapons within the US Congress, support that could translate into opposition to a START treaty that banned them. In the Spring of 1988 52 US senators demanded in a letter to President Reagan that START not 'compromise' long-range, conventional SLCMs and ALCMs.[34]

Means of Limiting SLCMs

This analysis leaves US negotiators with one of two choices: they can press for a total ban on long-range SLCMs and all nuclear SLCMs of whatever range, or merely a prohibition on the latter with limits on long-range conventional SLCM. Banning all long-range SLCMs would be easy enough, but either of those options calls for banning the nuclear version of a SLCM (either a short-range or a long-range) while allowing various numbers of the conventional version. Verifying nuclear versus conventional cruise missiles is difficult; indeed, then Secretary of Defense Caspar Weinberger testified during the INF Treaty debates that 'the Soviet ability to maintain an operational nuclear GLCM capability under the guide of a permitted conventionally armed GLCM program would be high and would provide a ready means of breaking out of the treaty'.[35]

The task of monitoring nuclear SLCM deployments is not impossible, however.[36] A variety of options exists to prevent deployment of nuclear SLCMs. Initially it is important to codify some of the steps that the United States has taken unilaterally: its Tomahawk SLCM is encased in a pressurized cannister that cannot be opened and resealed aboard most ships, and its warhead cannot be changed from conventional to nuclear aboard ship. A SLCM arms control regime should require both sides to deploy weapons with similar characteristics. Inspectors could then observe the construction of SLCMs on both sides, watch the warheads being loaded and the cannisters sealed, and applying a 'tag' to identify the missile. On-site inspections in ports as SLCMs were loaded and aboard ships could later match tags with specific missiles. In addition, special locks could be developed that would emit warnings if the seals on any completed SLCMs were broken.[37]

Other potential verification measures could be pursued. National technical means could be useful in identifying operational procedures aboard ships, SLCMs as they are loaded in port, numbers of SLCM carriers at sea, and other facts that would help build confidence in the security of the overall ban on nuclear SLCMs. A total ban on SLCMs would, for this reason and others, be easier to verify than a mere limit on allowed numbers of nuclear SLCMs. Deployments of long-range SLCMs could be limited, as the Soviets have suggested, to a handful of platforms to reduce the potential for cheating.

In a crisis or even after a war had begun, one or both sides might believe it to be in their interests to refit their conventional SLCMs with nuclear warheads, even though they would be detected. If the two sides reach agreement on deploying non-interchangeable warheads, however, this process would be lengthy, and the port facilities where it would take place would be subject to attack. Even if conversion could take place aboard ships, they too could be attacked; and space on the only relatively invulnerable SLCM carriers – submarines – probably is too limited to permit the installation of equipment allowing warhead exchange and re-pressurisation.

These remarks also pertain to the low risk of cheating in such a regime. The arguments that cheating on a nuclear SLCM ban would be unlikely and would not be significant are persuasive. First, given the relatively intrusive verification measures proposed above, the risk of being caught would be high; the general incentives to adhere to a START accord were examined above. Second, the Soviets have alternatives to cheating on a nuclear SLCM ban – they could use aircraft or long-range nuclear ALCM to deliver nuclear strikes; ii. leed, Soviet anti-ship ALCM carried by Bear bombers are quite advanced.[38] Third, even if the Soviets cheated and managed to deploy a few dozen nuclear warheads on SLCM, the United States could deter nuclear strikes against its naval forces with pledges of retaliation against Soviet ships or ports with ALCMs, aircraft or SLBMs. Fourth and finally, given the limited number of platforms carrying SLCMs and limits on long-range conventional SLCMs, the strategic implications of cheating would be rather small, provided the United States had modernised its nuclear forces as outlined above.

One additional measure could be appended to a ban on nuclear SLCMs: a total ban on all sea-based nuclear weapons with the exception of SLBMs. This option has been proposed by Paul Nitze,[39] and offers a number of advantages. It would render verification of a nuclear SLCM ban that much easier, since devices designed to detect nuclear materials could be added to other verification measures. It would magnify the advantages held by the US navy, which could be nullified during war by Soviet naval nuclear weapons. It would also help resolve the increasing controversy over the navy's policy of neither confirming nor denying the presence of nuclear weapons aboard ships.

ISSUES READY TO BE RESOLVED

It should by now be apparent that none of the three issues discussed above is likely to constitute a serious barrier to either a START accord or stability under such an accord. Only general strategic defences would destabilise the balance, but it is highly unlikely, especially given defence budget pressures within the United States, that deployment of such defences would be seriously contemplated. Verification concerns will undoubtedly be significant, especially for mobile missiles; provided the United States modernises its nuclear forces, however, the incentives for the Soviets to cheat, and the potential implications of Soviet cheating, will remain extraordinarily small. Finally, limits of some sort will be required for sea-launched cruise missiles, but such limits are both likely (either in START or a subsequent agreement) and reasonably easy to formulate.

In terms of central or simple nuclear deterrence, the case of this volume is now complete: START and other developments in the strategic environment will allow and encourage the superpowers to establish a situation of stable, consensual, co-operative mutual vulnerability-based deterrence through stategies like the co-operative reciprocal deterrence notion outlined earlier. This chapter has suggested that neither strategic defences, nor verification, nor SLCMs will stand in the way of such a result, provided the superpowers exercise some common sense with regard to each system or issue. The next chapter will discuss non-nuclear strategic weapons to determine whether they offer the potential to do so.

8 Non-Nuclear Strategic Weapons

When Soviet analysts refer to a 'revolution in military affairs', they are discussing what they perceive to be a sea-change in the nature of warfare. The Soviet acceptance in the late 1950s of the implications of nuclear weapons ushered in one such revolution. Soviet analysts determined that nuclear weapons would dominate the next war, which would quickly escalate to an all-out strategic exchange between the superpowers.

As the Soviets seem to recognise, it may well be that the implications of advanced conventional weapons are already ushering in another revolution in military affairs. In the coming decades, it is likely that non-nuclear strategic weapons (NNSW), weapons with the strategic reach of nuclear weapons and the precision and limited destructive power of conventional arms, will assume a crucial role in international military planning. Various evolving technologies – powerful tracking and targeting devices, cruise and ballistic missiles of great range and accuracy, stealth technologies, and precision-guided warheads – combine to make it possible for nations to strike across the globe very quickly and accurately with virtual impunity and, most importantly, without crossing the nuclear threshold.

This is especially true because of the remarkable improvements in destructive power that can be achieved with better accuracy. An improvement in accuracy by four times augments destructive power as much as an improvement in yield of 64 times; similarly an increase of ten times in accuracy is equal to a thousandfold increase in yield.[1]

At the same time, political and military incentives are arising to put that technology to use. Public disgust with and the military useless-ness of nuclear weapons both recommend non-nuclear means for achieving goals traditionally reserved for nuclear strikes. (This is especially true in Europe, as we saw in chapter 5.) A growing recognition that deterrence has worked and that the risks of nuclear use are so great that even large-scale conventional conflicts might not escalate to the nuclear level has also reaffirmed the importance of conventional deterrence. Militaries also possess incentives to replace nuclear weapons with conventional ones, and nuclear winter may mandate the use of conventional weapons for nuclear tasks.[2]

In sum, as Carl Builder, probably the most prolific writer on Non-Nuclear Strategic Weapons (NNSW) to date, has recognised, 'Nuclear-armed states in conflict will increasingly have the incentives and the means for attacking the enemy's sources of power without resorting to nuclear weapons'.[3] The Scowcroft Commission similarly argued that 'In time even non-nuclear weapons with excellent accuracy may be able to attack effectively some fixed targets previously thought to be vulnerable only to nuclear weapons'.[4] The implications for warfare, Builder and others contend, involving the superpowers as well as regional powers and smaller states, are quite simply staggering.[5]

As the United States enters into critical – and unprecedentedly promising – new rounds of conventional and strategic nuclear arms talks, it must consider carefully the implications of NNSW for the future of warfare. If unchecked, NNSW hold the potential to destabilise the most carefully constructed deterrent balances. Properly channelled and controlled, however, NNSW could serve as useful deterrent tools.

This chapter examines the emergence of NNSW and defines and describes evolving NNSW technologies, such as precision-guided munitions (PGMs). It considers the potential of NNSW to transform relations between the West and both the USSR and regional powers. Finally, the chapter lays out some of the direct implications of the emergence of NNSW. The conclusion is that NNSW, as with any weapons technology, will work both to augment and to undermine US security, and that only by developing superior technology and tactics in the field and by attenuating the more destabilising features of NNSW in arms accords can the United States avoid damage to its security.

DEFINITIONS: WHAT ARE NNSW?

Defining NNSW is not as easy as it would first appear. Taken literally, 'non-nuclear strategic weapons' could refer to a vast panoply of systems, from lasers to non-nuclear missile defences to chemical/biological weapons to strategic-range PGMs. Some discipline must be imposed on these categories.

Initially it is necessary to define what one means by 'strategic'. This chapter will consider NNSW only those weapons with inherently strategic (that is, intercontinental) range or the capability of attaining it. Emerging technologies have a wide variety of applications in theatre, air, naval and even low-intensity conflict scenarios.[6] Here, however, our focus is on strategic weapons and scenarios.

Neither chemical weapons nor energy beams, for the reason of range and others, fall under the rubric of what are commonly known as NNSW. Chemical weapons are not truly conventional, in that their use carries unique implications of its own (so much so that, despite their existence, they were essentially not used during World War II); and they are not revolutionary, in the sense that they could always have been carried by strategic-range delivery vehicles. Energy beams such as lasers and charged particle-beams are not of strategic range – they would have to be carried by satellites or other platforms that would allow them to attack strategic targets.

What is left? As the RAND Study on NNSW concluded, NNSW cover 'a broad spectrum of weapon technologies: high explosives, shaped charges, hypervelocity and self-forging projectiles, fuel-air explosives, or fragmentation bombs,' that are delivered to the target 'by standard delivery vehicles: long-range bombers, with or without cruise missiles, and by cruise and ballistic missiles launched from sea, land, air, or space platforms'.[7] As the same study recognised, these weapons achieve their results, not by the overwhelming destructive power of nuclear weapons, but through several other devices; precise placement of the weapon; focusing its destructive energy; 'coupling' that energy to the target; and 'exploiting target systemic vulnerabilities'.[8]

This chapter will not treat anti-submarine warfare (ASW) as a form of non-nuclear strategic warfare, despite the fact that attacks on missile-carrying submarines (SSBs or SSBNs) can have strategic implications. Again, the ships and planes that participate in ASW are not themselves of strategic range (although they conceivably could be, as could missiles developed for the same purpose). Therefore ASW systems themselves are not treated as types of NNSW.

More traditional conventional weapons could be considered NNSW as well. As the RAND Study suggested, bombers can possess strategic range (with refuelling capabilities) and can carry stand-off weapons such as cruise and attack missiles. The analysis that follows will assume that bombers, particularly using stealth technology, can fulfill many of the NNSW roles discussed, though it will not discuss bomber characteristics at length. Another conventional weapon that could be termed an NNSW is an aircraft carrier. When used in Maritime Strategy-type roles of attacking the USSR, carriers can certainly be treated as strategic weapons, and the Soviets apparently consider them so. Once again, in the following analysis it should be assumed that carrier aircraft could fulfill some of the NNSW roles being discussed.

NNSW warheads can also be carried by a number of different types of delivery systems within inherently strategic range or the potential to possess it. One such system is ballistic missiles. Since intermediate range weapons (300–3000 miles) have been banned, two classes are left: tactical ballistic missiles (TBMs) with ranges from under 100 to 300 miles, and intercontinental ballistic missiles (ICBMs) with ranges above 3000 miles. Circular errors probable (CEPs) for these systems range from tens of metres for tactical systems to hundreds of metres for ICBMs, but with terminal guidance even ICBM CEPs will be brought down under 100m.[9]

Cruise missiles can also deliver NNSW, and the accuracy of cruise missiles is generally much higher than their ballistic counterparts. Already CEPs of 3m or less can be achieved with terminal homing guidance systems.[10] The major drawback of cruise missiles is their range – existing missiles with nuclear warheads can fly about 2500 miles, but heavier conventional payloads reduce that range to about 800 miles. Longer-range versions are under study, including intercontinental range cruise and propfan-powered long-range cruise.[11] Of course, the range of cruise missiles can be extended by launching them from mobile platforms such as aircraft, surface ships and submarines.[12]

Using conventional munitions, these delivery vehicles can carry a number of emerging-technology warheads. For penetrating hard underground bunkers they can use 'needle rounds', more officially known as 'bunker target munitions' (BTMs); eight 200-pound BTMs can be carried on a missile with a one-ton re-entry payload and, with a CEP of 20m, can destroy underground command posts or other reinforced assets with a very high degree of probability.[13] Airfield attack munitions include various forms of penetrating bombs and bomblets, some with time delay fuses. One missile touted for a conventional role, for example, is the Pershing: modified as the Conventional Attack Missile (CAM-40), it carries a 1200-pound payload; 130 could close 40 Warsaw Pact airfields for a full day, using only conventional airfield attack munitions. Smart land mines can be dropped across expected lines of advance; such weapons can detect movement and launch mines or missiles at nearby armoured vehicles. Laser-guided bombs can be brought to a particular sector by a delivery vehicle and guided to their target by troops on the ground.

The effectiveness of such weapons relative to nuclear weapons can be illustrated by examining the Skeet system of smart 'pucks'. These are small, independently-guided anti-vehicular explosive devices; 12 multiple launch rocket system (MLRS) missiles can carry 73 dispensers with 288 Skeet pucks, enough to destroy a 13-vehicle unit. 'MLRS missiles equipped with terminally-guided weapons are just as effective as one missile equipped with a low-yield nuclear weapon.'[14]

Other emerging technologies will support NNSW with command, control, tracking, targeting and other services. Advanced surveillance systems such as the AWACS, Boeing's new joint Surveillance and Target Attack Radar System (JSTARS), and the Battlefield Intelligence Collection and Exploitation System (BICES) can help identify targets and guide NNSW to them. The advances in satellite surveillance are well-documented, and advanced satellites can perform both targeting and command/control for NNSW. Battlefield systems such as laser markers will allow soldiers to guide NNSW down in the last phases of their courses.[15]

The key barrier to widespread adoption of such systems has been their cost. One recent estimate suggests that the emerging technology weapons used to support the Defense Department's Competitive Strategies effort, which makes use of many such technologies, will cost between $20 and $60 billion annually.[16] But some cheaper weapons are already available – the CAM-40, for example, only costs $2 million, only $3 billion for a full set of 130. Eventually, costs can be expected to come down significantly, although the precision guidance required suggests that NNSW will cost no less, and perhaps significantly more, than comparable strategic nuclear weapons.

This short section was not meant to provide an exhaustive catalogue of existing NNSW technologies and their capabilities.[17] Rather, it was intended merely to outline a few examples of emerging technologies. More important than the characteristics of existing systems, however, is the fact that the state of technology today and its rate of advance make it inevitable that major powers will one day be able to launch extremely destructive conventional strikes across the globe with pinpoint accuracy. The balance of this chapter is devoted to discussing the implications of this fact.

SOVIET MILITARY DOCTRINE AND NNSW

Soviet military doctrine has long appreciated the potential of high-technology conventional systems, both in theatre and strategic applications. Their enthusiasm for such weapons provides a backdrop against which American development of NNSW must be judged. Soviet interest in non-nuclear means of warfare appears to have originated in their decision that nuclear war could not reliably be won and therefore that the means to fight a conventional war must be acquired. Brookings analyst Michael MccGwire places this decision at about 1966.[18]

Conventional weapons, meanwhile, have acquired new levels of accuracy and destructiveness. The Soviets viewed the growing power of conventional weapons as part of a revolution in warfare, which also included certain characteristics of nuclear weapons and the implications of emerging technologies. Marshal Nikolai Ogarkov has been the leading proponent of the view that advanced conventional weapons will revolutionise the modern battlefield. New technologies, he explains, 'increase (by an order of magnitude) the destructive power of conventional weapons, bringing them closer, so to speak, to weapons of mass destruction in terms of effectiveness'. This allows conventional munitions to take over many jobs previously assigned to nuclear warheads, and in such an environment combat operations 'will be strikingly different in nature from the last war'.[19] These effects will not be felt immediately, but only when the new weapons 'begin to be used in such quantities that they inevitably create a new qualitative condition'.[20]

While the first effects of these technologies will be felt at the conventional level, Ogarkov argues, eventually non-nuclear strategic weapons will emerge. Such systems will make it possible 'to immediately extend active combat operations, not just in border regions, but to the whole country's territory, which was not possible in past wars'.[21] By replacing nuclear systems, they will 'make nuclear war unnecessary',[22] and they suggest that a turn 'in the full sense revolutionary' is taking place in military affairs.[23]

This sort of thinking accounts for the Soviet investment in emerging technologies. Soviet tactical ballistic missiles armed with conventional or chemical warheads were thought to have assumed many targeting missions previously assigned to nuclear weapons. Soviet interest in lasers and other high-technology weapons systems, moreover, is long-standing.

Soviet emphasis on emerging conventional technologies and the reasons for that interest also provide a solid explanation for Soviet military interest in the INF Treaty and potential subsequent Triple

Zero options. The historical Soviet propensity to delay the introduction of new technologies, in which they recognise their political-economic system cannot compete, is clear. By banning all ballistic and cruise missiles in Europe in a Triple Zero accord, Moscow would achieve two ends: it would reduce the chance that any war in Europe would go nuclear, and it would seriously impair NATO's ability to pursue high-technology options for its AirLand Battle and Follow-On Forces Attack (FOFA) doctrines.

IMPLICATIONS FOR NUCLEAR DETERRENCE

What effects might NNSW have on conflict between the superpowers? As with any weapons systems when considered in the abstract, the effects of NNSW on the superpowers will be ambivalent. Only by analysis of specific scenarios can one begin to see what the practical implications of NNSW might be.

There are clear tactical uses for such weapons, in either high- or medium-intensity conflict. They could be used for theatre missions against the USSR or against minor powers. NNSW, for example, could have been used by the British to good effect in the Falklands War. While those applications will affect the nature of conventional war, however, they will not revolutionise conflict; 'it is in the strategic arena . . . [that] the introduction of enhanced capabilities for conventional weapons could be revolutionary'.[24]

It is important to recognise from the start that NNSW will not eliminate the need for nuclear weapons. The unique ability of nuclear weapons to annihilate societies, and the corresponding need to deter their use, mean that present nuclear powers will in all probability feel the need to retain nuclear weapons (although perhaps in smaller numbers, as we will see below).[25] The existing MAD relationship will therefore continue.

Would large-scale NNSW deployments threaten to upset this balance? Some analysts suggest that NNSW are suitable for attacks against strategic nuclear targets (that is, counterforce attacks). They could be targeted against silos, submarine pens, command and control systems and mobile missiles.

The potential counterforce use of NNSW creates other problems. If one side threatened to attack the other's strategic forces with NNSW alone, would the threat of retaliation with nuclear weapons alone be credible? Or is the conventional/nuclear firebreak so robust that the side being attacked would hesitate? It may be that if one side began deploying NNSW, the other would have to match it to maintain a credible deterrent.[26]

Moreover, if one side's nuclear forces came under non-nuclear attack, would it feel required to 'use them rather than lose them'? The RAND Study seems to think not. 'While this was a valid argument before the present size and parity of the nuclear arsenals', it contends, 'the mutual reluctance to cross the nuclear firebreak may now be so great that the belligerents will be very reluctant to use nuclear forces even if those forces are under direct attack'.[27]

That may be, but there is reason to doubt such reliance on deterrence at the nuclear level, both before a war begins and after. Every weapon that places either side's retaliatory forces in jeopardy hurts crisis stability.[28] Especially insofar as they might promise to render vulnerable the most survivable assets of the superpower arsenals, mobile missiles and SSBNs, NNSW could do serious damage to crisis stability. Fearing that its weapons were vulnerable – to nuclear weapons, NNSW, or (most probably) a combination of both – one side might strike first to avoid being taken by surprise.

NNSW might also spark a nuclear strike after hostilities had begun. As one side's nuclear forces are worn down by repeated NNSW attacks, and if the attacking opponent held a large nuclear reserve as well, the side being attacked might feel compelled to launch what was left of its nuclear arsenal rather than be disarmed. Certainly, the prospect of initiating a nuclear war would not be taken lightly; but neither would the potential for eventual nuclear devastation at the hands of an opponent. And both sides might distrust the other enough to believe that a counterforce attack undertaken with NNSW would eventually be escalated to nuclear weapons once enough of the defender's deterrent had been worn away.

These questions point to the problem of 'escalation ambiguity'. The opportunity would exist to destroy critical targets in an opponent's homeland without nuclear weapons. One key question is 'what drives escalation and retaliation, the weapon used or the target destroyed?'[29] The RAND Study came to no firm conclusion, for example, on whether the use of NNSW or INF against Soviet homeland targets would be more escalatory.

Imperfect Counterforce Tools

While NNSW could hurt crisis stability, however, a number of considerations suggest that the potential for NNSW attacks on nuclear forces is in fact not so clear. The superpowers possess a vast array of countermeasures to deploy against, say, a smart munition carried atop a super-accurate ICBM: jamming of the flight systems and targeting radar; dispersal, mobility, and hardening of targets; concealment; and others. NNSW, moreover, due to the stringent accuracy requirements dictated by less powerful warheads, are much more susceptible to countermeasures than nuclear weapons. Coupled with the vast number of strategic nuclear targets and the huge cost of high-technology NNSW, these are difficult problems for a military planner attempting to target silos or mobile ICBMs with NNSW.[30]

NNSW are also subject to many of the same uncertainties that plague nuclear weapons. Fired at such long ranges, small perturbations in weather could disrupt the flight path. Missiles fired over the poles are subject to unknown magnetic effects. If a large number of weapons are fired at closely-spaced silos, they could exercise a fratricidal effect on one another.

Certain forms of arms control treaties, moreover, could be used to shelter nuclear forces against the effects of NNSW. Numerical limitations on ballistic and cruise missiles, restricting their deployment to a few thousand at most, would reduce each side's ability to target the opponent's forces, and submarine approach rules could prevent either side from bringing SLCM-carrying subs close enough to be of much use in finding mobiles.

Defences against NNSW are also easier than against nuclear weapons. If a defender is willing to detonate nuclear weapons far above or out from his territory, for example, he can throw finely-tuned NNSWs off course just enough to guard his deterrent; such defences would not be as relevant against nuclear weapons since they would allow detonations on the defender's soil. Simple weapons such as cannon and anti-missile missiles, and more exotic weapons such as lasers, have already proven their effectiveness against cruise missiles, and could guard deterrent forces against NNSW attacks. For these reasons and others, the RAND Study concludes that NNSW may not be adequate counterforce weapons.[31]

The barriers to using NNSW as counterforce weapons are thus legion. Say, for example, a targeter is trying to knock out an SS-18 silo in the Soviet Union with a shaped-charge warhead guided by a PGM carried by an ICBM. First he must find the target – and not just the missile field, but specific silo doors, false copies of which could easily be made. He must hit it squarely with the projectile – carried over the earth's surface, across the unknown effects of magnetic fields and other disturbances, with a missile whose guidance could be jammed, whose flight plan could be disrupted by mid-course defences, carrying a PGM that could be similarly jammed and knocked off course. The warhead – probably a shaped charge along the lines of existing anti-tank warheads – must land on the silo at the proper angle; it could be defeated by angled or reactive armour.

NNSW and Mobile Missiles

These arguments must be qualified; NNSW might be useful against certain counterforce targets.[32] They might be particularly deadly against mobile missiles which, while difficult to find and track, are relatively easy to destroy. The tracking and command and control systems developed to permit super-accurate targeting of NNSW, moreover, would be useful to attack mobiles in a nuclear exchange when combined with nuclear warheads. The ability of mobiles to stabilise the nuclear balance under START is critical to the deterrent framework outlined in this volume; if NNSW rendered mobiles vulnerable, the implications for deterrence could be unfortunate.

Stephen Rosen treats the issue of NNSW attacks on mobiles extensively.[33] Rosen admits that large-scale NNSW ballistic missile strikes on mobiles would probably fail because the defender would be granted warning time and, unsure of what type of warhead the attacking missiles carried (and presumably doubtful about whether it really mattered), would launch under attack or immediately before it hit. Rosen sees the real threat to mobiles in stealthy cruise missiles, which could sneak up on their targets and either attack them directly (perhaps performing a search pattern to find them) or limit their mobility with mines or other means. To attack rail-mobile missiles, cruise could be programmed to fly along sections of track looking for certain types of trains.

Yet there are problems with such targeting; mobiles are not completely vulnerable to NNSW attacks. Vast numbers of cruise missiles would be required to find and destroy mobile missiles – probably thousands.[34] The range, fuel and payload constraints of cruise mean that each missile, launched from perhaps hundreds of miles off the US coast, would have only limited search capabilities once ashore. This points to a real limitation of cruise: they would have to be launched so close to the US shore as to place their carrying vehicles in jeopardy. US planners would possess many opportunities for the concealment of targets – they could put mobiles in caves or under roofs or in false homes. Regarding rail mobiles, just what sort of train would the cruise attack, if a missile-carrying train looked like all others? Point defence of mobiles, moreover, with cannon or emerging technologies like lasers, would also be very effective against one or two cruise missiles.

NNSW and the Speed of Conflict

So it seems that NNSW do not pose a particularly worrisome threat to nuclear forces. One qualification is a class of weapons not treated here as NNSW – ASW. Ballistic missile submarines might become vulnerable after a time to NNSW that represent evolutions of existing ASW technologies. The Soviets apparently consider ASW a form of NNSW.[35] NNSW could prove highly destabilising insofar as they rendered vulnerable the two most survivable portions of both sides' arsenals – mobile ICBMs and submarine-based SLBMs. But that is a separate subject.

Yet opportunities for counterforce applications of NNSW might perhaps be more likely during protracted conflicts, and NNSW could themselves encourage longer wars.[36] While NNSW do not pose a severe unique threat to deterrent forces, during a conventional war both sides might be tempted to begin attacking the other's deterrent and achieving a head start on damage limitation. Such tactics might be especially expected of the Soviets, for whom offensive damage limitation is a habit. If no nuclear weapons were employed at first, strategic non-nuclear exchanges could last over a period of days, weeks or even longer. Strategic nuclear systems could then come under long-term tracking and attack.[37] In this case, too, cost issues would be less relevant, since the two nations would be at war; both would begin furious production of NNSW, insofar as NNSW strikes by the opponent(s) against their own NNSW production facilities allowed them to do so.

There are limits to long-war possibilities for NNSW, however. One is satellite vulnerability. Presumably, NNSW would be controlled primarily by satellites, which are extremely vulnerable. NNSW would ideally have pre-set targeting, but as a war progressed and forces were moved this method would be less useful. Tracking and targeting the other side's forces would be difficult; in this case mobile missiles would be much more stable than silos, which could not be moved. NNSW thus increase the importance of satellite communication and hence anti-satellite (ASAT) technologies.[38] And the limitations described above on their potential as counterforce weapons would persist.

On the other hand, Carl Builder takes the trend toward shorter wars fought with weapons at hand as a spur toward NNSW. Such wars would place a premium, he believes, on precision strikes, not indiscriminate societal attacks. Most analysts, indeed, feel that the speed of war is increasing and that NNSW would encourage this trend by placing targets all over the globe at risk of conventional attack. In fact, NNSW might work both ways: they both increase the pace of conventional warfare[39] and slow the overall pace and destructive rate of war compared to nuclear conflict. NNSW would thus raise further the nuclear threshold while beginning to introduce a variant of assured destruction at the conventional level.

NNSW would also provide another means of response to attack, one that might make immediate nuclear retaliation unnecessary. Strategic analyst Peter deLeon has pointed out that

> one should not cavalierly dismiss the (perhaps) intuitive sense that any move away from the nuclear option is a move toward greater conflict control and, at base, long-run stability and security. To be relieved from the responsibility of immediate nuclear response . . . undercuts the destablizing and retaliatory tensions imposed by the fragility of the nuclear balance of terror and the mechanical frailties of the current command and control structures.[40]

NNSW could therefore provide important flexibility as part of the conditional delayed retaliation policy outlined in chapter 3.

Counterpower Targeting Options

One key question, then, is what NNSW will be used to attack. As we have seen, they are clearly too expensive for societal massive retaliation. Yet they might also be unsuited for counterforce attacks against nuclear weapons. What is left, it seems, are non-nuclear military and key industrial and political targets, which are both concentrated enough and soft enough to invite the use of NNSW.[41]

These targeting decisions carry crucial implications for the import-ance of NNSW. The most radical effect of NNSW on the nuclear balance would occur if they could take over the counterforce target-ing chores currently assigned to nuclear weapons; this would obviate the need for large nuclear arsenals, since only a few hundred warheads would be required to promise societal destruction and preserve deterrence.[47] If NNSW cannot assume that function, however, its effect on the size of nuclear arsenals might be marginal, especially since worst-case planning would encourage both sides to keep nuclear warheads as an insurance against the failure of untried NNSW.

An evolution of American targeting doctrine, however, might change these facts. With the continued modernisation of Soviet forces, and given a prospective START accord, US planners might have to give up planning to retaliate against Soviet nuclear weapons to reduce damage to the United States in a war; Soviet mobile missiles and SSBNs, probably the only forces left after a hypothetical Soviet first-strike, would be difficult if not impossible to track and destroy, especially given that an American leader might have well under 2000 warheads (out of a START force of 6–9000) with which to retaliate.[43] Therefore, US nuclear targeting might adopt a counter-power approach – retaliating against non-nuclear targets of military value – to achieve deterrence before war and damage limitation through coercive war termination once hostilities had begun. In this case, if they are useful for counterpower targeting, NNSW could assume most of the deterrent roles of nuclear weapons.

This trend would be accelerated by the speed-of-war considerations noted above. If wars are short, urban-industrial targets would be almost irrelevent since there would be insufficient time to mobilise assets not already in place; in that case, the only targets of priority value are military ones, and if nuclear forces are exempted, military-related non-nuclear targets might provide a promising role for NNSW.[44] Such targets include standing armies, command and control facilities, military bases and ports, reserve mobilisation centres, equipment stockpiles, transportation nodes and military industries.

Attacks on command and control assets would probably not be wise missions for NNSW, just as they are unprofitable for nuclear weapons. The reason is simple: attacking an enemy's leaders forces the opponent to make quick decisions on a retaliation, and leaves it without clear leadership to terminate a conflict. Strikes against C3 targets subvert escalation control and damage limitation, and should be avoided.

Using NNSW to attack standing military forces could be extraordinarily useful, however. Such attacks offer limited, discriminating responses to enemy provocations. They preserve an enemy's nuclear forces and command and control facilities, thus avoiding incentives for spasm launches. And they begin to encourage a perception of assured destruction on the conventional level – the notion that, just as has been the case with nuclear conflict, a state cannot achieve its objectives in conventional war because its opponent possesses the means to annihilate its forces. If the Soviets knew, for example, that 10 000 highly destructive NNSW would rain down on their major military units and installations in the first hour after they initiated hostilities, their calculus of the advisability of conventional war would be significantly affected.

NNSWs will render logistical, resupply and transportation targets especially vulnerable. The ports and airfields used to embark and disembark US reinforcements for Europe, for example, would be subject to destruction in the first hours of a war, as would major Soviet transportation hubs, mobilisation points, and equipment stocks. Once again, NNSWs undermine the notion that a traditional, drawn-out conventional war could be fought.

NATO may be more vulnerable to such attacks than the Warsaw Pact. Deployed in fixed military camps as they are, NATO units are highly vulnerable to a no-warning first strike by thousands of non-nuclear weapons (in this case they need not be of strategic range, though the weapons used might be from classes designated as NNSW, especially since the range of tactical NNSW is restricted by the INF Treaty). NATO reinforcement depends on secure sea and air lanes over the Atlantic, luxuries that might not survive in an NNSW era. US POMCUS (prepositioned overseas material configured in unit sets) sites in Europe are inviting targets for precision-guided weapons. And the US defence industrial base, dependent as it is on carefully made high technology items produced by only a few sources, is highly vulnerable to NNSW strikes.

Larger strikes on general industrial capacity, however, are highly unlikely; NNSW are simply too expensive to deploy on such a large scale. As the Allies discovered to their dismay in World War II, even huge, continuing, coordinated strategic bombing efforts will not by themselves eliminate enemy productive capacity. If thousands of bombers flying daily sorties could not achieve that goal, it is unlikely that a one-time attack of a few thousand NNSW would.[45] Particularly important industrial targets, such as sources of high-technology equipment, could certainly be attacked, however.

Even if the option to replace nuclear weapons with NNSW were open, there are reasons why the superpowers might not be particularly tempted to take it. Nuclear weapons are far cheaper than NNSW and achieve the same effect. The doubts about NNSW's effectiveness – given that they would never be able to be tested over the poles or against realistic fascimiles of the opponents forces – would recommend continued reliance on nuclear weapons. And the risks that one's own forces would become vulnerable mitigate against widespread deployment of NNSW. The fragility of American society relative to that of the USSR also create unique motives for the United States to worry about the implications of NNSW. The nuclear balance has proven reasonably stable; both superpowers might make strong arguments for arms limitation treaties on NNSW.

Still, even if adopted in part for counterpower targeting, NNSW could have a significant effect on deterrence by raising the threshold for nuclear use to very high levels – even strategic war could be conducted without crossing the nuclear threshold. Nuclear weapons would be required for nothing other than deterrence of the opponent's nuclear arsenal. This would result in an interesting fusing of the minimum deterrence and war-fighting schools of nuclear doctrines – nuclear weapons themselves are not usable war-fighting tools, but conventional NNSW are.

NNSW and 'Thinkability'

On the war-fighting side of that equation, some commentators have suggested that NNSW could help reduce damage to populations and therefore to achieve a 'cleaner' escalation. Fred Iklé has argued that

> By taking advantage of modern technology, we should be able to escape the evil dilemmas that the strategic forces on both sides must either be designed to kill people or else jeopardize the opponent's confidence in his deterrent. The potential accuracy of 'smart' bombs and missiles and the current choices in weapon effects could enable both sides to avoid the killing of vast millions and yet to inflict assured destruction on military, industrial, and transportation assets – the sinews and muscles of the regime initiating war.[46]

Yet such a development would seem to make strategic war more 'thinkable'. The fear of general destruction in nuclear conflict has deterred major war for 40 years. NNSW offer the potential to destabilise that balance by establishing far less destructive means of waging war. It is certainly true, moreover, that once a conflict had begun, NNSW might make strikes against the opponent's homeland more attractive; thus, while not making *war* more thinkable, NNSW do seem to make *escalation to strategic exchanges* more palatable.

Some analysts doubt this logic. Chapter 2 argued that discriminate options would neither degrade crisis stability nor contribute to the perception that major war would be significantly less destructive. The risk of unintended escalation to nuclear war will always exist, meaning that the deterrent to conflict itself would not be undercut. Moreover, as the RAND report points out, 'both the United States and the Soviet Union have possessed many options for limited conflict for years without any apparent lessening of deterrence'.[47]

Moreover, NNSW would exercise its own deterrent effects, since each superpower is vulnerable in its own ways to the unique advantages of NNSW. The Soviets stress rapid conventional victory with massed forces; their attacks could be annihilated by theatre applications of NNSW, which could also provide a powerful support to existing US AirLand Battle and follow-on forces attack (FOFA) tactics. Soviet political and military control of their various republics might also prove profitable targets for NNSW in case of war, massively raising the stakes of conventional conflict. The United States, similarly, depends on a small number of critical sources for high-technology war *matériel* such as computer chips. Its reinforcements for NATO are dependent upon static POMCUS equipment sites. And the continental United States, we must remember, is not accustomed to the experience of war or even moderate social dislocation; a few hundred well-placed NNSW strikes could throw the country into chaos.

Once again, however, the implications of NNSW could be severely limited by arms agreements. A START accord would restrict the potential to use ballistic missiles as NNSW, and subsequent agreements on cruise missiles would effectively restrain the potential for strategic-range conventional weapons. Under such a regime, such weapons could indeed be produced, and might be useful for theatre or Third World applications. But their implications for strategic deterrence, when nuclear weapons placed atop the same missiles would achieve much greater results, would be less than dramatic.

Regarding strategic deterrence, several things therefore seem apparent about NNSW. Provided their delivery systems are restrained in arms accords, they will not pose a unique threat to deterrent forces; indeed their counterforce capabilities are questionable. If unique NNSW delivery systems are not controlled and eventually proliferate, however, they could degrade crisis stability.

NNSW could be used as part of a counterpower targeting strategy, and in this sense (and others) offer the opportunity to significantly raise the nuclear threshold. It is in the assumption of counterpower targeting goals, in fact, that NNSWs would have their greatest impact on deterrence. And they offer huge tactical opportunities.

NNSW AND ALLIANCES

The implications of NNSWs for US alliance policy are far from clear. On the one hand, they offer the potential to bolster flexible response by substituting conventional escalation for incredible nuclear pledges. 'In an environment characterized in the West by concern that NATO's "seamless web" of conventional, theater nuclear and strategic nuclear forces has unraveled', the RAND Study notes, 'NNSW might make a significant contribution to the credibility of NATO's escalatory threats'.[48] NNSW might also make escalation unnecessary by improving significantly the alliance's conventional capabilities.[49]

The counterpower targeting strategy described above could provide profitable targets for NNSWs used as flexible response tools. US officials could threaten to escalate, not necessarily to nuclear weapons, but to strategic conventional strikes against critical Soviet war-making industries and conventional force deployments. This pledge would be significantly more credible than the current flexible response doctrine of nuclear first use.

On the other hand, large-scale deployment of NNSWs could complicate US-NATO relations in a number of ways. Substitution of conventional for nuclear strategic escalation might not be welcome among European leaders still accustomed to the American nuclear umbrella. Europeans might also fear that third-party conflicts started with easier-to-use NNSW might escalate and cause war on the Continent. US reinforcement plans would also be complicated by NNSWs that could destroy US forces at their bases in the United States, in ports as they embarked and disembarked and at sea or in the air along the way.[50]

Perhaps most significantly, however, some analysts contend that NNSW threaten to reopen many long-defunct alliance debates over conventional versus nuclear deterrence and conventional defence. Carl Builder points out that NNSW 'seems more likely to loosen than to strengthen the alliance bonds ... They will make all too evident the cracks that have been papered over for decades by the enormous potential of nuclear weapons for both destruction and ambiguity'.[51] Other trends in international relations are already having the same effect – the gradual shift to a 'post-nuclear age', for example, will undoubtedly resurrect arguments over no-first-use pledges – and NNSW will undoubtedly accelerate them.

NNSW also hold the potential to *increase* the dangers of escalation of a European war. While the fear of assured destruction might keep either side from initiating the use of nuclear weapons, resort to NNSW could be made more easily. Yet once strategic targets, including deterrent forces, come under attack, the urge to escalate to nuclear conflict might be irresistible.

NNSW might also affect US-Japanese alliance relations. Japan, with its high-technology industries, would seem a logical candidate for development of NNSW.[52] Such weapons would provide Japan a means to improve its military capabilities and, in particular, the global reach of those capabilities, while at the same time creating new products for export. The United States and Japan might establish joint research projects in these areas. However, if Japan chose to pursue such ventures independently, alliance relations could become strained as US producers lost markets and, potentially, as the Japanese sold the technologies to nations out of US favour.

NNSW AND ARMS CONTROL

Large-scale deployment of NNSW seems likely to affect superpower arms control efforts in a number of ways. Initially, if NNSW were perceived to have replaced nuclear weapons as an adequate strategic deterrent, the calls for further reductions in nuclear stocks would become ever more insistent.[53] The superpowers could adopt a version of minimum deterrence, keeping a few hundred nuclear warheads apiece to preserve a semblance of assured destruction while pursuing most of their current targeting requirements with NNSW. The side that achieved a significant lead in NNSW, moreover, might feel confident enough to lead such arms control efforts. Yet at the same time, as mentioned before, NNSW will not allow complete disarmament because they will not, for a time at least, promise the utter societal destruction that nuclear weapons suggest.

Yet NNSW also hold the potential to complicate arms control efforts. An example is provided by discussions of arms control for cruise missiles. It is virtually impossible to design a reliable verification method to determine whether deployed cruise missiles carry nuclear or conventional warheads, imagine the difficulties of verifying the armament of thousands of small, intercontinental ballistic or cruise missiles. If NNSW eventually become as accurate and powerful as some suggest, these distinctions may no longer be relevant; an NNSW might be just as good for first-strike counterforce missions as a nuclear warhead, and only a few hundred nuclear warheads would be enough to promise destruction of an aggressor's society. But the revelation in a crisis by one side that ten thousand of its NNSW are actually armed with nuclear warheads might provide significant bargaining leverage, and the knowledge of this fact might encourage 'cheating' on strategic warheads.

All of this analysis points to the necessity for arms control limits on NNSW themselves. These limits would be both numerical and operational. For example, all ballistic missiles could be counted under existing or prospective arms control treaties; if, for example, the START treaty allows both sides 4900 ICBMs and SLBMs, no exceptions would be made for conventional ballistic missiles. If one side decided to convert some of its missiles to NNSW, the effects on stability would be less than catastrophic. Operationally, the superpowers could establish approach rules for submarines to ensure that cruise-missile firing boats could not approach closer than, say, 500 miles from the coasts of either country.

REGIONAL CHALLENGERS AND NNSW

A number of analysts have highlighted the emerging danger from largely non-communist regional powers that possess increasingly powerful conventional – and perhaps nuclear – weaponry. Military analyst Jeffrey Record, among others, stresses the shift in threats to US interests from Soviet to non-Soviet origins as one of the outstanding trends of the present era.[54] What implications would NNSW have for large power-small power relationships?

Potential to Augment US Capabilities

In fact, NNSW present excellent opportunities for the United States to deal with regional challengers. The militaries and political power of developing states tends to be 'softer' and more vulnerable than those of developed countries. The economies of Third World states are generally at a delicate stage between primitive agricultural stages and development, and are hence vulnerable to strikes on such critical societal targets as power and communication hubs, food distribution centres and the like. And their relative poverty and military backwardness (especially in technology) renders regional powers less able to deploy sophisticated countermeasures to NNSW.[55]

NNSW would also satisfy well the requirements for strikes on regional powers. The *Discriminate Deterrence* report spelled out the need:

> We must diversify and strengthen our ability to bring discriminating, non-nuclear force to bear where needed in time to defeat aggression. To this end, we and our allies need to exploit emerging technologies of precision, control, and intelligence that can provide our conventional forces with more selective and more effective capabilities for destroying targets.[56]

A more apt description of the capabilities of NNSW could hardly be imagined.

The military forces of Third World states would also become extremely vulnerable with the large-scale deployment of superpower NNSW. NNSW could be employed against military forces, airfields, bases or other fixed targets. Because of their expense, however, and the ability of military assets accustomed to attack to reconstitute themselves, such use might not prove cost-effective. More promising might be opportunities to use NNSW against targets that are especially difficult to replace, such as radars, air defences and communication facilities.

Thus used, NNSW could reduce requirements for spending on projection forces. The United States, in order to punish a Middle Eastern state, would not need to deploy a $3-billion-plus aircraft carrier; it could merely dispatch a few dozen NNSW from bases in the continental United States. As the cost of NNSW come down and as US bases overseas come under increasing political pressure, such options will become increasingly attractive.

Potential Problems

Yet the story regarding NNSW and US-Third World power relationships is not quite so simple. Most obviously, NNSW offer the potential to Third World states to increase their capabilities *vis-à-vis* major powers.[57] Examples of how such technologies might be acquired are provided by recent sales of ballistic missiles to Third World states by such nations as China and Argentina. To date such weapons have been restricted to tactical systems, but in the long term the acquisition of strategic missiles seems an inevitability.

Still, the incentives of Third World states to use such weapons against US targets are far from great. The United States could always retaliate with more force, up to and including the use of nuclear weapons. In a pitched battle, US conventional forces would win. The knowledge of this would seemingly deter the use by Third World states of NNSW. The threat of American NNSW use would exercise its own unique deterrent effect, especially as the United States might obtain these technologies a decade or more before such states as Libya and Syria.

Third World acquisition of NNSW would carry ambiguous implications for nuclear proliferation among developing states. NNSW might slow proliferation by providing developing states with an interim option, but other factors would work to undermine this effect: there is a prestige attached to nuclear weapons, for example, that is particularly attractive to nationalistic Third World states. NNSW delivery platforms would also provide any states previously incapable of strategic nuclear delivery with that means. Moreover, the destructive power of NNSW will not be close to that of large-yield nuclear warheads; a state with nuclear weapons could deter and cow a state with NNSW, but it is not at all clear that a state with a few dozen NNSW could deter a nuclear power. Moreover, non-nuclear *strategic* forces are not of great use to Third World powers, most of whose adversaries lie close at hand; strategic weapons would only allow them to attack more distant nations, many of which are powerful enough to deter such use.

The introduction of NNSW-type weapons, even of only theatre range, might also hurt crisis stability between developing states. The potential for pre-emption offered by such highly accurate and destructive weapons can be destabilising. For example, in the Arab-Israeli conflict, acquisition of hundreds of NNSW by Arab states would force Israel both to harden existing military facilities and to go to a virtual hair-trigger response policy.[58]

The existence of NNSW in a world of gradually proliferating weapons systems, however, might have one salutary implication. Countries that know from the start that static military facilities are vulnerable to precise attacks will be encouraged to harden such facilities or make them mobile. Thus, states that might otherwise have deployed somewhat vulnerable first-generation nuclear systems might pursue more survivable ones, even at the price of a delay in deployment. Once deployed, if such systems are essentially invulnerable to existing NNSW, and if both sides possess them, the balance would essentially have been preserved.

On the other hand, NNSW in the Third World might drag the superpowers into local crises. As the sophistication of regional wars and their potential to spray violence across the globe increase, it seems inevitable that such conflicts will pose greater risks of drawing in the superpowers.[59] For example, if the Soviet Union were supplying Arab states in a war and Israel decided to hit Soviet merchant ships or even ports with NNSW (a radical step but one that might not be unthinkable if Israel were losing), the pressure for escalation would be acute.

Finally, NNSW hold the potential to exacerbate existing US political difficulties in dealing with the Third World. As the RAND report notes,

> the diverse impacts and consequences of NNSW proliferation would generally exacerbate current U.S. political dilemmas involving regional balances and confrontations. NNSW proliferation would raise anew questions of whether to extend security guarantees as well as arms and technology transfers to various regional powers. U.S. and Soviet transfer and guarantee policies may play important roles in spurring or delaying NNSW proliferation, as well as in stabilizing or destabilizing post-proliferation balances.[60]

China and NNSW

NNSW might carry special implications for China's deterrent posture. Beijing subscribes to a variant of minimum deterrence in which it pledges, not to be able under any circumstances to win a nuclear exchange, but only to do enough damage to an aggressor's homeland to render an attack unattractive. Some analysts suggest that NNSW hold some potential to disrupt this strategy by placing at risk China's small deterrent force.[61]

This is not likely, however. China's force, hidden as it is in caves and other inaccessible places, is not susceptible to reliable targeting, by NNSW or other devices. The Chinese have begun deployment of missile-carrying submarines, which will remain essentially invulnerable until better ASW technologies emerge. And the clearly minimal nature of China's deterrent increases the significance of each remaining warhead, minimising threats to the arsenal as a whole.

NNSW could put China at an additional conventional disadvantage, however. Its high-technology industries are still in their infancy and are not well placed to compete in an NNSW arms race. China's security could thus decline relative to many of its neighbours – even smaller states like South Korea and Japan that possess thriving high-tech industries.

IMPLICATIONS

The development of NNSW carry a number of implications for US force structure and military policy. These are spelled out below.

The Requirement for High Technology Research. The United States must make a much more concerted effort to examine potential NNSW technologies. The SDI programme has developed certain systems potentially applicable to NNSW, and the Soviets recognise this. But a more specialised research effort is required. One promising idea might be a 'Strategic Research Programme' that would replace SDI. It would do research on strategic defences, NNSW and new nuclear technologies. It would incorporate the SDI budget and additional R&D funds from existing programmes related to other strategic areas. The effort would be an integrative synergy meant to ensure that all potential cross-applications of each technology are examined.

Bases Become Less Important. The United States would acquire the potential to project power with NNSW, and its dependence on overseas bases would decline correspondingly.[62] Indeed, resources currently devoted to base upkeep and base rights payments could be put to work directly on the development of NNSW.

Areas of Control. The potential for launching NNSW from submarines and aircraft near each superpower's homeland increases the premium on control of the air and sea areas around their borders. Increased ASW and anti-aircraft capabilities would seemingly be called for, as would better early warning systems.[63]

Stealth Technologies. The importance of stealth technologies would grow with widespread reliance on NNSW.[64] With nuclear weapons, stealthy delivery platforms perhaps pose less of a first-strike threat because of the huge natural disincentives to conflict contained in nuclear weapons. The advent of strategic conventional capabilities could change this equation, and render stealthy offensive systems important. The implications for crisis stability, as noted above, could be unfortunate.

Intra-War Negotiation and Coercion More Important. NNSW would extend (perhaps very much) the period of conventional-only war during which coercion and bargaining would remain critical, and before nuclear weapons had fallen, ruining communications and perhaps ending all thoughts of war termination. Coercion and negotiation thus become more important.[65]

Need for More Survivable Forces. NNSW, by placing US strategic forces even more at risk, would increase the already significant premium on survivable forces.

Air and Missile Defences. With the potential for conventional cruise and ballistic missile and bomber attacks on the United States, the role of defences of all sorts would grow.[66] The United States must examine such defences, especially air defences, more carefully. A more promising way to eliminate the threat of ballistic NNSW would be to include all ballistic missiles under START or post-START counting rules, thus reducing the incentive to deploy NNSW. Air defences could then be deployed to defend against air-breathing threats such as bombers and cruise missiles.

The most important task now is to control NNSW at the strategic level. If START and subsequent agreements on cruise missiles restrain the delivery platforms, it is unlikely that NNSW would disrupt the strategic balance by threatening deterrent forces. Meanwhile, new technologies deployed at the tactical level would significantly increase deterrence, and might even begin to introduce the notion of 'assured destruction' to conventional warfare. And NNSW would provide the superpowers with new means to deal with Third World challengers.

The only significant effect remaining for NNSW would be as part of a counterpower strategy, and it is in this sense that non-nuclear weapons will have their real effect on the strategic balance. They may serve to raise the nuclear threshold and to make war more thinkable in some ways, since the threat of escalation would have been reduced still further. But the ability of NNSW to annihilate standing armies, coupled with the ever-present risk of nuclear escalation, should be sufficient to deter wars. In the long-term, the implications of such a higher nuclear threshold are ambiguous.

9 Summary

Where, then, is deterrence headed in the 21st century, shaped as it will be by the START treaty and other events and trends? The foregoing analysis has hopefully made clear that the stability of nuclear deterrence should grow considerably in the years ahead, provided a START treaty is signed and ratified and the trends under consideration continue. This chapter will summarise the argument to this point, make a series of recommendations based on that argument, and propose a number of arms control treaties to supplement START.

THE PROSPECTS FOR STABLE DETERRENCE

This volume has argued both that deterrence will probably evolve in the manner suggested above and that such an evolution would be a good thing. The superpowers should therefore take measures designed to encourage this evolution. If, however, some of the preconditions are not met – if the START treaty is not concluded, for example, or if the United States fails to modernise its nuclear forces adequately – the sanguine picture painted here might fail to materialise.

(1) *The Future of Deterrence.* The next decade should witness more of the same – that is, deterrence based on mutual vulnerability and the security of retaliatory forces. Such deterrence has proven stable for over 40 years and will become even more so, thanks to several developments in the strategic environment. Deterrence will therefore continue to disprove the thesis that 'all the evidence shows that the U.S.-Soviet strategic relationship never conformed to the theory of stable consensual vulnerability – either before or since the ABM Treaty'.[1] This analysis also rejects the potential for or the likelihood of a transition to a 'defence-dominant environment'.

Such a future is not at all bad. One should hestitate to characterise the situation of assured destruction as a pejorative thing. Critics of assured destruction lament the notion that both sides are vulnerable to the other's attacks. In fact, however, as long as survivable forces exist, each side is primarily vulnerable, not to a first strike, but to a retaliation. Neither side is vulnerable to a first strike precisely *because* both are vulnerable to a counterblow. And this is not an entirely bad situation: neither side enjoys the freedom to initiate conflict because both are subject to punishment.

Deterrence will also evolve into a much more co-operative system than has been the case. Denied the realistic potential either to attack or to be attacked by the other, the superpowers ought to find it more and more in their interest to maintain stability. Their mutual enthusiasm for the START treaty is one example of this process. Others, including an increasing reliance on such stable weapons such as mobile ICBMs, should continue to bolster the stability of deterrence. The result will allow the superpowers to avoid the 'paradox of deterrence', which had previously rendered almost impossible the near-simultaneous deterrence of both general and limited war. Two RAND analysts have recognised this fact, pointing out that 'If U.S. policymakers believe in enhancing first-strike stability, the United States should spend money to alleviate the vulnerabilities of U.S. strategic nuclear forces rather than to increase the vulnerabilities of Soviet strategic nuclear forces. The vulnerabilities of Soviet forces are not necessarily in the U.S. interest, nor are U.S. attempts to create further vulnerabilities in these forces. Survivable forces on both sides remain the key to the shared objective of enhancing first-strike stability'.[2]

The two developments outlined earlier that are particularly critical to this process are the START treaty and US strategic modernisation. Both help eliminate beliefs in the ability to conduct effective nuclear strikes: capping strategic arsenals at levels significantly below those currently deployed prevents either side believing it can achieve a usable advantage by building many weapons, while US strategic modernisation (to parallel Soviet efforts) is required to deprive the Soviets of a counterforce capability against US land-based nuclear forces. Without either a START treaty or US modernisation (the latter critically comprising Midgetman or some similar weapon), the foregoing analysis would be seriously, though not fatally, undermined.

Other trends will affect this process as well. Public opinion and the potential for nuclear winter will continue to defeat arguments for extensive war-fighting schemes. Increasing accuracy, speed and lethality of nuclear weapons and their delivery vehicles will mandate arms reductions and better methods of passive defence, such as mobility and concealment. Most significant, the overriding fact of the post-war age will continue to obviate thoughts of nuclear conflict: largely due to the advent of nuclear weapons but partly for other reasons, large-scale conflict is today obsolete as a political, military or economic tool.

(2)   *US Nuclear Strategy.*   Partly in response to these trends, US nuclear strategy might begin a slow return from countervailing strategies emphasising war-fighting, counterforce strikes against Soviet nuclear targets, and extended conflicts to 'co-operative re-ciprocal deterrence', a strategy combining strikes against Soviet non-nuclear military, industrial and, to a limited degree, political targets to achieve deterrence. Deterrence could be based on retaliation against critical military-industrial targets, augmented by the ever-present danger of escalation to general war, in which given the vulnerability of societies, both nations would be destroyed as advanced nations.

Today, the United States appears to be moving in the opposite direction with SIOP-7, its new nuclear war plan. Initial reports have suggested that the new SIOP calls for a total – and perhaps ruinously expensive – pursuit of counterforce targeting. As this book has suggested, such a course could not be more misguided; but the fact remains that it appears to be US policy, and that fact disputes some of the trend analysis contained here. Still, good reason remains to believe that US policy will eventually turn back from this course. US planners are already aware of the tensions between counterforce and many strategic developments. One can only hope that this awareness will translate itself into policy.

Extended deterrence of conventional conflict in such areas as Europe will not withstand the various pressures outlined in preceding analysis. Trends are at work that will encourage and require the United States to drop its pledge of escalation in the defence of NATO or other allies. Extended deterrence of nuclear blackmail by the USSR or another country could remain for a time but seems destined to wither away as well.

Finally, US nuclear planners must retain clearly enunciated and refined plans and capabilities to engage in limited nuclear options. Such plans and capabilities are critical to deter the use of limited nuclear operations (LNOs) by other states. Previously attaining such a capability might risk instability (through the analysis of the paradox of deterrence), but in the stable environment of a START world such a result can be avoided.

(3) *Other Threats to Stability.* Other potentially destabilising weapons systems or doctrines also appear not to pose a threat to the stable environment sketched out above. Soviet military doctrine has never recently called for nuclear trouble-making, and in the future Soviet leaders – increasingly, military as well as political – should be less and less likely to believe that nuclear conflict could serve any Soviet national interests. Strategic defences will probably not be deployed on any significant scale, and limited, point defences of nuclear assets would augment deterrence. Verification of the START accord should be sufficient to prevent destabilising amounts of cheating, and in any case, given US nuclear modernisation, Soviet planners would have little motive to cheat in the first place. Agreements on SLCMs seem likely to be reached, either in START or afterward, that would prevent SLCMs from undermining the stability crafted in an accord. Finally, neither non-nuclear strategic weapons nor low-yield nuclear weapons are likely to increase either the risk of conflict or of nuclear war.

The analysis of the three preceding sections is graphically represented in Figure 9.1.

DETERRENCE AND 'NUCLEAR LEARNING'

Many barriers to these changes exist, of course. Some were summarised in chapter 4; the institutional and doctrinal barriers to an abandonment of counternuclear targeting are particularly severe. There may be little reason to expect either superpower to edge toward a more co-operative form of deterrence.

It is possible, however, for the superpowers to recognise that stable deterrence of the sort outlined in the preceding chapters of this volume is in their interests. Indeed, in many ways they already have. Their changing impressions have been characterised by what Joseph S. Nye, Jr terms 'nuclear learning'.[3] Nye agrees with Robert Jervis that a 'security regime' of co-operative behaviour to protect mutual safety does not exist in regard to the US-Soviet security relationship as a whole. Nye suggests, however, that a series of regime-like accommodations have been reached on a number of specific issues, such as strategic arms control, accidental nuclear war prevention, and non-proliferation. They have evolved because the superpowers have learned over time that destabilising forces and doctrines are in neither side's interests.

Nye's analysis also points to the direction in which the balance could evolve in the future. Learning by both sides requires a shared body of experience, and he outlines four 'areas of common knowledge' that have led to partial security regimes. These include the destructive power of nuclear weapons (resulting in the condition of

Trends

Nuclear Arms Control (START)   Public Opinion
                                  Domestic
                                  International

Nuclear Winter   Weapon Technologies
                                  Accuracy
                                  Weapon Effect

Infeasibility of Major War   Counterforce Infeasible

US-Soviet Détente   Cuts in US Nuclear
                                  Forces in Europe

Conventional Arms Control   European Integration

'Co-operative Reciprocal Deterrence'

Central Deterrence of Major War:
Countervailing-type strategy with reciprocal retaliation;
Co-operative stability through mobile missiles and
other means; 'dynamically-stable deterrence';
Partial delayed response to nuclear attack;
Mutual improvements in C3I, including survivable Hotline;
Counterpower targeting; .
Extended deterrence of conventional war given up,
of nuclear blackmail preserved for a time;
LNOs deterred through escalation matching

Risks
Discriminate Options
Bolstered Counterforce Strategies (SIOP-7)
General Strategic Defences
Non-Nuclear Strategic Weapons

A 'Happy Ending'?

FIGURE 9.1   *Deterrence Regime for the 1990s*

assured destruction and general deterrence), the problem of control of the weapons (leading to PALs, accidents and crisis management agreements, and the like), the dangers of proliferation (spurring mutual efforts at non-proliferation), and (to a lesser extent) the risks of arms race instability (leading to arms control accords). Nye also suggests a fifth area of knowledge which has not yet been formalised in a regime of any sort: the optimal form of deterrent force structure, which he suggests would involve 'invulnerability for crisis stability, counterforce for credible threat, [and] conventional [forces] for credibility'.[4]

In the context of Nye's concept of nuclear learning, this volume would contend that the next decade will witness a firming up of the fourth area of knowledge (manifest in arms control) and the beginnings of shared ideas on the fifth. The result will be mutual adoption of more stable systems, along the lines of the 'dynamically stable deterrence' discussed earlier. As time goes on, moreover, the process of nuclear learning should continue, leading to increasingly co-operative dealings on such issues as arms reductions and operational arms control measures.

RECOMMENDED FORCE STRUCTURES

Given the requirements outlined earlier (primarily in chapter 3) for a stable force structure, what actions ought the United States to take to bolster its strategic deterrent? Several options appear particularly promising.

Land-Based Modernisation. Procurement of improved land-based deterrent forces is perhaps the most critical step the United States must take to ensure the evolution of stable deterrence along the lines suggested above. Without it, the possibility for at least partial counterforce targeting will remain; and if the US SSBN force – reduced in size to perhaps 18 boats – were rendered vulnerable by a technological breakthrough or similar development, the United States would possess virtually no survivable nuclear forces. The dangers of such a situation are clear.

The United States ought therefore to purchase and deploy Midgetman (at least 300, preferably 500), deploy its 50 MX missiles in rail garrison, and (eventually) obtain a carry-hard system for remaining Minuteman missiles. To fund these weapons, the B-2 bomber programme should be substantially slowed or completely cancelled. The weapons, moreover, need not be purchased with undue haste; an initial procurement of 200–300 Midgetmen, perhaps deployed at first in silos, would provide enough of a hedge until the remaining forces could be obtained, which might occur as many as five to ten years later.

Submarine and Bomber Forces. The United States ought to plan on eventually deploying a new generation of SSBN, one that might carry just six or eight missiles rather than the 20 to 24 common on existing boats. The new submarines should be designed for optimum quietness. Significant new efforts should be made in research on new techniques for communicating with submarines before, during or after an attack. These systems need not be deployed for 10–15 years; they would constitute another step toward absolute stability after the deployment of better land-based forces.

Strategic bombers would have the lowest modernisation priority. Until a new bomber can be built, existing B-52 and B-1 aircraft should be used as ALCM-carriers that would not necessarily penetrate Soviet airspace at all. The B-2 should be gutted, with only a few B-2s purchased, the technologies reapplied to all new generations of aircraft. The next generation of bomber should not be designed primarily as a penetrator, since missions for such systems would be largely obviated by a counterpower strategy; although if possible the bomber should possess the capability to track and target large Soviet *conventional* forces moving throughout Eastern Europe or the Western USSR. The recommended type of bomber would be an uncomplicated, stealthy ALCM carrier.

Strategic Defences. The United States should investigate and eventually deploy promising ground-based defensive technologies around any fixed nuclear targets – command and control centres, remaining Minuteman silos, MX garrison sites, Midgetman control centres, and the like. Prohibitions against more general deployments should be included in a reaffirmed, modified ABM Treaty.

US Nuclear Strategy. The United States ought to enunciate a new strategy, to be entitled 'co-operative reciprocal deterrence' or something similar. It should include (1) a reorientation of the SIOP away from counternuclear targeting and toward counterpower; (2) a pledge of no-first-use against Soviet nuclear assets; (3) carefully designed limited nuclear options; and (4) a prescribed pause in the event of a very limited nuclear attack. The strategy should also begin the task of renouncing the US pledge to escalate in response to Soviet conventional aggression, while reaffirming (for a time) the US intention to respond to Soviet nuclear blackmail of US allies. More details of the strategy can be drawn from chapters 2 and 4.

Command, Control and Communications In addition to the efforts mentioned above in regard to SSBN communications, the United States should invest several tens of billions of dollars in the improvement of its general nuclear C3I programmes. The superpowers should also establish a survivable Hotline for the reasons and on the order suggested in chapter 3.

Public Relations Efforts. Successive US administrations must make a concerted effort to justify these programmes to what will undoubtedly be an increasingly sceptical public. Some assistance can be obtained from the promise of an 'end' to the quantitative and, eventually, the qualitative arms race: US governments could appeal for a last set of expenditures for programmes that will allow the 'nuclear question' to be answered almost indefinitely. The critical point must be continually made that peace does not come without a price – and that that price, at the nuclear level at least, involves force modernisation.

WHERE DO WE GO FROM HERE?

If Joseph Nye is right and the superpowers are indeed in the midst of a learning process about nuclear weapons, what consensuses might they reach in the future? A number of arms accords might usefully supplement a START treaty and enhance stability, cementing in place the stable balance achieved through arms reductions and strategic modernisation.

ASAT Restrictions. Anti-satellite weapons are uniquely destabilising insofar as they threaten the primary superpower means of command and control. This is especially true for American nuclear and conventional forces, which rely more heavily on satellites than do their Soviet counterparts. An ASAT ban would help protect both sides' communications and would assist in ensuring retaliation and allowing escalation control and war termination.[5]

Missile Flight-Test Ban. After the currently-conceived generation of missiles is deployed, the superpowers could agree to a ban on any flight tests of intercontinental weapons. This would effectively preclude the development of new, more accurate systems, since they could never be adequately tested. A more narrow approach might be a ban on flight tests of depressed-trajectory SLBMs, weapons that hold particular dangers because of their ability to hit targets within several minutes of being launched if fired from close offshore.[6]

Submarine Approach Limits. The superpowers already adhere to unwritten understandings that prohibit missile-carrying submarines from approaching closer than several hundred miles from each others' coasts. These understandings could be codified in agreements that would prohibit approaches closer than, say, 500 miles by any SSB or SSBN. Such an agreement would reduce the opportunities for short-warning attacks.[7]

Comprehensive Test-Ban Treaty. This accord would essentially ban all testing of new nuclear devices. Its advantage is obvious – by preventing development of more powerful or uniquely destructive weapons, it would help remove the potential for destabilising developments. The debate about the verifiability and wisdom of such an accord is volatile, but in the proper context – at the right moment on the superpower 'learning curve' in relation to nuclear weapons – a CTBT could be useful. Some exemptions to the prohibition could be made to test existing weapons to ensure the efficacy of both sides' deterrents.

SSBN Arms Control. Several steps could be taken to augment the survivability of SSBNs. Undersea command posts could be established, protected by mutual treaty, that would facilitate communication with SSBNs. In a crisis period or during the early stages of war, such command posts would be exempt from attack; if either side did attempt to destroy the other's posts, it would provide a reasonably unambiguous signal of aggressive intent at the nuclear level. Ocean sanctuaries could also be established in which ASW activities are prohibited which would increase the survivability of both sides' submarine-based deterrents. The Soviets already pursue such tactics to avoid American ASW. SSBNs should not be restricted to patrolling such sanctuaries, to avoid either side using barrage tactics to attack them.

Controlling Nuclear Alerts. The dangers of mutually escalating nuclear alerts have been pointed out by a number of analysts. Paul Bracken, for example, has emphasised the danger of 'nuclear Sarajevos' rather than 'nuclear Munichs', and concludes that the most likely route to war is a series of escalating crisis alerts.[8] The need to control such alerts is clear, and mutual procedures governing crisis procedure can be worked out.[9] A number of important steps have already been taken in this direction: such communication facilities as the Hot Line and Nuclear Risk Reduction Centers will help the superpowers clarify actions during crises. As recommended in chapter

5, similar systems ought to be set up for NATO, an idea brought to the forefront by the failure of warning after a Soviet MiG-23 flew pilotless into NATO airspace in July 1989.[10]

Ban Multiple-Warhead Mobile Missiles. One addition that the United States ought to make to its position on a potential START II treaty relates to mobile missiles. There would be merit in a proposal to allow only single-warhead mobile missiles.[11] This would enhance stability by encouraging de-MIRVing and the deployment of survivable weapons. The Soviets, for their part, might well be willing to give up the SS-24 for the MX, especially given that they would continue to possess a significant SS-18 force; they would bargain away one mobile missile to obtain the prohibition of the most powerful American weapon. From the US standpoint, such an accord would save money, obviating the need to spend $9–12 billion on rail garrison MX. That missile, moreover, is the least stabilising of the mobile weapons insofar as it would have to be generated in a crisis.

Incentives for de-MIRVing. Additional incentives could be created to encourage each side to deploy single-warhead missiles. The Midgetman and SS-25 could be exempted from the treaty limit of 1600 launchers, while leaving the limit of 6000 warheads intact.[12] This would allow each side theoretically to deploy as many targets as the other side has weapons, the most stable situation of all. (The accord should not allow existing missiles to be down-loaded to single-warhead configuration; that situation would create real risks of cheating or crisis breakout – imagine a force of 1600 'single-warhead' SS-18s suddenly boosted up to 15 warheads apiece.)

Reducing Premium on Bomber Weapons. The current loophole in the treaty regarding gravity bomb- or short-range attack missile (SRAM)-carrying bombers should be dropped. Bombers may be more stabilising weapons than ICBMs, but in the regime contemplated here that consideration would be less important. Enunciation of a counterpower strategy would reduce the premium on penetrating bombers, moreover. And dropping the loophole would reduce the number of strategic weapons actually held by each side to 6000, rather than 8–9000 if the loophole remains.

A PROMISING FUTURE – IF WE WANT IT

The preceding analysis has hopefully made clear two facts about the balance under a potential START treaty: it would not be safe without

US modernisation and other guarantees of stability, but it would most definitely be stable and in the US interest with them. The resulting agreement will save the United States money in the long term, but saving money is not the purpose of arms control. The goal is to restrain, channel and end in certain areas the nuclear arms race in ways that augment stability. A modernised US force under START would serve those goals admirably.

Commitment to modernisation is important in a number of regards. It is required for stability. It would immeasurably bolster US credibility in the eyes of foreign leaders watching hopefully for a sign that the United States is not using arms control to avoid its defence responsibilities. It would eliminate the incentive for Soviet cheating, as we saw in chapter 7. And it would be crucial to the ratification process in the United States, a process whose importance is difficult to exaggerate; the failure of another treaty in the US Senate would ruin world confidence in the arms control process.

Henry Kissinger, though dubious of a START accord, has provided an outstanding suggestion to ensure such modernisation: an 'executive-legislative summit' in which 'the administration outlines how it proposes to compose post-START U.S. strategic forces and congressional leaders agree to fund the programs needed to improve their survivability'.[13] Such a summit – held before a US president signed an accord – would offer several advantages: it would virtually ensure Senate ratification of the treaty, since Senate leaders would have been reassured about post-START deterrence; it would destroy any notion, in the minds of Soviet planners or third parties, that the US deterrent would be degraded after an accord; and most crucially, it would actually guarantee the sorts of nuclear force modernisation described above. The process is already underway with Bush administration proposals for nuclear modernisation.

Finally, the foregoing analysis takes seriously the much-repeated axiom that arms control in itself is not a panacea. One analyst of the treaty has pointed out that 'While START therefore should not be held responsible for making U.S. forces vulnerable, neither can it be expected by itself to ensure their survivability ... The responsibility for maintaining survivable forces must rest primarily not on arms control, but on U.S. defence programmes'.[14] The prospective START treaty is an excellent example of an arms control agreement that could help augment security by complementing its modernisation programme, but that, when viewed in isolation, could be destabilising. Only if the United States is prepared to develop its strategic nuclear deterrent will the START accord be in the West's interests; but if it is prepared to do so, the agreement would be very sound.

Many of those who have traditionally pursued arms control for its own sake, in fact, have not been 'wooly-headed arms control advocates', but hard-nosed politicians in Europe, the Soviet Union and the United States. Arms control is a distinctly political process, driven by political requirements and dictated by political timing. SALT I was arguably a far less worthy accord than its successor SALT II, but the political context surrounding the latter was not conducive to an agreement. Many thorny issues in the INF negotiations were quickly resolved to meet the timetable of the December 1987 Reagan-Gorbachev summit. Barriers to an MBFR agreement could have been similarly overcome had the political will existed.[15]

To a great degree, this book exists only because the political incentives for a strategic arms reduction treaty have coalesced in both Washington and Moscow. START is happening, not because strategic arms reductions suddenly became a good idea, but because they have become a political imperative. The preceding chapters have concentrated mainly on the strategic and technical, rather than political, aspects of the treaty, and this was by design; political forces were already impelling START to a finish. Where relevant, of course, political influences – on the future of nuclear weapons in Europe or US nuclear strategy or the potential for US strategic modernisation – have been considered. But the general political environment has made START almost inevitable, and our task now is to ensure that it creates a stable strategic balance.

That goal is eminently achievable, as outlined in preceding chapters. The START regime would not entail a radical departure from existing deterrent procedures and doctrines – no massive transition to a 'defence-dominant world', no sudden 'abolition'. It would, rather, represent perhaps the best incremental steps toward 'perfect' deterrence for which we could hope. This volume has begun and ended on related themes: major war is obsolete, it argued early on, and has become so largely due to the implications of nuclear weapons; and partly as a result the superpowers have learned, it followed Joseph Nye in recognising in this chapter, that deterrence benefits their mutual security and that stable deterrence is the best situation. These twin realities form the anchor-posts between which are strung the rest of the propositions of the argument of the volume.

'Will stable deterrence last forever?', Joseph Nye has asked somewhat rhetorically. 'Human fallibility suggests that it will not.'[16]

While Nye does not necessarily agree with that pessimistic conclusion, many analysts of the nuclear balance, of both left and right, have done so through the years. Those on the left cry for disarmament; those on the right, mostly for technological solutions such as strategic defence or counterforce. This volume is dedicated to the propositions that neither of those approaches offers a real solution to the 'nuclear danger' (or should), and that neither will characterise the future of deterrence in the 1990s and beyond. Rather, we are essentially in for more of the same – deterrence through mutual vulnerability. But that basic core of deterrence which has worked so well can be supplemented: by nuclear forces and doctrines and by the START treaty (as documented in previous chapters), and by subsequent numerical and operational arms accords (summarised above). That is about the best we can hope for – and it is about all that can reasonably be expected. Most important of all, it will probably continue to *work*.

Notes

1 The Status of Deterrence: START and Other Factors

1. Andrew Goldberg, project director, *Securing Strategic Stability* (Washington, DC: Center for Strategic and International Studies, December 1988), p. 3.
2. Richard K. Betts, *Cruise Missiles and U.S. Policy* (Washington, DC: Brookings, 1982), p. 11.
3. Edward L. Warner III and David Ochmanek, *Next Moves: An Arms Control Agenda for the 1990s* (New York: Council on Foreign Relations, 1989), p. 24n.
4. Warner and Ochmanek, *Next Moves*, pp. 25–7.
5. Max M. Kampelman, 'START: Completing the Task', *The Washington Quarterly* 1 (Summer 1989), 7.
6. See, for example, Peter DeLeon, *The Altered Strategic Environment Toward the Year 2000* (Lexington, MA: D.C. Heath and Co., 1987), pp. 59–66, and Michael Howard, 'The Forgotten Dimensions of Strategy', *Foreign Affairs* 57 (Summer 1979).
7. Philip Bobbitt, *Democracy and Deterrence: The History and Future of Nuclear Strategy* (New York: St Martin's Press, 1988), pp. 110, 284.
8. Market Opinion Research, Marttila and Kiley Inc., *et al.*, *Americans Talk Security*, Full Survey Report. No publication location, various dates. The figures come from No. 9, October 1988; the quotation is from No. 6, June 1988, p. 41. Emphasis mine.
9. *Americans Talk Security*, No. 9, October 1988; No. 6, June 1988.
10. For good summaries of the issue, see DeLeon, *The Altered Strategic Environment*, pp. 7–25; and Thomas Powers, 'Nuclear Winter and Nuclear Strategy', *The Atlantic* 254 (November 1984).
11. Herbert A. Simon, 'Mutual Deterrence and Nuclear Suicide', *Science* 23 (4 February 1984), 775.
12. Klaus Knorr, *On The Uses of Military Power in the Nuclear Age* (Princeton, NJ: Princeton University Press, 1966), p. 23.
13. Knorr, *On the Uses of Military Power*, pp. 38–115.
14. John Mueller, *Retreat From Doomsday: The Obsolescence of Major War* (New York: Basic Books, 1989), pp. 59–60.
15. Knorr, *On the Uses of Military Power*, pp. 87–9.
16. Knorr, *On the Uses of Military Power*, p. 90.
17. Mueller, *Retreat From Doomsday*, pp. 4–5.
18. Mueller, *Retreat From Doomsday*, pp. 227–35.
19. Mueller, *Retreat From Doomsday*, pp. 236–40.
20. Robert Jervis, 'The Nuclear Revolution and the Common Defense', *Political Science Quarterly* 101 (1986), 689, 694.
21. Edward L. Warner and David Ochmanek, *Next Moves: An Arms Control Agenda for the 1990s* (New York: Council on Foreign Relations, 1989), p. 19.

22. Robert Jervis, 'Strategic Theory: What's New and What's True', *Journal of Strategic Studies* 9 (December 1986), 158–9.

2 The Requirements of Deterrence

1.   The author is indebted to Dr William Kincade for some of the ideas in these paragraphs.
2.   Cited in Philip Bobbitt, *Democracy and Deterrence: The History and Future of Nuclear Strategy* (New York: St Martin's Press, 1988), p. 283.
3.   See Glenn Snyder, 'The Balance of Power and the Balance of Terror', in Paul Seabury (ed.), *The Balance of Power* (San Francisco: Chandler, 1965).
4.   Richard K. Betts, 'NATO Deterrence Doctrine: No Way Out', CISA Working Paper No. 51 (Center for International and Strategic Affairs, UCLA: June 1985), p. 66.
5.   Richard K. Betts, 'Nuclear Peace and Conventional War', *Journal of Strategic Studies* 11 (March 1988): 94.
6.   Martin Griffiths, 'A Dying Creed: The Erosion of Deterrence in American Nuclear Strategy', *Millennium: Journal of International Studies* 15 (No. 1, 1988): 226.
7.   Michael MccGwire, 'Dilemmas and Delusions of Deterrence', *World Policy Journal* 1 (Summer 1984), 750.
8.   Mueller, *Retreat From Doomsday*, pp. 250–1.
9.   Scott D. Sagan, *Moving Targets: Nuclear Strategy and National Security* (Princeton, NJ: Princeton University Press, 1989), pp. 4–5.
10. John Steinbruner has argued that if deterrence fails 'then it would not be rational actually to carry out the threat of massive retaliation . . . [because] once attacked, a rationally calculating player has nothing to gain by massive retaliation'. Quoted in Griffiths, 'The Erosion of Deterrence', p. 227.
11. Quoted in Daniel Charles, *Nuclear Planning in NATO: Pitfalls of First Use* (Cambridge, MA: Ballinger, 1987), frontispiece. Jonathon Schell's *The Fate of the Earth* (New York: Knopf, 1982) is essentially an extended argument dedicated to proving exactly this point by demonstrating that the effects of nuclear attacks are so horrendous that retaliation would be brutal and pointless, which if true would undercut deterrence.
12. Lawrence Freedman, 'I Exist; Therefore I Deter', *International Security* 13 (Summer 1988), 177.
13. See Spurgeon M. Keeny and Wolfgan Panofsky, 'MAD versus NUTS: Can Doctrine or Weaponry Remedy the Mutual Hostage Relationship of the Superpowers?', *Foreign Affairs* 60 (Winter 1981–82).
14. Freedman, 'I Exist', p. 177.
15. See Morton Halperin, *Nuclear Fallacy: Dispelling the Myth of Nuclear Strategy* (Cambridge, MA: Ballinger, 1987); and for a description of these views, Philip Bobbitt, *Democracy and Deterrence*, pp. 138–44.

16. Freedman, 'I Exist', p. 189.
17. For a description, see Bobbitt, *Democracy and Deterrence*, pp. 136–8.
18. Bobbitt, *Democracy and Deterrence*, p. 102.
19. Richard Betts, *Cruise Missiles and U.S. Policy* (Washington, DC: The Brookings Institution, 1982), pp. 11–12.
20. The following quotations come from Department of Defense *Annual Report, Fiscal Year 1981* (Washington, DC: DoD, 29 January 1980), pp. 65–8.
21. Lawrence Freedman, 'I Exist, Therefore I Deter', *International Security* 13 (Summer 1988): 184–5. See also Robert McNamara, 'The Military Role of Nuclear Weapons: Perceptions and Misperceptions', *Survival* 25 (November–December 1983), and Thomas Schelling, *Arms and Influence* (New Haven: Yale University Press, 1960), p. 98.
22. Robert Jervis, 'The Nuclear Revolution and the Common Defense', *Political Science Quarterly* 101 (1986), 690, 693.
23. Therefore, even many minimum deterrence advocates recognise the need for strategic modernisation to ensure the survivability of US forces; see Halperin, *Nuclear Fallacy*, p. 76.
24. Richard Betts, 'Nuclear Peace and Conventional War', *Journal of Strategic Studies* 11 (March 1988), 79.
25. Hence Robert Jervis argues that 'the side that is "losing" by various measures of military capability can inflict unprecedented destruction on the side that is "winning" as easily as the "winner" can do this to the "loser"'. Jervis, 'The Nuclear Revolution and the Common Defense', pp. 692–4.
26. Michael MccGwire has a very good discussion of Soviet motives and the lack of a need to deter them by denying their 'war aims' in 'Dilemmas and Delusions of Deterrence', pp. 750–67.
27. Freedman, 'I Exist', p. 185.
28. Some would suggest that a defender could count on an attacker's fear of a spasm or revenge-based response to bolster deterrence; even if it is not logical for a victim to respond, he might anyway, intentionally or not. But this is not a robust notion on which to hang the peace, and during a crisis might prove insufficient. If more deterrent power could be acquired without damage to stability – avoiding the paradox – it probably should.
29. Of course, minimum deterrent proponents would say he would have quite a few options, from retaliating with a few bombs against Warsaw Pact installations to attacks with conventional weapons like aircraft carriers or bombers. It seems undeniable, however, that if one side possessed a minimum deterrent and the other did not, in a crisis the side with superiority might well succeed in deterring any nuclear response. It is only under such extreme conditions that notions like the 'suicide or surrender' dilemma become relevant.
30. Certain mobile weapons can have ambiguous implications for crisis stability. If they are not secure in a day-to-day environment and must be 'flushed' to become stable weapons, they may contribute to crisis escalation; the process of flushing may be interpreted as an aggressive

act. As chapter 3 will make clear, the United States needs mobile weapons that are secure on a day-to-day basis.

31. Lt. Col. Fred J. Reule, USAF, *et al.*, *Dynamic Stability: A New Concept for Deterrence* (Maxwell APB, AL: Air University Press, September 1987), p. 1; see also the statement regarding the paradox by Maj. G. E. Myers on p. 77, *ibid.* The quotes below come from pages 1–14.

32. Gregg Herken, 'The Not-Quite-Absolute Weapon: Deterrence and the Legacy of Bernard Brodie', *Journal of Strategic Studies* 9 (December 1986), 19.

33. Quoted in David W. Tarr, 'Avoiding Nuclear War by Other Means', in Stephen J. Cimbala (ed.), *Strategic War Termination* (New York: Praeger, 1986), p. 45. See also Wohlstetter, 'Between an Unfree World and None', *Foreign Affairs* 63 (Summer 1985).

34. Quoted in Peter deLeon, *The Altered Strategic Environment Toward the Year 2000* (Lexington, MA: D.C. Heath, 1987), p. 47.

35. deLeon, *The Altered Strategic Environment*, pp. 51–2.

36. This would appear to contradict the argument, made above and in chapter 3, that weapons *do* in fact cause instability of themselves, but on closer examination the conflict seems to disappear. If one side enjoys a potential first-strike advantage with nuclear weapons, then the resulting crisis instability can create tensions independently of any political desire to go to war. The mere ability to wage a more discriminate nuclear war would not create the same pressures, unless it undermined crisis stability still further; but the lack of unique counter-force applications for discriminate weapons suggests that that outcome is unlikely.

3 Stability

1. For a detailed explication of this notion, see Philip Bobbitt, *Democracy and Deterrence: The History and Future of Nuclear Strategy* (New York: St Martin's Press, 1987), pp. 161–2. See also Glenn A. Kent and David E. Thaler, *First-Strike Stability: A Methodology for Evaluating Strategic Forces* (Santa Monica, CA: RAND Corporation, August 1989).

2. In part, conservatives deny that fact because they believe Soviet analysts deny it. Chapter 5 refutes that argument.

3. These and following quotes come from Fred Charles Iklé, 'Nuclear Strategy: Can There Be a Happy Ending?', *Journal of Strategic Studies* 9 (December 1986), 48–9 and 52–3.

4. Richard Betts, *Cruise Missiles and U.S. Policy* (Washington, DC: Brookings Institution, 1982), p. 18 n33.

5. Michael MccGwire, 'Dilemmas and Delusions of Deterrence', *World Policy Journal* I (Summer 1984), 764.

6. MccGwire, 'Dilemmas and Delusions of Deterrence', p. 765.

7. For a more detailed examination of attack scenarios and the current balance, see Congressional Budget Office, *Modernizing U.S. Offensive Nuclear Forces* (Washington, DC: GPO, November 1987).

8. Zbigniew Brzezinski concludes that 'Under prevailing conditions, it is unlikely that any Soviet military planner could confidently expect that

a Soviet nuclear attack would so disarm the United States as to prevent an extremely damaging retaliatory response'. *Game Plan: How to Conduct the U.S.-Soviet Contest* (New York: Atlantic Monthly Press, 1987), p. 105. Stephen J. Cimbala agrees that 'the balance of terror . . . is basically not delicate'. *Nuclear War and Nuclear Strategy: Unfinished Business* (New York: Greenwood Press, 1987), p. 19.

9. This is not to say that the *absolute* numbers of superpower weapons have been increasing; in fact, the US nuclear stock has declined. But as both sides proceed with modernisation, the numbers of counterforce weapons increases.

10. CBO, *Modernizing U.S. Offensive Nuclear Forces*.

11. David Hendrickson, *The Future of American Strategy* (New York: Holmes and Meier, 1987), p. 135.

12. Flexibility in targeting – obtained from single-warhead missiles rather than submarines, which give their position away with single launches – is an important justification for modernisation.

13. Panel on the Future of Strategic Systems, *Securing Strategic Stability* (Washington, DC: Center for Strategic and International Studies, December 1988).

14. On the vulnerability of US ICBMs in a START world, see Brent Scowcroft, 'Strategic Arms in the Balance', *The East-West Papers* No. 11 (May/June 1988), and Charles Krauthammer, 'The End of Arms Control', *The New Republic*, 29 August 1988.

15. Some analysts, such as Colin Gray, have contended that ICBMs are not in fact vulnerable because they could be launched on warning or under attack. But nuclear doctrines that call for such launches are destabilising insofar as they risk accidental launch. Nor can we be certain that the United States adheres to them, and in case it does not we ought to plan forces capable of withstanding a blow.

16. Bombers are not totally vulnerable to a first strike, but they are partly vulnerable both to that and to interception and destruction once airborne. The cruise missiles they carry are also subject to interception by modern Soviet aircraft. For a short argument on why US retaliation should not be based on bombers, see the arguments below about immediate versus delayed responses.

17. For two qualified 'yeses', see Barry Blechman, 'Triad, Schmiad', *The New Republic*, 6 February 1989, pp. 15–17; and Fred C. Iklé, 'Riding ICBMs Into the Past', *New York Times* 27 March 1989.

18. Statement in *Strategic Force Modernization and Arms Control* (Cambridge: MA: Institute for Foreign Policy Analysis, 1986), p. 25. Admittedly, however, there is little prospect of SSBN vulnerability; see Donald C. Daniel, 'Antisubmarine Warfare in the Nuclear Age', *Orbis* 28 (Fall 1984), 527–52; and Michele A. Flournoy, 'START Thinking About a New U.S. Force Structure', *Arms Control Today* 18 (July/August 1988), 12–13. 'The first indicator [sic] of a Soviet breakthrough' in ASW, moreover, 'could be the loss of a U.S. submarine'; Panel on the Future of Strategic Systems, *Securing Strategic Stability* p. 37.

19. As Robert McFarlane has argued, while SLBMs are survivable and

can reach their targets rapidly, 'the difficulties in discrete, dispersed targeting inherent in any multiple-warhead missile, when combined with the problematic communications characteristics of submarines, make this a poor weapon of choice. If the goal is high confidence of assuring rapid initial response as well as measured responsiveness through the course of the battle, SLBMs do not fill the bill'. McFarlane, 'Effective Strategic Policy', *Foreign Affairs* 67 (Fall 1988), 41–2. See also Michael Altfeld and Stephen Cimbala, 'Trident II for Prompt Counterforce: A Critical Assessment', *Defense Analysis*, December 1987; Francis P. Hoeber and Robert M. Dannenberg, 'Are Land-Based Missiles Obsolete?', *Journal of Contemporary Studies* VI (Autumn 1983), 25–44; Michael Nacht, *The Age of Vulnerability: Threats to the Nuclear Stalemate* (Washington, DC: The Brookings Institution, 1985), pp. 61–2; Bobbitt, *Democracy and Deterrence*, pp. 181–90; and Desmond Ball, 'U.S. Strategic Forces: How Would They Be Used?', *International Security* 7 (Winter 1982–83), 48–50.

20. Lt. Col. Fred J. Reule, USAF, *et al.*, *Dynamic Stability: A New Concept for Deterrence* (Maxwell AFB, AL: Air University Press, September 1987), p. 7.

21. James L. George, 'The "Two-Track" Dilemma in the START Negotiations', *Strategic Review* XVI (Winter 1988), 40; Alexander H. Flax, 'The Impact of New Technologies and Noncentral Systems on Offensive Force Reductions', in *Reykjavik and Beyond: Deep Reductions in Strategic Nuclear Arsenals and the Future Direction of Arms Control* (Washington, DC: National Academy of Sciences, 1988), p. 30.

22. A number of analysts have recognised these dangers. See Brent Scowcroft, John Deutch and R. James Woolsey, 'Come and Get Us', *The New Republic*, 18 April 1988, p. 16; James L. George, 'The "Two-Track" Dilemma'; and Henry Kissenger, 'START: A Dangerous Rush for an Agreement', *Washington Post*, 24 April 1988, p. D7.

23. The Discussion Group on Strategic Policy, *Deterring Through the Turn of the Century* (Washington, DC: Center for Strategic and International Studies, January 1989), p. 4. Scowcroft resigned from the study when he accepted the post as George Bush's national security adviser.

24. See, for example, Michael Getler, 'A Mobile Milestone: Bush can Build a Stable, Survivable Nuclear Force', *Washington Post*, 26 March 1989, p. D1.

25. *Report of the President's Commission on Strategic Forces* (Washington, DC, April 1983), p. 15.

26. Getler, 'A Mobile Milestone'; Paul Mann, 'Defense Leaders Line Up with Scowcroft on Midgetman and Carry-Hard Basing', *Aviation Week and Space Technology*, 6 February 1989, pp. 23–4; and CSIS Discussion Group on Strategic Policy, *Deterring Through the Turn of the Century*, pp. 7–10.

27. On the case for silo-basing SICBMs, see Jan Lodal, 'SICBM Yes, HML No', *International Security* 12 (Autumn 1987); Sidney D. Drell, 'Good Start on START Promises Reductions in Long-Range Missiles',

San Jose Mercury-News 17 April 1988, p. 7-C; and my 'Midgetman and Arms Control', *Defense Analysis* 4 (No. 2, 1988).

28. Flournoy, 'START Thinking', p. 11; Bennendijk, 'START: A Preliminary Assessment', pp. 14–15; and Bobbitt, *Democracy and Deterrence*, p. 165. McFarlane has pointed out a serious flaw in the concept of downloading Minuteman IIIs to single-warhead configuration: the missile has the capability to carry three warheads, and verification of the downloading would require extremely intrusive measures. The Soviets would also be sure to insist on single-warhead counting rules for missiles they would claim to download, and as he notes, 'even if agreed, the larger throw-weight of Soviet missiles would give them an enormous breakout advantage, were they to cheat by reverting to multiple warheads'. The prospect of 1000 SS-18s lying around, ostensibly carrying one warhead apiece but with the capability to carry ten, is disquieting, to say the least. McFarlane makes the obvious conclusion – both sides can best verify de-MIRVing by introducing wholly new missiles, such as the Midgetman and SS-25. He also notes that silo-basing Midgetman could be an effective interim, cost-saving option. McFarlane, 'Effective Strategic Policy', pp. 45–6.

29. See Barry R. Schneider, 'U.S. National Security Implications of Superhard ICBM Silos', in Schneider, Colin S. Gray and Keith B. Payne, *Missiles for the Nineties: ICBMs and Strategic Policy* (Boulder, CO: Westview Press, 1984), pp. 42–60. Joshua Epstein, *The 1988 Defense Budget* (Washington, DC: The Brookings Institution, 1987), p. 29, calculates that silos able to withstand 50 000 psi of overpressure (as opposed to current levels around 2000 psi) would require the Soviets to triple the accuracy of warheads just to maintain the same kill probabilities they now enjoy.

30. Stephen Weiner, 'Systems and Technology', and Ashton B. Carter, 'BMD Applications: Performance and Limitations', in Carter and David N. Schwartz (ed.), *Ballistic Missile Defense* (Washington, DC: The Brookings Institution, 1984), pp. 49–181.

31. Robert Einhorn, 'The Emerging START Agreement', *Survival* 30 (September-October 1988), 397. Einhorn also disputes the claim that once the Midgetmen were mobile, limitations on their movement would render them vulnerable; currently agreed-upon rules provide for more than enough space for Midgetmen to roam, both in peacetime and in crisis situations; Einhorn, pp. 397–9.

32. Robert Jervis, *The Illogic of American Nuclear Strategy* (Ithaca: Cornell University Press, 1984), pp. 168–9.

33. Tom Shanker, 'U.S. Plays Cloak-and-Boxcar', *Chicago Tribune*, 14 June 1989.

34. See the 'International Media' summary in US Air Force, *Current News*, Early Bird, 14 June 1989, p. 15.

35. Richard Nixon, 'Letter to the Editor', *Foreign Affairs* 68 (Summer 1989), 162. See also Nixon, 'American Foreign Policy: The Bush Agenda', *Foreign Affairs* (America and the World, 1988/89).

36. R. James Woolsey, 'The Future of NATO's Deterrent Posture: An

American Perspective', *Atlantic Community Quarterly* 26 (Summer 1988), 126–8.

37. CSIS Discussion Group on Strategic Policy, *Deterring Through the Turn of the Century*, p. 4; CSIS Panel on the Future of Strategic Systems, *Securing Strategic Stability*, p. 32.
38. Bobbitt, *Democracy and Deterrence*, p. 167.
39. Maj. G. E. Myers, 'A Force Structure for Stability', in Reule, *Dynamic Deterrence*, p. 85.
40. James Rubin, 'Getting Off to the Right START', *Defense News*, 16 January 1989, p. 28, argues that 'Cutting Soviet barrage capacity also pays a dividend for overall survivability, because barrage attacks can also theoretically threaten submarines in open ocean areas and bombers shortly after leaving the bases'.
41. It must be admitted that the prospect of having to employ 30 000 or more nuclear warheads in an attack – a number that might be powerful enough actually to split the earth in half, or at a minimum to wipe it clean of civilisation – must encourage caution in even the most hard-hearted Kremlin planner. See also Edward Warner and David Ochmanek, *Next Moves: An Arms Control Agenda for the 1990s* (New York: Council on Foreign Relations, 1989), p. 59; and CSIS Panel on the Future of Strategic Systems, *Securing Strategic Stability*, p. 23.
42. Jack Mendelsohn, 'START is a Good Beginning', *Arms Control Today* 18 (May 1988), 10.
43. Robert Jervis, 'The Nuclear Revolution and the Common Defense', *Political Science Quarterly* 101 (1986), 702, stresses the importance of this result.
44. See, for example, Michael Howard, 'On Fighting a Nuclear War', *International Security* 5 (Spring 1981), 16–17; and Richard K. Betts, *Nuclear Blackmail and Nuclear Balance* (Washington, DC: The Brookings Institution, 1987).
45. Einhorn, 'The Emerging START Agreement', p. 396. See also Warner and Ochmanek, *Next Moves*, esp. pp. 17–23 and 63; and Max M. Kampelman, 'START: Completing the Task', *Washington Quarterly* 12 (Summer 1989).
46. C3I is the most comprehensive term of command, control, communications and intelligence, and is distinguished from C2, which involves only command and control.
47. Bruce G. Blair, *Strategic Command and Control: Redefining the Nuclear Threat* (Washington, DC: Brookings, 1985), pp. 4–5, 89; cf. pp. 83–96; see also Appendix B.
48. Kurt Gottfried and Bruce G. Blair (eds), *Crisis Stability and Nuclear War* (New York: Oxford University Press, 1988), pp. 92–3.
49. Blair, *Strategic Command and Control*, p. 4; on command system vulnerability, see pp. 96–115, 184–207.
50. See 'U.S. Uses '50s Radar to Track '80s Missiles', *Washington Times* 16 June 1989, p. 5.
51. Blair, *Strategic Command and Control*, p. 285.
52. Some have said that C3I can never withstand even a limited nuclear

environment; Bobbitt, *Democracy and Deterrence*, pp. 144–7, for example, contends that C3I vulnerabilities doom a countervailing strategy. New advances in communications technology promise at least partial wartime C3I, however, and in any case this volume accepts only a very limited version of the countervailing strategy, not one that calls for extended war-fighting capabilities.

53. Some propose limited BMD systems to guard against accidental attack. While they might be useful for various purposes, chapter 7 will make a strong case against any significant space-based defensive systems. Moreover, survivable communications can address threats BMD cannot – suitcase bombs, pleasure-boat carried bombs and other non-missile delivery systems.

54. US Senate, Subcommittee on Arms Control, International Law and Organizations, Committee on Foreign Relations, *Hearing on U.S. and Soviet Strategic Doctrine and Military Policies*, 93rd Congress, 2nd session, 4 March 1974 (Washington, DC: GPO, 1974), p. 13; emphasis mine.

55. William Langer Ury and Richard Smoke, *Beyond the Hotline: Controlling a Nuclear Crisis* (Cambridge, MA: Nuclear Negotiation project, Harvard Law School, 1984), p. v.

56. Desmond Ball, 'U.S. Strategic Forces: How Would They Be Used?', *International Security* 7 (Winter 1982/83), 45.

57. Desmond Ball, *et al.*, *Crisis Stability and Nuclear War* (AAAS and Cornell Peace Studies Program, January 1987), p. 25.

58. Warner and Ochmanek, *Next Moves*, p. 2n.

59. Kurt Gottfried and Bruce Blair (eds) (many joint authors), *Crisis Stability and Nuclear War* (New York: Oxford University Press, 1988), pp. 110–11.

60. Ball *et al.*, *Crisis Stability and Nuclear War*, p. 25; Gottfried and Blair, *Crisis Stability and Nuclear War*, p. 111; Bruce G. Blair, *Strategic Command and Control: Redefining the Nuclear Threat* (Washington, DC: The Brookings Institution, 1985), p. 302.

61. Ury and Smoke, *Beyond the Hotline*, p. v.

62. William C. Martel and Paul L. Savage, *Strategic Nuclear War: What the Superpowers Target and Why* (New York: Greenwood Press, 1986), p. 189.

63. See, for example Morton Halperin, *Nuclear Fallacy: Dispelling the Myth of Nuclear Strategy* (Cambridge, MA: Ballinger, 1987), p. 5–20.

64. Stephen Cimbala, *Rethinking Nuclear Strategy* (Wilmington, DE: Scholarly Resources Books, 1988), p. 198.

65. Blair, *Strategic Command and Control*, pp. 288–9.

66. Scott D. Sagan, *Moving Targets: Nuclear Strategy and National Security* (Princeton, NJ: Princeton University Press, 1989), p. 90. See also Halperin, *Nuclear Fallacy*, pp. 76ff.

67. Sagan, *Moving Targets*, p. 157. Sagan's advocacy of a slower, bomber-based counterforce retaliation on pp. 90–2 does seem to contradict this later analysis.

4 Targeting Policy

1. Walter Slocombe, 'The Countervailing Strategy', *International Security* 5 (Spring 1981), 18.
2. The question, as Francis Hoeber phrased it in 1979, is 'whether a capability and doctrine for a U.S. attack on the Soviet (nuclear) forces would enhance deterrence and provide some damage limitation, should deterrence fail'. Hoeber, 'How Little is Enough?', *International Security* 3 (Winter 1978–9), 57. See also Scott D. Sagan, *Moving Targets: Nuclear Strategy and National Security* (Princeton, NJ: Princeton University Press, 1989), pp. 6–7.
3. Desmond Ball, 'Targeting for Strategic Deterrence', *Adelphi Papers* No. 185 (London: International Institute for Strategic Studies, Summer 1983), and the essays by Ball and David Allan Rosenberg in Ball and Jeffrey Richelson (eds), *Strategic Nuclear Targeting* (Ithaca, NY: Cornell University Press, 1986), pp. 35–83.
4. Panel on the Future of Strategic Systems, *Securing Strategic Stability* (Washington, DC: Center for Strategic and International Studies, December 1988), p. 7.
5. Michael Nacht, *The Age of Vulnerability* (Washington, DC: Brookings Institution, 1985), p. 85; Robert Jervis, *The Illogic of American Nuclear Strategy* (Ithaca: Cornell University Press, 1984), p. 24; and Morton Halperin, *Nuclear Fallacy: Dispelling the Myth of Nuclear Strategy* (Cambridge, MA: Ballinger, 1987).
6. Sagan, *Moving Targets*, p. 17.
7. Ball, 'Targeting for Strategic Deterrence', pp. 2–6; Lawrence Freedman, *The Evolution of Nuclear Strategy* (New York: St Martin's Press, 1981), pp. 1–224.
8. Ball, 'Targeting for Strategic Deterrence', p. 6. See also Sagan, *Moving Targets*, p. 11.
9. Nacht, *The Age of Vulnerability*, p. 86. See also David Allan Rosenberg, ' "A Smoking Radiating Ruin at the End of Two Hours": Documents on American Plans for Nuclear War with the Soviet Union, 1954–1955', *International Security* 6 (Winter 1981–82), 3–38. Benjamin S. Lambeth and Kevin N. Lewis, 'Economic Targeting in Nuclear War: U.S. and Soviet Approaches', *Orbis* 27 (Spring 1983), 127–50, stress the importance of industrial targets during this phase.
10. Sagan, *Moving Targets*, pp. 20–2.
11. Ball, 'Targeting for Strategic Deterrence', p. 8.
12. Scott Sagan refers to the 'stunning inflexibility' of this plan, which called for retaliation against all Sino-Soviet bloc nations 'on an utterly massive scale'. Sagan, *Moving Targets*, p. 24.
13. Quoted in Ball, 'Targeting for Strategic Deterrence', pp. 9–10.
14. See the outstanding essays by David Allan Rosenberg and Desmond Ball in Ball and Jeffrey Richelson (eds), *Strategic Nuclear Targeting* (Ithaca, NY: Cornell University Press, 1986), pp. 35–83. Part and parcel with the continued shift to counterforce came a gradual public rejection of that concept, and McNamara publicly declared that Assured Destruction (with its implication of countervalue targeting)

was the only proper strategy. Michael Nacht has noted the secret nature of the conversion: 'In retrospect it was clear by 1963 that declaratory policy and actual guidelines for nuclear weapon use as translated into war plans conveyed very different impressions of where a U.S. nuclear strike would hit. The former stressed countervalue targets – population – and the latter stressed counterforce targets'. Nacht, *The Age of Vulnerability*, p. 88.

15. Sagan, *Moving Targets*, pp. 12–13.
16. Ball, 'Targeting for Strategic Deterrence', p. 12.
17. Ball, 'Targeting for Strategic Deterrence', pp. 13–15; Freedman, *Evolution of Nuclear Strategy*, pp. 225–56.
18. Jervis, *Illogic of American Nuclear Strategy*, p. 65. Indeed, the notion of damage limitation was a form of counterforce in disguise. As noted, it called for strikes against Soviet nuclear forces in case of war; the only difference was that it appeared to favour *retaliation* against Soviet war-making facilities rather than pre-emption of them. But since US nuclear strategy was always defensive in nature, and the counterforce options discussed were forwarded in such a context, the distinction between general counterforce and post-attack damage limiting counterforce was, at best, rhetorical. Michael Intriligator noted in 1968 that McNamara merely appended a renewed emphasis on assured destruction (countervalue strikes) onto existing counterforce, damage-limitation strategies. 'The counterforce strategy', Intriligator concluded, 'is one of damage limitation'. 'The Debate Over Missile Strategy: Targets and Rates of Fire', *Orbis* 11 (Winter 1968), 1140.
19. Ball, 'Targeting for Strategic Deterrence', pp. 17–20; Freedman, *Evolution of Nuclear Strategy*, pp. 331–71.
20. These lists betray an apparent contradiction: if US targeting strategy emphasised counterforce targets, why did so many countervalue targets remain? Two analysts commented as late as 1986 that the SIOP 'to this day appears to be dominated by urban-industrial targets'. William C. Martel and Paul L. Savage, *Strategic Nuclear War: What the Superpowers Target and Why* (New York: Greenwood Press, 1986), p. 175.

   As noted in chapter 1, dissonance continues to exist between US nuclear strategy and procurement policy and US target lists. It can be fairly claimed that US policy has become a counterforce one to the greatest degree allowed by technology, and that the SIOP seems to have become increasingly counterforce-dominated over a number of years. This chapter, moreover, recognises that many value targets remain on the SIOP, that counterforce is not an all-or-nothing proposition; its argument is for abandoning any residual targeting of nuclear weapons.
21. PD-59, influenced by the Nuclear Targeting Policy Review (NTPR) of 1978–79, sought to increase Soviet apprehension by targeting food supplies, military units facing the PRC in the East, and additional political control institutions. Importantly, it de-emphasised targeting Soviet economic recovery assets, called for targeting of mobile Soviet command and control and weapons systems, and authorised NUWEP-

2, which also decreased the priority given to hitting Soviet economic recovery potential. This shift away from targeting recovery assets marked a significant change from pre-Carter doctrine.

22. Thus Michael Nacht has concluded that flexible response options 'were extensions of the basic ideas long embedded in actual war plans. The modifications of Schlesinger and Brown were incremental ... rather than significant departures from existing practice'. Nacht, *The Age of Vulnerability*, p. 90. See also Freedman, *Evolution of Nuclear Strategy* pp. 372–400.

23. Sagan, *Moving Targets*, pp. 44–8.

24. See Desmond Ball, 'The Development of the SIOP, 1960–1983', in Ball and Richelson, p. 81; and Ball, 'Targeting for Strategic Deterrence', p. 26. See also Study Group on the Future of Strategic Systems, *Securing Strategic Stability* (Washington, DC: Center for Strategic and International Studies, December 1988), p. 18.

25. Carl H. Builder, 'Strategic Conflict Without Nuclear Weapons' (Santa Monica, CA: RAND Corporation, April 1983), p. 33.

26. Desmond Ball, 'U.S. Strategic Forces: How Would They Be Used?', *International Security* 7 (Winter 1982–83), 44–7.

27. Bobbitt, *Democracy and Deterrence*, p. 8.

28. Andrew C. Goldberg, 'Offense and Defense in the Postnuclear System', *Washington Quarterly* XX (Summer 1988); Robert Jervis, *The Ilogic of American Nuclear Strategy* (Ithaca: Cornell University Press, 1984), p. 71.

29. On START, see Hans Bennendijk, 'START: A Preliminary Assessment', *Washington Quarterly* 11 (Autumn 1988); Michael Mazarr, 'On Strategic Nuclear Policy', *SAIS Review* 9 (Winter-Spring 1989); Brent Scowcroft, James Woolsey and John Deutch, 'Come and Get Us', *The New Republic*, 18 April 1988, p. 16; Walter Slocombe, 'Force Posture Consequences of the START Treaty', *Survival* 30 (September-October 1988); and Strobe Talbot, 'Why START Stopped', *Foreign Affairs* 67 (Autumn 1988).

30. This analysis is supported by the official US government estimate of surviving warheads needed. The MX programme was based on an imputed need for 1000 warheads to retaliate just against Soviet silos; Bobbitt, *Democracy and Deterrence*, p. 159. Under START a US planner might not even have that many retaliatory warheads, and meanwhile Soviet strategic modernisation would increase US retaliatory requirements through the deployment of mobile missiles and other systems.

31. See Peter Claussen *et al.*, *In Search of Stability: An Assessment of New U.S. Nuclear Forces* (Cambridge, MA: Union of Concerned Scientists, 1986), pp. 15–21; Congressional Budget Office, *Modernizing U.S. Strategic Offensive Forces: Costs, Effects, and Alternatives* (Washington, DC: CBO, 1987) pp. 57–8.

32. See Bruce G. Blair, *Strategic Command and Control: Redefining the Nuclear Threat* (Washington, DC: Brookings Institution, 1985).

33. McNamara recognised as early as 1964 that 'as time goes on and the Soviet Union continues to harden its missile sites and continues to

build missile-firing submarines, it will become increasingly difficult to destroy a substantial portion of the residual forces' in a retaliation. McNamara, FY 1965 statement, 27 January 1964; quoted in Intriligator, 'The Debate Over Missile Strategy', p. 1144. See also Sagan, *Moving Targets*, pp. 25–6, 28–9 and 32–3 for evidence that US planners recognised all along that their counterforce strikes would be imperfect.

34. Michael Brower, 'Targeting Soviet Mobile Missiles: Prospects and Implications', *Survival*, 31 (September-October 1989), 433–4. See also Robert R. Ropelewski, 'USAF Backpedaling on B-2 Relocatable Target Mission', *Armed Forces Journal International*, July 1989, p. 14. Center for Strategic and International Studies, *Securing Strategic Stability* (Washington, DC: CSIS, 1988), pp. 34–7. This point has been implicitly acknowledged by the Defense Department, which has gradually de-emphasised the B-2s role of targeting SRTs, knowing it cannot do the job.

35. Panel on the Future of Strategic Systems, *Securing Strategic Stability*, pp. 10–11.

36. It is unlikely that strategic defences will be deployed, however, for at least two reasons: a START accord will probably ban large-scale defences, and US budget pressures will prevent them. This avenue of escaping from the shortcomings of counterforce will therefore probably not prove feasible.

37. For an extended argument on that score, see Charles-Philippe David, *Debating Counterforce: A Conventional Approach in a Nuclear Age* (Boulder: Westview Press, 1987).

38. Study Group on the Future of Strategic Systems, *Securing Strategic Stability*, p. 10.

39. Purely industrial targeting is of questionable credibility and utility; Ball, 'U.S. Strategic Forces', pp. 52–5, and Lambeth and Lewis, 'Economic Targeting in Nuclear War', pp. 148–9. The last two analysts do approve of counter-military/industrial targeting, however, which would be part of counterpower.

40. Defense Department and CIA estimates have placed these numbers as high as 1500 to 2000; Sagan, *Moving Targets*, pp. 51–2.

41. Ball, 'Targeting for Strategic Deterrence', pp. 31–2; Colin Gray, 'Targeting Problems for Central War', in Ball and Richelson, *Strategic Nuclear Targeting*, pp. 183–6; and Beres, 'Tilting Toward Thanatos', p. 30. Jervis, *Illogic of American Nuclear Strategy*, pp. 119–20, makes the same arguments, and also notes that, for the same reason, the countervailing strategy's targeting of leadership contradicts its express intention to fight an extended war.

42. Bernard Brodie, *Strategy in the Missile Age* (Princeton, NJ: Princeton University Press, 1978), p. 136.

43. David T. Cattal and George H. Quester, 'Ethnic Targeting: Some Bad Ideas', in Ball and Richelson, *Strategic Nuclear Targeting*, pp. 267–84; Quester, 'Ethnic Targeting: A Bad Idea Whose Time Has Come', *Journal of Strategic Studies* 5 (June 1982). It should be pointed out that

counterpower targeting, by annihilating Soviet military deployments in the republics, might achieve virtually the same effects without the problems inherent in targeting specifically for ethnic reasons.

44. See Richelson, 'The Dilemmas of Counterpower Targeting', in Ball and Richelson, p. 163, and Hoeber, 'How Little is Enough', p. 58. Other articles that discuss counterpower strategies include Bernard Albert, 'Constructive Counterpower', *Orbis* 20 (Summer 1976), 343–66; Bruce Russett, 'Assured Destruction of What? A Countercombatant Alternative to Nuclear MADness', *Public Policy* XXII (Spring 1974), 121–38; and Russett, 'Sensible Deterrence as Arms Control', in *American Security in a Changing World* (ed.), Joseph Goldman (Washington, DC: University Press of America, 1987).

45. Jervis, *Illogic of American Nuclear Strategy*, p. 139.

46. Stephen Cimbala's notion of a 'sensitive target base' sheds light on these ideas. As he writes, 'A sensitive target base/attack force relationship means that small changes in the attacking force will make important differences in the prelaunch survivability of the defending force'. Cimbala, *Nuclear War and Nuclear Strategy: Unfinished Business* (New York: Greenwood Press, 1987), p. 31. In this case, the sensitive relationship is between an attacker's reserve force and a defender's retaliation. Counterforce increases that sensitivity by establishing the need for thousands of retaliatory warheads; counterpower would render the balance very insensitive.

47. See, for example Stephen Cimbala, *Rethinking Nuclear Strategy* (Wilmington, DE: Scholarly Resources, 1988); and Leon Wieseltier, 'When Deterrence Fails', *Foreign Affairs* 63 (Spring 1985), 827–47; Ball, 'U.S. Strategic Forces', pp. 44–7; Cimbala (ed.), *Strategic War Termination* (New York: Praeger, 1986). Limiting a conflict and promoting rational thinking during the early stages of one was seen as one of the primary goals of counterforce; Intriligator, 'The Debate Over Missile Strategy', p. 1141. Counterpower would preserve this ability by offering various non-urban targets for early destruction.

48. Bernard Brodie, the father of much of the theory of nuclear deterrence, once remarked that 'the main war goal up to the beginning of a strategic nuclear exchange' was 'to terminate it as quickly as possible and with the least amount of damage possible – on both sides'. Quoted in Michael Howard, 'On Fighting a Nuclear War', *International Security* 5 (Spring 1981), 4. On termination and targeting, see George Quester, 'War Termination and Nuclear Targeting Strategy', in Ball and Richelson, *Strategic Nuclear Targeting*, pp. 285–306.

49. Blair, *Strategic Command and Control*, pp. 289–95; Sagan, *Moving Targets*, pp. 21, 24, 90–7.

50. Bruce Russett, 'Extended Deterrence with Nuclear Weapons: Now Necessary, How Acceptable?', *The Review of Politics* 50 (Spring 1988), 298, 300.

51. Russett, 'Extended Deterrence', p. 282.

52. This contention provided much of the motivation for counterforce; see Colin Gray, 'Nuclear Strategy and the Case for a Theory of Victory',

International Security 4 (Summer 1979), and Gray and Keith Payne, 'Victory is Possible', *Foreign Policy* No. 39 (Summer 1980).
53.   Thus Colin Gray has concluded: 'These three goals – victory denial, defeating the enemy, and winning . . . all require a serious U.S. effort to achieve a worthwhile measure of damage limitation'. Gray, 'Targeting Problems for Central War', pp. 174–5. Michael R. May's 'Some Advantages of a Counterforce Deterrence', *Orbis* 14 (Summer 1970) is a persuasive case for that strategy. May argues that 'if a nuclear war occurs, what we will want to do most immediately will be to destroy our opponent's ability to wage war further . . . the targets comprising his residual military capability would assume pre-eminent importance, to him as well as to us' (pp. 279–80). See also Sagan, *Moving Targets*, pp. 49–50, 67–9, 80.
54.   Beres, 'Tilting Toward Thanatos', pp. 27–9; Jervis, *The Illogic of American Nuclear Strategy* pp. 105–9.
55.   Howard, 'On Fighting a Nuclear War', p. 10.
56.   Department of Defense, *Soviet Military Power 1987* (Washington, DC, 1987), p. 18.
57.   Gray, 'Targeting Problems for Central War', pp. 187–8.
58.   Nacht, *The Age of Vulnerability*, p. 93. An aide to McNamara once reportedly said that 'there could be no such thing as primary retaliation against military targets after an enemy attack'; Ball, 'Targeting for Strategic Deterrence', p. 12.
59.   George Quester, 'The Difficult Logic of Terminating a Nuclear War', in Cimbala (ed.), *Strategic War Termination*, p. 71.
60.   Richard Betts wonders 'whether it is wise to threaten Soviet ICBMs even under the logic of the countervailing strategy. The rationale for doing so is rather convoluted. Escalation control might argue against a threat large enough to provoke launch on warning'. Betts, *Cruise Missiles and U.S. Policy* (Washington, DC: Brookings Institution, 1982), p. 18.
61.   Bobbitt, *Democracy and Deterrence* p. 174.
62.   Sagan, *Moving Targets*, pp. 52, 77.
63.   See Bruce Blair, *Strategic Command and Control: Redefining the Nuclear Threat* (Washington, DC: Brookings Institution, 1985), pp. 219–20.
64.   Gray, 'Issues in Strategic Nuclear Targeting', p. 188.
65.   Panel on the Future of Strategic Systems, *Securing Strategic Stability*, pp. 20, 35.
66.   Damage limitation, therefore, is only contemplated for limited conflicts; the prospect of it is surrendered completely for major nuclear war.
67.   Ball, 'Targeting for Strategic Deterrence', p. 28.
68.   Goldberg, 'Offense and Defense', p. 62.
69.   Jervis, *Illogic of American Nuclear Strategy*, p. 114, contends that the speed of OMT retaliation is irrelevant; 'cruise missiles, if not gravity bombs, should be sufficient'. Initially, this contradicts his argument that OMT targets move, which would recommend prompt strikes and retargeting abilities. Second, the more capable American retaliatory assets, the more credible the threat.

70. Russett, 'Extended Deterrence', p. 300. Sagan, *Moving Targets* p. 92 argues the opposite, but he assumes that the United States would want to target all OMT; it need not, and as we have seen counterpower, since it does not demand damage limitation, is an inherent more warhead-flexible strategy than counterforce.
71. There are, however, reasons to doubt how quickly this would happen; Sagan, *Moving Targets*, pp. 61–6.

5 Extended Deterrence

1. This essay will use the term 'flexible response' rather than 'extended deterrence' simply because the former is most often associated with NATO policy. In terms of overall US deterrent strategies, however, the US nuclear guarantee is, of course, a form of extended deterrence.
2. Daniel Charles, *Nuclear Planning in NATO* (Cambridge, MA: Ballinger, 1987), p. 15 explains that McNamara viewed flexible response as a way to deter war, if necessary, 'without resorting to the use of nuclear weapons'.
3. The relevance of this fact can be traced back for decades – one observer has commented on the 'deep underlying tension between [Secretary of Defense] McNamara's statements on mutual nuclear deterrence and NATO military doctrine'. Scott D. Sagan, *Moving Targets: Nuclear Strategy and National Security* (Princeton, NJ: Princeton University Press, 1989), p. 40. The chief statement of this thesis, and the most important, was made by Henry Kissinger in 1979. See Kissinger, 'The Future of NATO', *Washington Quarterly* 2 (1979).
4. Eckhard Lubkemeier, 'Current NATO Strategy and No-First-Use', in Frank Barnaby and Terence Hopmann (eds), *Rethinking the Nuclear Weapons Dilemma in Europe* (London: Macmillan, 1988), pp. 120–2.
5. Philip Bobbitt, *Democracy and Deterrence: The History and Future of Nuclear Strategy* (New York: St Martin's Press, 1988), pp. 107–8.
6. Bruce G. Blair, *The Command and Control of U.S. Nuclear Forces* (Washington, DC: Brookings Institution, 1983). See especially his chapter on flexible response.
7. Paul Bracken, *The Command and Control of Nuclear Forces* (New Haven: Yale University Press, 1983), pp. xx–ff.
8. Leon V. Sigal, 'No First Use and NATO's Nuclear Posture', in John Steinbruner and Leon Sigal (eds), *Alliance Security: NATO and the No-First-Use Question* (Washington, DC: Brookings, 1983), p. 111.
9. John B. Harris, 'From Flexible Response to No Early First Use', in Barnaby and Hopmann (eds), *Rethinking the Nuclear Weapons Dilemma*, pp. 96–101.
10. Fred Iklé, 'Nuclear Strategy: Can There Be a Happy Ending?', *Journal of Strategic Studies* 9 (December 1986), 51.
11. Cimbala, 'Extended Deterrence and Nuclear Escalation: Options in Europe', *Armed Forces and Society* 15 (Autumn 1988), 6 and 27.
12. Paul Warnke, 'The Illusion of NATO's Nuclear Defense', in Andrew Pierre (ed.), *Nuclear Weapons in Europe* (New York: Council on Foreign Relations, 1984), p. 80.

13. Paul Bracken, *The Command and Control of Nuclear Forces* (New Haven: Yale University Press, 1983), pp. 163–4. Bruce Russett agrees that this threat of 'inadvertent' nuclear response 'is in fact what the NATO nuclear deterrent has become, partly by design and partly without intent or general awareness'. Russett, 'Extended Deterrence With Nuclear Weapons: How Necessary, How Acceptable?', *The Review of Politics* 50 (Spring 1988) 294.
14. Russett, 'Extended Deterrence', pp. 294–5.
15. Sagan, *Moving Targets*, p. 74. See also Russett, 'Extended Deterrence', pp. 295–6; Earl Ravenal, 'Counterforce and Alliance: The Ultimate Connection', *International Security* 6 (Spring 1982); and Bobbitt, *Democracy and Deterrence*, pp. 10, 99–109. George Quester agrees that 'the problem of achieving an extended nuclear deterrence to shield West Germany' and the rest of Europe is 'probably the single problem which, more than anything else, activates the entire strategic discussion'. Quester, review of Charles-Philippe David, *Debating Counterforce*, in *International Journal* XLIII (Autumn 1988), 685–6.
16. George H. Quester, *The Future of Nuclear Deterrence* (Lexington, MA: Lexington Books, 1986), pp. 84–93.
17. Quester, *The Future of Deterrence*, p. 100.
18. Richard Betts, 'Compound Deterrence vs. No-First-Use: What's Wrong is What's Right', *Orbis* 28 (Winter 1985), 702.
19. Bobbitt, *Democracy and Deterrence*, p. 282.
20. Earl Ravenal, 'Coupling and Decoupling: The Prospects for Extended Deterrence', in Barnaby and Hopmann, *Rethinking the Nuclear Weapons Dilemma*, p. 59, points out that although a 64 per cent chance of retaliation might deter the Soviets, 'those odds will probably not convince the allies of their protection'.
21. P. Terence Hopmann and Frank Barnaby, 'Rethinking the Nuclear Weapons Dilemma in Europe', in Hopmann and Barnaby (eds), *Rethinking the Nuclear Weapons Dilemma*, pp. 1–2.
22. Richard K. Betts, 'NATO Deterrence Doctrine: No Way Out', CISA Working Paper No. 51 (UCLA: Center for International and Strategic Affairs, June 1985), pp. 65–6.
23. See the testimony of Phillip Karber, 'Soviet Implementation of the Gorbachev Unilateral Military Reductions: Implications for Conventional Arms Control in Europe', statement to the House Armed Services Committee, 14 March 1989, pp. 5, 8, 11.
24. See especially John J. Mearsheimer, 'Why the Soviets Can't Win Quickly in Central Europe', *International Security* 7 (Summer 1982).
25. Helmut Sonnenfeldt, 'The European Pillar: The American View', *Adelphi Papers* No. 235 (London: IISS: Spring 1989), p. 97.
26. Demographics do pose a problem for the Alliance; as military forces on both sides are reduced, however, and as emerging technologies and territorial defence concepts emerge as useful adjuncts to NATO's conventional posture, demographic shortfalls – from which the USSR also suffers – should not prove crippling.
27. Gert Krell, Thomas Risse-Koppe, and Hans-Joachim Schmidt, 'The

No-First-Use Question in West Germany', in Steinbruner and Sigal, *Alliance Security*, p. 156.

28. Pierre Lellouche, 'Nuclear Deterrence and European Security: Towards a Not So "Happy Ending"?', *Journal of Stratetic Studies* 9 (December 1986), 67. See also Harris, 'From Flexible Response to No Early First Use'.

29. 'After Lance', *Economist*, 11–17 March 1989, p. 13.

30. Jack Mendelsohn, 'Gorbachev's Preemptive Concession', *Arms Control Today* 19 (March 1989), 14. See also Stephen Szabo, 'European Opinion After the Missiles', *Survival* 27 (November-December 1985).

31. Bobbitt, *Democracy and Deterrence*, p. 117.

32. 'After Lance', p. 13.

33. Bobbitt, *Democracy and Deterrence*, p. 157.

34. Andrew Goldberg, 'Offense and Defense in the Postnuclear System', *Washington Quarterly* 11 (Spring 1988), 61.

35. Sonnenfeldt, 'The European Pillar', p. 94.

36. Perhaps the strongest argument for this proposition is made by a Greek scholar, Panayiotis Ifestos, in *Nuclear Strategy and European Security Dilemmas* (Aldershot: Gower, 1988). Ifestos recognises that the US guarantee is fading, but contends that it is irreplaceable in any case. 'As European leaders remind us time and again', he contends, 'Europe is not in a position ... to substitute the American nuclear guarantee with a European nuclear deterrent force'. The Soviet reaction to European independence, Ifestos argues, 'would undoubtedly be automatically negative if not actively hostile' (p. 324). He concludes regarding European defence co-operation that all that can be said is 'this is a matter fraught with difficulties which should be handled with extreme caution' (p. 392). This may be true today; the argument of this essay is that several years from now it may not.

37. Lellouche, 'Nuclear Deterrence and European Security', pp. 68–9. See also the review of Lellouche's recent book by David S. Yost, 'Radical Change in French Defense Policy?', in *Survival* 28 (January-February 1986), 53–68.

38. Gregory Treverton, 'Managing NATO's Nuclear Dilemma', *International Security* 7 (Autumn 1983), 115.

39. Ifestos, *Nuclear Strategy and European Security Dilemmas*, pp. 383–4. See also his comments quoted in n. 22 above.

40. Lawrence Freedman, 'U.S. Nuclear Weapons in Europe: Symbols, Strategy, and Force Structure', in Pierre (ed.), *Nuclear Weapons in Europe*, p. 51.

41. Bertram, 'Europe's Security Dilemmas', pp. 953–4.

42. Gregory Treverton, 'Managing NATO's Nuclear Business: The Lessons of INF', in Barnaby and Hopmann, *Rethinking the Nuclear Weapons Dilemma*, pp. 15–17.

43. At least not as the result of well-thought out, declaratory policy. In the 1960s, pilots from Germany and other NATO states sat in the cockpits of quick response aircraft on NATO runways, with only a rifle-armed sentry present to stop them should they attempt to take off. Sagan, *Moving Targets*, p. xx.

44. Extended deterrence is in fact a two-part task: deterrence of Soviet conventional and nuclear attacks on NATO; Lawrence Freedman, 'I Exist, Therefore I Deter', *International Security* 13 (Summer 1988), 191. Indeed, as long ago as May 1962, McNamara, when giving NATO defence ministers in a confidential session on US flexibile response strategy, distinguished between US escalation in response to Soviet nuclear and conventional attack; Sagan, *Moving Targets*, p. 37.

45. Sagan, *Moving Targets* p. 81. The French have recently cut back on their nuclear strike forces, eliminating two strike squadrons of aircraft for budgetary reasons; Giovanni de Briganti, 'French Eliminate 2 Nuclear Strike Squadrons to Slow Defense Costs', *Defense News*, 12 June 1989, p. 12. Other planned modernisations, however, will continue.

46. Leon Sigal is more sanguine about the prospects for an independent nuclear deterrent; see Sigal, 'No-First-Use and NATO's Nuclear Posture', pp. 119–27. See also Edward A. Kolodziej, 'British-French Nuclearization and European Denuclearization: Challenge for American Policy', *Atlantic Community Quarterly* 26 (Autumn-Winter 1988), 318, who foresees a 'decreasing European dependence on the United States' achieved in part through the 'gradual emergence of a European nuclear deterrent'.

47. Bobbitt argues that nuclear multipolarity is dangerous; see *Democracy and Deterrence*, pp. 19–218, 283. He fears that 'the recission of extended deterrence would yield multipolarity with its profound and malignant effects on central stability (p. 273). This volume, however, does not contemplate nuclear multipolarity; mine is not Bobbitt's image of a 'third nuclear superpower' (p. 144) but only of an increasingly assertive NATO within a bipolar framework – at least for the time being.

48. Treverton, 'Managing NATO's Nuclear Dilemma', p. 115.

49. Fred Iklé, 'Nuclear Strategy: Can There Be a Happy Ending?', p. 51.

50. Edward Luttwak, 'The Alliance, Without an Enemy', *New York Times*, 3 February 1989.

51. See Market Opinion Research, Marttila and Kiley, Inc., *et al.*, *Americans Talk Security*, Full Survey Report, no publication location; No. 6, June 1988, and No. 9, October 1988; and *Old Doctrines vs. New Threats: Citizens Look at Defense Spending and National Security* (Washington, DC: Roosevelt Center for American Policy Studies, April 1989).

52. Theresa Hitchens, 'NATO Shifts Philosophy on Short-Range Weapons', *Defense News*, 12 June 1989, p. 1.

53. See, for example, the analysis in International Institute of Strategic Studies, *Strategic Survey 1989–90* (London: IISS, 1989).

54. Karber, testimony before House Armed Services Committee, p. 34.

55. See Keith A. Dunn, 'NATO's Enduring Value', *Foreign Policy* No. 71 (Summer 1988), 156–75.

56. Freedman, 'I Exist, Therefore I Deter', p. 195.

57. Sonnenfeldt, 'The European Pillar', pp. 92–3.

58. Sonnenfeldt, 'The European Pillar', pp. 103–4.
59. See Phil Williams, 'NATO Crisis Management: Dilemmas and Trade-Offs', *Washington Quarterly* 12 (Spring 1989).

6 Soviet Nuclear Doctrine

1. Harriet Fast Scott and William Scott, *The Armed Forces of the USSR* (Boulder, CO: Westview Press, 1984), pp. 38–9.
2. John M. Caravelli, 'The Role of Surprise and Preemption in Soviet Military Strategy', *International Security Review* VI (Summer 1981), 209–36; Yossef Bodansky, 'The Initial Period of War – Surprise and Special Operations', *Global Affairs* I (Spring 1986); Mark E. Miller, 'Soviet Strategic Thought: the End of an Era?', *International Security Review* V (Winter 1980–81), 491–6. James McConnell has qualified the Soviet dedication to pre-emption by noting that Soviet planners 'value surprise and will do what they can to get it', but that they also place a high value on being able to conduct long-term operations; 'they are counting on stamina', he argues, 'more than surprise and blitzkrieg'. 'SDI the Soviet Investment Debate and Soviet Military Policy', *Strategic Review* XVI (Winter 1988).
3. Albert L. Weeks, 'The Garthoff-Pipes Debate on Soviet Doctrine: Another Perspective', *Strategic Review* XI (Winter 1983), 59; Douglas M. Hart, 'The Hermeneutics of Soviet Military Doctrine', *Washington Quarterly* 17 (Spring 1984), 80–2.
4. Weeks, op. cit., pp. 61–2; Miller, op. cit., pp. 482–91.
5. Fritz Ermarth, 'Contrasts in American and Soviet Strategic Thought', in Derek Leebeart (ed.), *Soviet Military Thinking* (Boston: Allen & Unwin, 1981), p. 56.
6. Jack H. Nunn, 'A Soviet Disarming First Strike: How Real is the Threat?', *Parameters* XIII (March 1983), 69–72; Weeks, op. cit., p. 62.
7. Richard Pipes, 'Why the Soviet Union Thinks it Can Fight and Win a Nuclear War', *Commentary* 64 (July 1977); and Pipes, 'Soviet Strategic Doctrine: Another View', *Strategic Review* X (Autumn 1982), 53.
8. Ibid.
9. This distinction was emphasised by retired Soviet Gen. Valentin Larionov of the Institute of US and Canadian Studies at the Academy of Sciences of the USSR at a presentation to the Center for Strategic and International Studies, Washington, DC, 8 May 1989. Larionov argued that the purposes of the Soviet military build-up and of military doctrine had been different: the former (guided by political priorities) was designed to deter war through preparedness, the latter to provide a plan to win a war if it nevertheless came.
10. Cimbala, op. cit., p. 75.
11. Scott and Scott, op. cit., p. 65; cf pp. 65–8.
12. William Lee and Richard Staar, *Soviet Military Policy Since World War Two* (Stanford, CA: Hoover Institution Press, 1986), pp. 1–9.
13. Pipes, 'Why the Soviet Union Thinks...', op. cit., p. 26.
14. Leon Goure *et al.*, *The Role of Nuclear Forces in Current Soviet*

Strategy (Miami: University of Miami Center for Advanced International Studies, 1974), pp. 65, 3.

15. Ermath, op. cit., pp. 67–8.
16. Paul Dibb, *The Soviet Union: The Incomplete Superpower* (Urbana: University of Illinois Press, 1986), p. 141. Dibb is characterising a view to which he does not subscribe.
17. Nathan Leites, *The Operational Code of the Politburo* (New York: Rand/McGraw Hill, 1951).
18. Singer is quoted in Zbigniew Brzezinski, *Game Plan: How to Conduct the U.S.-Soviet Contest* (New York: Altantic Monthly Press, 1986), p. 20.
19. Seweryn Bialer, *The Soviet Paradox: External Expansion, Internal Decline* (New York: Vintage Books, 1986), p. 263.
20. Ibid, p. 268.
21. Dibb, op. cit., pp. 15–16.
22. This conclusion has been reached by, among others, Stephen Cimbala, who notes that

> It is sometimes said that the Soviets have been given by Marx and Lenin a precise road map of where they are going ... However, what the Kremlin has is comparable to a series of statements that history is on the side of Communism instead of capitalism, statements having important value for mobilizing society and exporting propaganda and statements to be taken seriously at that level. But Marx and Lenin, not having foreseen weapons of mass destruction, could not possibly have provided guidance about the sensitivity of U.S. and Soviet arsenals to one another ... Getting oneself blown up in the process of promoting the revolution is unrevolutionary.

See Cimbala, p. 32.
23. Vernon Aspaturian, 'The Stalinist Legacy in Soviet National Security Decisionmaking', in Jiri Valenta and William Potter (eds), *Soviet Decisionmaking for National Security* (Boston: Allen & Unwin, 1984), p. 31.
24. N. S. Khrushchev, *Khrushchev Remembers* (Boston: Little, Brown & Co., Vol. 1, 1970), p. 11. It should be noted that some analysts see the decision-making of this period as more complex, with institutions possessing more influence relative to Stalin.
25. Pipes, 'Why the Soviet Union Thinks...', op. cit., p. 30.
26. Lt. Gen. A. Yavseyev, 'On Certain Trends in the Changing Substance and Nature of the Initial Period of War', *Military History Journal* No. 11 (1985), 10–20; translated and reprinted in USAF *Soviet Press*, September-October 1986, p. 155.
27. See Avner Yaniv, *Deterrence Without the Bombs: The Politics of Israeli Strategy* (Lexington, MA: Lexington Books, 1987).
28. Andrew C. Goldberg, 'Western Analysts Reappraise Soviet Strategic Policy', *Washington Quarterly* 12 (Spring 1989), 202–3.
29. Pipes, 'Why the Soviet Union Thinks...', op. cit., p. 34.
30. Dibb, op. cit., p. 110.
31. Quoted in Christopher Bellamy, 'What the New Warsaw Pact Military

Doctrine Means for the West', *Janes Defense Weekly*, 5 December 1987, p. 1310.

32. Emphasis mine; Ogarkov, *History Teaches Vigilance*, cited in Michael MccGwire, 'Rethinking War: The Soviets and European Security', *The Brookings Review* 6 (Spring 1988), 9.

33. Raymond Garthoff, 'A Rebuttal', *Strategic Review* X (Autumn 1982), 59. Robert Arnett agrees; see his excellent 'Soviet Attitudes Toward Nuclear War: Do They Really Think They Can Win?', *Journal of Strategic Studies* 2 (September 1979), 172–91.

34. Nunn, op. cit., p. 76.

35. See Martin F. Herz (ed.), *Decline of the West? George F. Kennan and His Critics* (Washington, DC: Ethics and Public Policy Center, 1978), p. 37.

36. Paul Stockton, 'Strategic Stability Between the Superpowers', *Adelphi Papers* 213 (Winter 1986), p. 31; and Andrew C. Goldberg, 'Moscow's New Military Doctrine: A Tamer Bear?' *The World and I*, October 1988, p. 143. Goldberg points out that 'The least contentious issues within Gorbachev's regime lie in the realm of nuclear arms control. Even during the Brezhnev era, it was generally recognized that stalemate – not meaningful superiority – would characterize nuclear relations with the West'. For an analysis of Soviet views on parity, see Robbin F. Laird and Dale R. Herspring, *The Soviet Union and Strategic Arms* (Boulder, CO: Westview Press, 1984).

37. Arthur Alexander, 'Modeling Soviet Defense Decisionmaking', in Potter and Valenta (eds), *Soviet Decisionmaking*, op. cit., p. 20.

38. Stockton, op. cit., p. 32.

39. See Brzezinski, op. cit.

40. Tsuyoshi Hasegawa, 'Soviets on Nuclear War-Fighting', *Problems of Communism* (July-August 1986); Raymond Garthoff, 'Mutual Deterrence and Strategic Arms Limitation in Soviet Policy', *Strategic Review* X (Autumn 1982); Lt. Gen. D. Volkgonov, 'Thus Spake Lenin', *Strategic Review* XIV (Winter 1986), 84–5.

41. Brezhnev quote is cited in Garthoff, 'A Rebuttal', op. cit. See also Dale R. Herspring, 'The Soviet Military in the Aftermath of the 27th party Congress, *Orbis* 30 (Summer 1986), 308–9; John Van Oudenaren, 'Deterrence, War-Fighting, and Soviet Military Doctrine', *Adelphi Papers* 210 (Summer 1986), p. 21.

42. Van Oudenaren, op. cit., pp. 13–15, 20–1; George Quester, 'On the Identification of Real and Pretended Communist Military Doctrine', *Journal of Conflict Resolution* 10 (June 1966); Tom Gervasi, *The Myth of Soviet Military Supremacy* (New York: Harper & Row, 1986), pp. 233–4.

43. Goure *et al.*, op. cit., p. 47. Goure is, of course, a hawkish critic of Soviet nuclear policies, and he would not necessarily agree with the implications drawn from his words.

44. Miller, op. cit., p. 481.

45. Van Oudenaren, op. cit., pp. 16–18.

46. Cimbala, op. cit., pp. 72–3.

47. John Erickson, 'The Soviet View of Deterrence: A General Survey',

Survival XXIV (November/December 1982), 4; Nunn, op. cit., pp. *15–6*.

48. Staar and Lee, op. cit., p. 27.
49. William Scott, 'Another Look at the USSR's "Defensive" Doctrine', *Air Force Magazine* 71 (March 1988).
50. In other words, the military/political side becomes operative *when the war has begun*, whereas political doctrine manages peacetime. Thus, offensive overtones in military/technical strategies say little about the risks that the Soviet Union would actually start a war.
51. Scott, 'Another Look', op. cit.
52. In fact, the West's own tradition of 'just' wars waged on behalf of some 'superior' moral or political ideology ought to restrain our willingness to engage in self-righteous finger-wagging about Soviet international behaviour.
53. Michael MccGwire, *Military Objectives in Soviet Foreign Policy* (Washington, DC: Brookings Institution, 1987), pp. 13–22.
54. David Holloway, 'The View From the Kremlin', *Wilson Quarterly* 7 (Winter 1983), 102–11, agrees, noting that the Soviet military build-up stems from fears dating back to the period of Mongol invasions.
55. MccGwire, op. cit., pp. 37–42.
56. Andrew C. Goldberg, 'Offense and Defense in the Postnuclear Era', *Washington Quarterly* 11 (Spring 1988), 58. See also Philip Bobbitt, *Democracy and Deterrence: The History and Future of Nuclear Strategy* (New York: St Martin's Press, 1988), 147–8.
57. Albert Weeks, 'Soviet Military Doctrine', *Global Affairs* 3 (Winter 1988), 172.
58. Dan and Rebecca Strode, 'Diplomacy and Defense in Soviet National Security Policy', *International Security* (Autumn 1983), 95–6; emphasis mine.
59. Ibid.
60. Rebecca Strode and Colin Grey, 'The Imperial Dimension of Soviet Military Power', *Problems of Communism* 30 (November-December 1981), 1.
61. Dibb, op. cit., p. 153.
62. International Institute of Strategic Studies, *The Military Balance 1986–87* (London: IISS, 1987), pp. 57, 63–4, 142–3.
63. Raymond Garthoff, 'The Soviet Military and SALT', in Potter and Valenta, *Soviet Decisionmaking*, op. cit., p. 147.
64. US Department of Defense, *Soviet Military Power 1987* (Washington: US GPO, March 1987), pp. 26–31.
65. This seems true even though Soviet START negotiators refuse to agree to a reorientation of their warheads to SLBMs and bombers. However, they have been relatively forthcoming in allowing limits on heavy ICBM warheads. The Soviet insistence on allowing mobile missiles, in the face of heavy (if gradually fading) US pressure, clearly speaks to a desire to prevent an attack rather than make one possible. If the Soviets had truly wanted a first-strike force they could have put many more resources into heavy ICBMs, which would have given them a much bigger counterforce arsenal than they now possess. That

they did not emphasises that the desire to fight a nuclear war is not the *primary* Soviet goal.

66. Dennis Ross, 'Rethinking Soviet Strategic Policy', *Journal of Strategic Studies* 1 (May 1978), 3–30.
67. William J. Broad, 'The Secrets of Soviet Star Wars', *New York Times Magazine*, 28 June 1987, p. 22, notes that the CIA believes the US and the USSR are in a 'dead heat' on SDI research.
68. Erickson, op. cit., p. 244.
69. Garthoff, 'Soviet Military and SALT', op. cit., p. 150.
70. See, for example, Les Aspin, 'Soviet Civil Defense: Myth and Reality', *Arms Control Today* 6 (September 1976), 1–4; Fred M. Kaplan, 'The Soviet Civil Defense Myth', *Bulletin of Atomic Scientists*, March and April 1978; and Kaplan, 'Soviet Civil Defense: Some Myths in the Western Debate', *Survival* 20 (May-June 1978), 113–20.
71. 'Civil Defence', *Krasnaya Zvezda*, in *Strategic Review* XIV (Autumn 1986), 94–5, and V. L. Govorov, 'Never to be Forgotten', in *Strategic Review* XV (Summer 1987), give good examples of how the Soviets view civil defence as a simple response to military realities.
72. Cimbala, op. cit., p. 35.
73. See Jack Snyder, 'The Gorbachev Revolution: A Waning of Soviet Expansionism?', *International Security* 12 (Winter 1987–88).
74. Ibid., p. 117.
75. Condoleeza Rice has also stressed the role of Soviet civilian scientists and research scientists in changing Soviet perspectives on security; see 'The Party, the Military, and Decision Authority in the Soviet Union', *World Politics* XI (October 1987), 70.
76. Cited in *Strategic Review* XV (Winter 1987), 87–9.
77. Cited in *Strategic Review* XIV (Winter 1986), 85–6.
78. Quoted in *Strategic Review* XIII (Autumn 1985), 86.
79. Quoted in *Disinformation* No. 7 (Autumn 1987), 7.
80. Quoted in Bellamy, op. cit., p. 1310.
81. Gorbachev's policies were formalised in a series of public pronouncements on the Soviet pledge not to use force against neighbours, presumably including Eastern European countries.
82. *Pravda*, 31 May 1987.
83. Weeks, 'Soviet Nuclear Doctrine'. Weeks also quotes a 'high MPA official' to the effect that 'War to the hilt between communism and capitalism is inevitable . . . The bourgeoisie will have to be put to sleep . . . As soon as their guard is down, we shall smash them with our clenched fist'. Weeks does not mention the date of this statement; only in the footnote do we find that it was made in 1931. It is, to say the least, questionable to apply a quotation from that time – pre-World War II, pre-nuclear era, let alone pre-Gorbachev – to the present situation.
84. *Disinformation* No. 7 (Autumn 1987), 1. See also Leon Goure's comments on sections of the doctrine in *Strategic Review* XV (Autumn 1987), 85, and William Scott, 'Another Look', who calls the doctrine 'one primarily of "pokazuka" (for show)'.
85. Lev Yudovich, 'The Warsaw Pact's New Military Doctrine: More

Velvet Glove, Less Iron Fist', *Armed Forces Journal*, February 1988, р. 38.

86. George C. Wilson, 'The Warsaw Pact's New Military Doctrine: More Velvet Glove, Less Iron Fist', *Washington Post*, 17 March 1988, p. 35.

87. Robert Legvold, 'Gorbachev's New Approach to Conventional Arms Control', Harriman Institute *Forum* 1 (January 1988); Strode and Strode, 'Diplomacy and Defense', pp. 100–1.

88. John J. Dziak, *Soviet Perceptions of Military Power: The Interaction of Theory and Practice* (New York: Crane, Russak, 1981), p. 67.

89. John Collins, 'What Have We Got for $1 Trillion', *Washington Quarterly* 9 (Spring 1986), 49.

90. Andrew C. Goldberg, 'New Developments in Soviet Military Strategy', Washington, DC: Center for Strategic and International Studies, Significant Issues Series, Vol. IX, No. 7, 1987, p. 1. On the US ability to shift Soviet policy, see also Dennis M. Gormley and Douglas M. Hart, 'Soviet Views on Escalation: Implications for Alliance Strategy', European American Institute for Security Research Paper No. 8, Summer 1984, pp. 14–17.

7 Other Issues: The Mechanics of the Nuclear Deterrent

1. See Theresa M. Foley, 'SDI Phase One System Will Meet Joint Chiefs' Minimum Defense Needs', *Aviation Week and Space Technology*, 26 June 1989, p. 30.

2. See the analysis by John Steinbruner in *Reykjavik and Beyond*, p. 17.

3. Harold Brown, 'Off to a Good START', *Washington Post*, 13 December 1987, p. M2.

4. Andrew Goldberg, 'Offense and Defense in the Postnuclear System', *Washington Quarterly* 11 (Spring 1988), 65.

5. Goldberg, 'Offense and Defense', p. 65.

6. See, for example, the critical discussion of limited BMD in 'Limited Missile Defenses – What Can They Protect?' *Arms Control Today* 19 (April 1989), 18–22.

7. On this need, and the Indigo-Lacrosse satellite that might fill it, see Rowland Evans and Robert Novak, 'The Indigo-Lacrosse Satellite'; Susan F. Rasky, 'U.S. Ability to Monitor Strategic Pact is Doubted', *New York Times* 17 February 1988, p. 8; and 'New Spy Satellites Urged for Verification', *Science*, 1 April 1988, p. 20.

8. John M. Collins, 'What Have We Got for $1 Trillion?', *Washington Quarterly* 9 (Spring 1986), 50.

9. 'Former Defense Official Defends Mobile ICBM Systems', *Washington Times*, 4 March 1988, p. F–5.

10. Quoted in Charles Krauthammer, 'The End of Arms Control', *New Republic*, XXXX, p. 30.

11. Discussion Group on Strategic Policy, *Deterring Through the Turn of the Century* (Washington, DC: Center for Strategic and International Studies, January 1989), p. 12. See also Lt. Col. Fred Reule, USAF, *et al.*, *Dynamic Stability: A New Concept for Deterrence* (Maxwell AFB, AL: Air University Press, September 1987), 23–4.

12. Discussion Group on Strategic Policy, *Deterring Through the Turn of the Century*, p. 12.

13. Another crucial issue is, of course, that of sea-launched cruise missiles or SLCMs. Space does not permit a close consideration of the issues surrounding SLCMs; for a discussion of them and of possible verification procedures, see . . .

14. James. P. Rubin, 'Limiting SLCMs – A Better Way to START', *Arms Control Today* 19 (April 1989), 10.

15. Superb background on this issue is provided by a number of the chapters in Richard K. Betts (ed.), *Cruise Missiles: Technology, Strategy, Politics* (Washington, DC: Brookings Institution, 1981), especially those by Ronald Huisken, Robert Art and Stephen Ockenden. See also Ronald Huisken, *The Origins of the Strategic Cruise Missile* (New York: Praeger, 1981).

16. For further information, see Thomas B. Cochran *et al.*, *Nuclear Weapons Databook, Vol I: U.S. Nuclear Forces and Capabilities* (Washington, DC: Natural Resources Defense Council, 1984), pp. 184–7; Kosta Tsipis, *Arsenal: Understanding Weapons in the Nuclear Age* (New York: Simon & Schuster, 1983), pp. 147–66; and Joel Wit, 'Soviet Cruise Missiles', *Survival* 25 (November-December 1983).

17. See, for example, two articles in *International Security* 13 (Winter 1988/89) – Henry C. Mustin, 'The Sea-Launched Cruise Missile: More Than a Bargaining Chip'; and Linton Brooks, 'Nuclear SLCMs Add to Deterrence and Security', esp. pp. 170–1.

18. Richard K. Betts, *Cruise Missiles and U.S. Policy* (Washington, DC: Brookings Institution, 1982), p. 12.

19. Theodore A. Postol, 'Banning Nuclear SLCMs: It Would Be Nice if We Could', *International Security* 13 (Winter 1988/89), 193.

20. See Brooks, 'Nuclear SLCMs', p. 171, and Terry Terriff, 'Controlling Nuclear SLCM', *Survival* XX (January/February 1989), 53–4. On the inadequacy of cruise missiles for prompt counterforce targeting requirements as part of a war-fighting strategy, see Betts, *Cruise Missiles*, pp. 13–17.

21. Terriff, 'Controlling Nuclear SLCM', p. 54.

22. Postol, 'Banning Nuclear SLCMs', p. 193.

23. Rubin, 'Limited SLCMs', p. 11.

24. Betts, *Cruise Missiles*, p. 47.

25. Betts, *Cruise Missiles*, pp. 22–3.

26. See Mustin, 'The Sea-Launched Cruise Missile', pp. 186–7, and Brooks, 'Nuclear SLCMs', pp. 171–2.

27. Terriff, 'Controlling Nuclear SLCM', pp. 56–7.

28. See, for example, Richard Burt, 'Local Conflicts in the Third World', in Betts (ed.), *Cruise Missiles*, pp. 213–30.

29. Postol, 'Banning Nuclear SLCMs', pp. 193 and ff. See also The Discussion Group on Strategic Policy, *Deterring Through the Turn of the Century* (Washington, DC: Center for Strategic and International Studies and Johns Hopkins Foreign Policy Institute, January 1989), p. 4.

30. Terriff, 'Controlling Nuclear SLCM', p. 58.
31. This last point is made by Detts in *Cruise Missiles*, p. 20.
32. Terriff, 'Controlling Nuclear SLCM', p. 65.
33. R. Jeffrey Smith and David Remnick, 'Soviet Urges Ban on Naval Cruise Missiles', *Washington Post*, 14 July 1989, p. A1.
34. *Aerospace Daily*, 2 May 1988, p. 172.
35. Cited in Rubin, 'Limiting SLCMs', p. 13.
36. These suggestions come from Rubin, 'Limiting SLCMs'; Gottemoeller, 'Finding Solutions to SLCM Arms Control Problems'; and Terriff, 'Limiting Nuclear SLCM'.
37. See Alton Frye and Peter Zimmerman, 'A Slick Trick for SLCMs', *Washington Post*, 21 February 1988, and Valerie Thomas, 'False Obstacle to Arms Control', *New York Times* 13 July 1989, p. A23.
38. Terriff, 'Controlling Nuclear SLCM', pp. 64–5.
39. See Michael R. Gordon, 'U.S. Aide Offers Plan to Cut Arms at Sea', *New York Times* 6 April 1988.

8 Non-Nuclear Strategic Weapons

1. Peter deLeon, *The Altered Strategic Environment Toward the Year 2000* (Lexington, MA: D. C. Heath, 1987), p. 47; Philip Bobbitt, *Democracy and Deterrence: The History and Future of Nuclear Strategy* (New York: St Martin's Press, 1988), p. 155.
2. deLeon, *The Altered Strategic Environment*, pp. 71, 75–76.
3. Carl H. Builder, *Strategic Conflict Without Nuclear Weapons* (Santa Monica, CA: RAND Corporation, April 1983), p. 3. A similar version of the same paper was published as 'The Prospects and Implications of Non-nuclear Means for Strategic Conflict', *Adelphi Papers* No. 200 (London: International Institute for Strategic Studies, Summer 1985). All Builder citations in this chapter will refer to the former work.
4. *Report of the President's Commission on Strategic Forces* (Washington, DC: April 1983), 9.
5. As Builder argues, 'A revolution in weaponry is on its way ... The morning of this revolution is coming in the 1980s with a new generation of nonnuclear theater weaponry capable of both mass and precision strikes. The turn of the century will see the revolution in its full light – the capabilities will have been developed for intercontinental strategic conflict without nuclear weapons'. Builder, 'Strategic Conflict Without Nuclear Weapons', p. 62.
6. See the various essays in Geoffrey Kemp *et al.*, (eds), *The Other Arms Race: New Technologies and Non-Nuclear Conflict* (Lexington, MA: Lexington Books, 1975).
7. Carl Builder *et al.*, 'The Rand Winter Study on Nonnuclear Strategic Weapons: Executive Summary' (Santa Monica, CA: RAND Corporation, December 1984), p. 2. Hereinafter referred to as 'RAND Study'.
8. RAND Winter Study, p. 4. See also Jacqueline Davis *et al.*, 'An Inventory of New Weapons Systems for Non-Nuclear Conflict', in Kemp, *The Other Arms Race*, pp. 151–92.
9. N. F. Wikner, 'Interdicting Fixed Targets with Conventional

Weapons', *Armed Forces Journal International*, March 1983, p. 80. On TBMs see Hugh De Santis, 'An Anti-Tactical Missile Defense for Europe', *SAIS Review*, Summer-Autumn 1986; Steven Meyer, 'Soviet Theater Nuclear Forces, Part I: Development of Doctrine and Objectives', *Adelphi Papers* No. 187 (London: IISS, Winter 1983–84); Dennis M. Gormley, 'A New Dimension to Soviet Theater Strategy', *Orbis*, Autumn 1985; and William A. Davis, *Regional Security and Anti-Tactical Ballistic Missiles: Political and Technical Issues* (Washington, DC: Pergamon Brassey's for the Institute for Foreign Policy Analysis, 1986).

10. Wikner, 'Interdicting', p. 80.
11. Anthony Ramirez, 'Secrecy Surrounding New Defense Projects Has Some Analysts Worried', *Philadelphia Inquirer*, 7 August 1983, p. 5; 'Boeing Studies Long-Range, Propfan-Powered ALCM', *Aviation Week and Space Technology*, 22 August 1988, p. 31.
12. For detailed data on cruise characteristics, see Richard K. Betts (ed.), *Cruise Missiles: Technology, Strategy, Politics* (Washington, DC: Brookings Institution, 1981), especially the essay by John Toomay; Betts, *Cruise Missiles and U.S. Policy* (Washington, DC: Brookings Institution, 1982); and Charles A. Sorrels, *U.S. Cruise Missile Programs* (New York: McGraw Hill, 1983). Yet none of these contain any significant discussion of NNSW – they examine strategic nuclear and tactical conventional weapons.
13. Wikner, 'Interdicting', p. 80. See also Wikner, 'Conventional Weapon Destruction of Hardened Targets: Penetrators New or Old?', *Armed Forces Journal International*, March 1983, pp. 91–5.
14. N. F. Wikner, ' "E.T." and the Soviet Union', *Armed Forces Journal International*, November 1984, p. 100.
15. See John G. Roos and Benjamin F. Schemmer, 'Revolution in NATO's Conventional Defense Looms from "Competitive Strategies" Initiative', *Armed Forces Journal International*, October 1988, pp. 114–21.
16. Barbara Amouyal, 'New Cost, Validity Expected to Dampen Fever for Competitive Strategies', *Defense News*, 16 January 1989, p. 8.
17. For a more extensive consideration of emerging technologies, see Anthony H. Cordesman, 'Technology and the Search for Conventional Options: Religion Versus Reality', paper presented at CSIS/Potomac Foundation Conference on Defense Economics, 31 October-1 November 1988.
18. Michael MccGwire, *Military Objectives in Soviet Foreign Policy* (Washington, DC: Brookings Institution, 1987). The connection between non-nuclear options and the 'suicidal' nature of nuclear war is drawn in the comments by Soviet Gen. Shabonev in 'Deadlier Conventional War', *Strategic Review*, Winter 1987, pp. 87–9.
19. Wikner, ' "E.T." and the Soviet Union', pp. 100–1.
20. Leon Goure and Michael J. Deane, 'The Soviet Strategic View', *Strategic Review*, Autumn 1985, p. 98. For an extensive discussion of these issues, see Mary C. Fitzgerald, 'Marshal Ogarkov on the Modern Theater Operation', *Naval War College Review* 34 (Autumn 1986), 6–25.

21. Wikner, '"E.T." and the Soviet Union'.
22. D. L. Smith and A. L. Meler, 'Ogarkov's Revolution. Soviet Military Doctrine for the 1990s', *International Defense Review* 20 (No. 7, 1987), p. 864.
23. John G. Hines, Phillip A. Petersen and Notra Trulock III, 'Soviet Military Theory from 1945–2000: Implications for NATO', *Washington Quarterly* 9 (Autumn 1986), 125–8.
24. deLeon, *The Altered Strategic Environment*, p. 51.
25. RAND Winter Study p. 2; Builder, 'Strategic Conflict', pp. 43–4.
26. RAND Winter Study, p. 8.
27. RAND Winter Study, p. 8.
28. For analysis of this point, see Glenn A. Kent and David E. Thaler, *First Strike Stability: A Methodology for Evaluating Strategic Forces* (Santa Monica, CA: RAND Corporation, August 1989).
29. RAND Winter Study, p. 18.
30. The RAND Winter Study reached no firm conclusions about countermeasures to NNSW; see pp. 2, 4–6.
31. RAND Winter Study, p. 6.
32. Carl Builder, while recognising that NNSW are more vulnerable to countermeasures than nuclear weapons, nevertheless is more sanguine than this analysis about the technical feasibility of counterforce NNSW. See 'Strategic Conflict', pp. 20–30.
33. Stephen Rosen, 'Conventional Combat and the Nuclear Balance', *Journal of Strategic Studies* 10 (March 1987), 48–50.
34. Indeed, a study of the first-strike requirements for NNSW against a given number of mobiles on a given amount of land would be interesting.
35. Rosen, 'Conventional Combat and the Nuclear Balance', pp. 39–44.
36. The converse is also true; NNSW are far less relevant in a short war. Builder notes that 'If strategic conflicts are fought only as a single spasm, nonnuclear capabilities will have little military significance until they can replace all strategic nuclear weapons'. 'Strategic Conflict', p. 31.
37. RAND Winter Study, p. 10.
38. For updated information on the status of ASATs and ASAT arms control, see the articles by Spurgeon M. Keeny, Jr., Senator Tom Harkin, and Matthew Bunn in *Arms Control Today*, March 1989, pp. 2–9.
39. James F. Digby, 'Precision-Guided Munitions: Capabilities and Consequences', in Kemp, *The Other Arms Race*, p. 12.
40. deLeon, *The Altered Strategic Environment*, p. 77.
41. For details of counterpower strategies, see Bernard Albert, 'Constructive Counterpower', *Orbis* 20 (Summer 1976), 343–66; Bruce Russett, 'Assured Destruction of What? A Countercombatant Alternative to Nuclear MADness', *Public Policy* XXII (Spring 1974), 121–38; and Jeffrey Richelson, 'Dilemmas of Counterpower Targeting', in Desmond Ball and Richelson (eds), *Strategic Nuclear Targeting* (Cornell: Cornell University Press, 1986).
42. Builder, pp. 31–3, 50; RAND Winter Study, p. 7.

43. Andrew C. Goldberg, 'Offense and Defense in the Postnuclear System', *Washington Quarterly*, Spring 1988, pp. 58–9. See also the study authored by Goldberg, *Securing Strategic Stability* (Washington, DC: Center for Strategic and International Studies, 1988).

44. On this issue, see the discussion in David W. Tarr, 'Avoiding Nuclear War By Other Means', in Stephen Cimbala (ed.), *Strategic War Termination* (New York: Praeger, 1986), pp. 45–6.

45. This raises an interesting point: enemy NNSW factories are likely to be among the first targets of NNSW themselves. Neither side can therefore count on continuing supplies of NNSW once hostilities begin, and the employment of existing weapons will involve extremely tough choices – a fact that might be true with all weapons systems in future wars.

46. From a 1973 presentation; quoted in Builder, 'Strategic Conflict', p. 5.

47. RAND Winter Study, p. 9.

48. RAND Winter Study, p. 15.

49. Geoffrey Kemp and Robert Pfaltzgraff, 'New Technologies and the Emerging Geo-Strategic Environment', in Kemp, *The Other Arms Race*, p. 142.

50. RAND Winter Study, pp. 20–1.

51. Builder, 'Strategic Conflict Without Nuclear Weapons', p. 60.

52. RAND Winter Study, p. 22.

53. Builder, 'Strategic Conflict Without Nuclear Weapons', pp. 47–51.

54. Jeffrey Record, 'Conventional Force Options for the 1990s', paper delivered at CSIS/Potomac Foundation Conference on Defense Economics for the 1990s, 31 October-1 November 1988, p. 1. See also Debra van Opstal and Andrew Goldberg, *Meeting the Mavericks: Regional Challenges for the Next President* (Washington, DC: Center for Strategic and International Studies, 1988).

55. The RAND report (p. 28) concludes that 'The cost of more capable NNSW may increase rather than decrease the gap between the superpowers and other nations'.

56. Fred C.Iklé and Albert Wohlstetter, co-chairs, *Discriminate Deterrence: Report of the Commission on Integrated Long-Term Strategy* (Washington, DC: January 1988), p. 2.

57. Kemp and Pfaltzgraff, 'New Technologies and the Emerging Geo-Strategic Environment', pp. 139–40.

58. Israel, for example, has also expressed great fears over the deployment of increasingly accurate tactical ballistic missiles (TBMs) by the Arab states, and is developing an ATBM to counter that threat. See W. Seth Carus, 'Israel and the Strategic Defense Initiative', report of the Fund for an American Renaissance, 1988; and Keith Payne and Marc Berkowitz, 'Anti-Tactical Missile Defense, Allied Security and the ABM Treaty', *Strategic Review* XVI (Winter 1988) 24–34.

59. RAND Winter Study, p. 30.

60. RAND Winter Study, p. 30.

61. RAND Winter Study, p. 29.

62. Kemp and Pfaltzgraff, 'New Technologies and the Emerging Geo-Strategic Environment', pp. 140–1.

63. Rosen, 'Conventional Combat and the Nuclear Balance', pp. 45–6.
64. Rosen, 'Conventional Combat and the Nuclear Balance', p. 47.
65. Rosen, 'Conventional Combat and the Nuclear Balance', pp. 57–8, 59–60.
66. RAND Winter Study, p. 10.

9 Summary

1. Fred C. Iklé, 'Nuclear Strategy: Can There Be a Happy Ending?', *Journal of Strategic Studies* 9 (December 1986), 47.
2. Glenn A. Kent and David E. Thaler, *First Strike Stability: A Methodology for Evaluating Strategic Forces* (Santa Monica, CA: RAND Corporation, August 1989), p. viii.
3. Joseph S. Nye, Jr, 'Nuclear Learning and U.S.-Soviet Security Regimes', *International Organization* 41 (Summer 1987), 371–402.
4. Nye, 'Nuclear Learning', p. 384.
5. Bruce G. Blair, *Strategic Command and Control* (Washington, DC: Brookings Institution, 1985), pp. 243–4.
6. Blair, *Strategic Command and Control*, pp. 300–1; Scott D. Sagan, *Moving Targets: Nuclear Strategy and National Security* (Princeton, NJ: Princeton University Press, 1989), pp. 160–1.
7. Blair, *Strategic Command and Control*, p. 300; Sagan, *Moving Targets*, pp. 162–4.
8. Paul Bracken, *The Command and Control of Nuclear Weapons* (New Haven: Yale University Press, 1983), esp. pp. 242–3.
9. Sagan, *Moving Targets*, pp. 166–73.
10. Peter Almond, 'Stray MiG Incident Prompts Talk of Military Hotline', *Washington Times*, 6 July 1989, p. A11.
11. Jan M. Lodal, 'A Treaty That Could Do Harm', *New York Times*, 14 June 1989, p. 27.
12. Lodal, 'A Treaty That Could Do Harm'.
13. Henry Kissenger, 'A Dangerous Rush Toward an Agreement'.
14. Einhorn, 'The Emerging START Agreement', p. 400.
15. This analysis owes much to the comments of career foreign service officer and CSIS adjuct fellow Leo Reddy at a CSIS conference on coventional arms control, Washington, DC, 14 November 1989.
16. Nye, 'Nuclear Learning', p. 371.

Index